CONTENTS

CW01498218

ROUTE 52

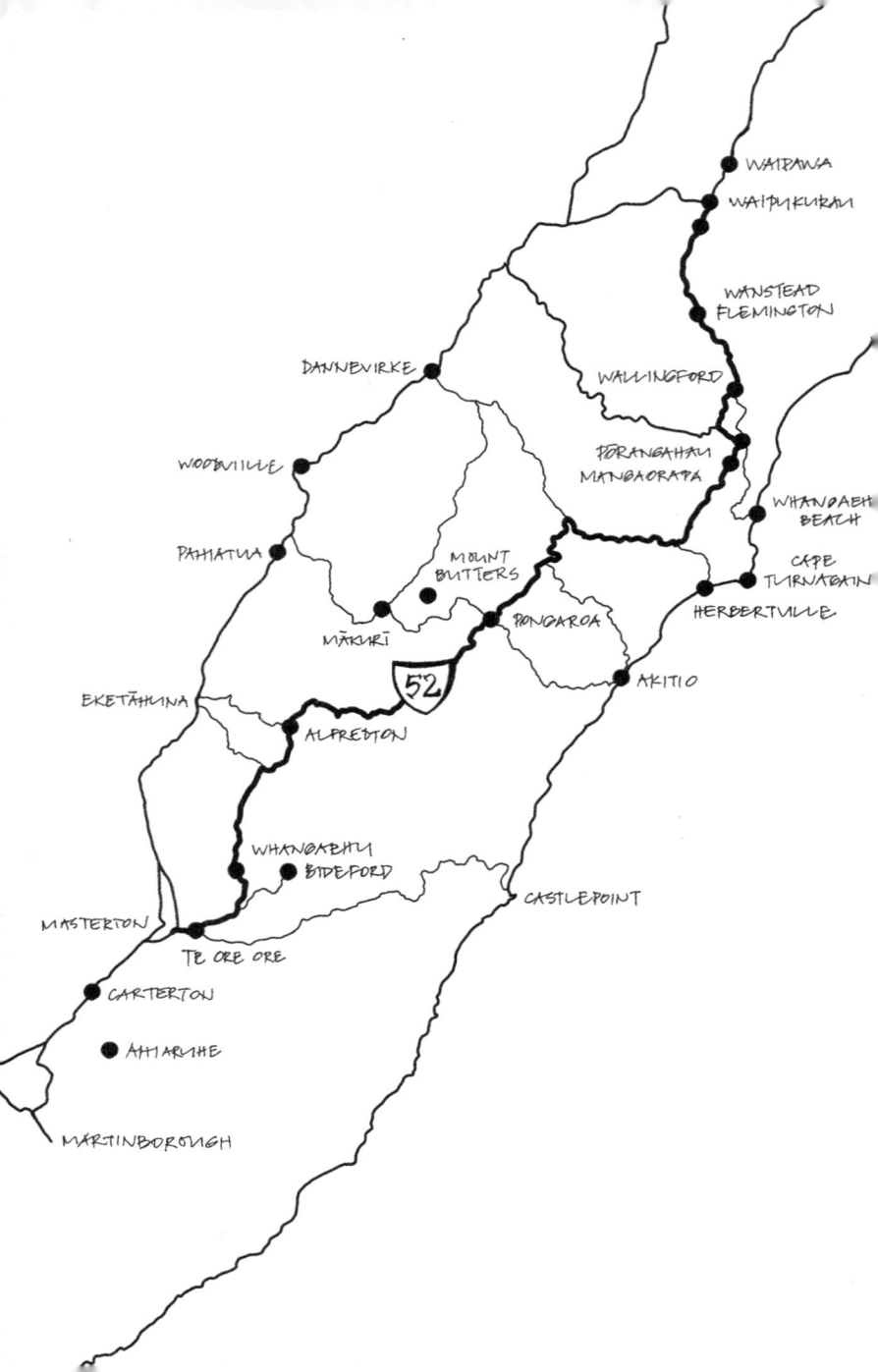

ROUTE 52

A BIG LUMP OF
COUNTRY UNKNOWN

Simon Burt

UGLY HILL PRESS

For Pip, Olly, and Lucien

A PLACE OF MY OWN

I'D HARDLY SET FOOT IN ONE, LET ALONE TOWED OR slept or boiled a whistling kettle in one, but after years of drooling over the pages of RV camping magazines and Trade Me I finally took the plunge a few years ago and bought a caravan. It was a Liteweight Vagabond 1100 with fading yellow paint. It was largely in original condition albeit with years of steady use, and a bit of neglect to remedy. It still had the badge from where it was bought new in 1978—White Heather Caravans, Normanby. It was classic '70s, all brown vinyl, plastic wood veneer and aluminium trim. It had orange curtains and nasty polyester upholstery with a swirly brown design. Three-berth at a squeeze, about as small as caravans come, it looked like a pumpkin on wheels. That little old 'van was not a 'she'. It had not been pimped or retro-ed or painted with high-gloss seven-pot lacquer. There was no hidden TV or microwave. It did not have a colour coordinated tow car with fluffy dice, and it wasn't decked out with reproduction period furnishings or accessories. And it most certainly did not have a name.

The kids weren't interested in my caravan, nor was my wife; they hardly stepped through its door. But the neighbourhood blokes were—it was parked up on the front lawn most Friday nights of every summer and a lot of each winter; awning erected, table set, fridge full, music, snacks—an open invitation. Many a global or personal problem was solved way past dinner time in my little 'van.

A few years later, the desire for a little more elbow room got the better of me and my tiny pride and joy was superseded by a very slightly bigger and older version of the same thing. Same make, grander model. Brown and copper interior. Copycat gas fridge. Hot water! Carpet! Badly applied olive-green paint, quickly re-sprayed its former burnt orange. Original features, no pimping. And if it ever had a name, it sure doesn't now.

A caravan is like a boat; it's all about storage, efficiency, layout, manoeuvrability . . . and style. Some are curvy architectural gems; others commit violent design crimes. One will look pretty on the exterior but be totally impractical inside; another will work like a dream while presenting a bit ugly. But however they look or function, caravans have a common value—they're able to be hitched up and taken for a spur-of-the-moment overnighter when the sunset is looking promising or a good book needs finishing. Like a bach on wheels.

There are some top caravan spots on and around Route 52. I've overnighted on wild Herbertville Beach, and at the equally blustery Herbertville Campground. In the moody Pongaroa

Parked up at home
AHIARUHE

Domain, and under clear Alfredton skies. I've spent starry nights at Akitio, parking as close to the tide as it's possible to be. Pōrangahau, too—just a grassy dune between pillow and pounding surf. I've ventured, albeit unintentionally, through the twisty Mākurī Gorge. I've checked out the Eketāhuna camping ground with its lovely riverside walk and uncatchable trout, and the abandoned garden and lily pond at Pahiatua's Carnival Park.

But almost as enjoyable are nights parked up in the paddock —a few dozen steps from my front door but feeling like a million miles away. I think that's what I love about my caravan, it's a little haven, a cocoon, a well-ordered space where I'll find stuff as I left it.

A place of my own.

TAKING THE WATERS

ON THE SIDE OF THE ROAD AT TE ORE ORE, A FEW short kilometres from central Masterton, a handwritten cardboard sign hangs in the window of a grey tin shed. It says *OPEN*, but even in the showery Sunday evening gloom no lights are evident. I press my nose to the window and can make out an elderly Chinese woman who has nodded off in a simple wooden chair.

I open the door and the woman wakes. She stands, smiles, and spreads her hands palms up across trays of courgettes, red peppers, celery, and pumpkins. I point to a few items which she wraps and bags. She totes up with spidery fingers on an abacus smoothed by lifetimes of use. I'm hoping to talk about her life here, but her little English makes conversation difficult. I hand her cash, thank her—'xiè xiè'—and leave.

Next to the shop, a small letterbox and a few bits of what used to be a Coca-Cola sign hang on a sagging wooden fence. A half-hinged gate leads to a faded weatherboard bungalow with a rust-tinged iron roof. The guttering is growing almost as much vegetation as the fields behind. Through the windows, white blinds are drawn.

Across the road a concrete lamppost displays a small black and red *Cycle Trail* emblem with an arrow pointing to Masterton. Above it, a cluster of yellow AA signs face away from town towards Castlepoint, Bideford, Whangaehu, and Pongaroa. An occasional vehicle hisses by on the mirror-wet bitumen.

There is nothing to announce it, but this unremarkable spot is where 184 kilometres of road called Route 52 begins. Or ends, depending on where you start.

*

Te Ore Ore is a mere blip on the vast Wairarapa landscape. Its name possibly refers to a time when a young man was entertaining a local woman while courting her; her hearty laughter—te ori ori—was heard far and wide. Another story has it that a visiting chief stepped out of the bush on the hills above and saw this fertile valley spread out below. Excited by his discovery he gave a deep chortle—ore ore, meaning 'to shake'.[1] Either way, Te Ore Ore is what Māori settlers called the place where they built their marae, a couple of kilometres along the road.

Māori settled by rivers, lakes, and the sea—sources of food. Te Ore Ore is on the banks of the Ruamāhanga (twin forks), the river which flows the length of the Wairarapa valley. The river provided the settlers with tuna (eels), koura (small crayfish), freshwater mussels, and native trout.

Caroline Hohua grew up in this settlement. She remembers the little vegetable shop and the market garden behind it on the fertile river flats. 'They've been there as long as I've been around.' There were other Chinese gardens, too, down Watsons Road where she lived. In the 1950s and '60s at Te Ore Ore School, opposite Watsons Road, her Māori friends and family mingled with the children from the gardens, as well as the Pākehā kids from the local farms and from along the road towards town. After school, they'd all go down to the river—swimming, eeling, trouting . . . 'At Christmas, the kids would pack up after lunch and spend the rest of the day down there.'

It's a beautiful Wairarapa morning when I meet Caroline and her fellow marae trustee, Robin Pōtangaroa. Caroline is about my age and quiet, thoughtful, welcoming. She wears a moko kauae. Robin is younger, more outgoing, energetic. He has already made a trip out to Castlepoint, Whakataki, by the time his plumber's van scrunches up the gravel drive past the courtyard of the marae, where I'm enjoying the sunshine in front of the wharenui.

Robin has thoughtfully brought coffee and cake and we've settled down to a milky cup and buttery slice in the wharekai. Robin is at pains to defer to 'Auntie' Caroline at every opportunity, saying she spends a lot more time here than he does. He's also concerned that as he's out and about doing the more high-profile work for their people—Treaty negotiations and Trust Board roles—he gets enough press. Despite that, he does most of the talking and speaks with authority as a descendant of the prophet Pāora Te Pōtangaroa, who played a key role in the development of the marae.

Te Ore Ore marae—Hine Mataki o te kata o Te Ore Ore—was established around 1878 at the encouragement of the chief Wi Waaka. Building the unusually large carved wharenui were Pāora Pōtangaroa and Te Kere, a master carver from Whanganui. Shortly after work commenced, the two men fell out and Te Kere moved away, telling Pōtangaroa: 'E Kore e taea te whakamutu i te whare i mua atu i ngā tau e waru.'—'It will not be possible for you to build this house in eight years.' This spurred on the team of carvers, and when the whare was completed in just over a year, Pōtangaroa called the house Nga Tau e Waru, The House of Eight Years, a pointed reminder of Te Kere's failed prophecy.[2]

The marae is affiliated to both Rangitāne and Kahungunu, the two major Wairarapa iwi. 'It's got to be shared because all of us are both,' Robin quips. 'But our role isn't iwi. The original trustees of the marae came from many different tribes anyway. We have to look past our own worldview and understand that we're just here to make sure the marae functions for the benefit of all.'

Caroline agrees. 'The marae is for everyone, not just us. Samoans, Rarotongans have used it for different events. Tomorrow, the Council is having a citizenship ceremony here— they're showing the new citizens there's more than just a town hall in Masterton. It's probably the first and last time most of them will come to a marae, but it's a great thing to do anyway.'

Caroline's grandmother was born at Hamua, ten kilometres north of Eketāhuna. With the associated Tutaekara pā, Hamua was an important Māori settlement between the 1830s and 1850s.

Hine Mataki o te kata o Te Ore Ore
TE ORE ORE, MASTERTON

It had a hotel, store, and school, but now consists merely of a picnic layby on State Highway 2. 'Grandma's land stretched from Pahiatua, north of Hamua, all the way to here, to Te Ore Ore. She ended up here and married our ancestor from the coast, who was a Pōtangaroa. We still have family land here, on the corner of Watsons Road, opposite the vegetable shop.' Hamua was a pre-eminent ancestor, Robin says. 'He's at the top of the tekoteko. A lot of our people consider themselves Hamua.'

Caroline says she spends a lot of time at the marae. 'I look after it, clean it, set it up for hui, tangi. Of course, Robin and others help—with the tables, mattresses. I live just down at Colombo Road so I'm not far away. Sometimes, I just come out here and sit by myself, have a talk to the old ones . . .'

*

In the second half of the nineteenth century, the land around Te Ore Ore was also being settled by Europeans. By 1874, around 2,700 acres five miles from the marae was in the ownership of Bennet Pascoe Perry, son-in-law of Joseph Masters (after whom Masterton is named). A photograph taken on the property that year shows a dwelling, a simple timber slab structure no bigger than a whare—maybe ten metres long and a couple wide. At one end a man stands, hands on hips, looking towards a nearby thatched barn, little bigger than the house. A horse and cow are tied to a railing fence while another figure strides away from the group. The scene takes place at the foot of a bush-covered hill.

A column in the *Wairarapa Daily Times* from 21 January, 1888 reports the following:[3]

Sulphur or iron Deposits near Masterton—
The Mineralized Springs

*Hearing that Mr. B. P. Perry has some intention of ascertaining
the nature of the deposits indicated by the so called sulphur springs,
which flow on his lately acquired property 'Sulphur Wells' a part
of the Woodlands estate, and situated on the Upper Taueru road,
about six miles from Masterton, a representative from this journal
waited upon that gentleman yesterday and obtained the following
description of these developments of nature: The main springs are
situated in streams which flow through the property, but there are
also others apart from all running water. The springs have the usual
bubbling up appearance similar to that of a pot boiling, and the
water which flows up is decidedly impregnated with sulphur or some
mineral substance which is deposited below. The fluid is also of quite
a dark color, except when taken up and examined in a tumbler, and
then it is only slightly discolored. There is a very perceptible smell on
approaching the openings, and the issue of the waters from the main
spring, has caused quite a hole, down which a stick can be placed for
about ten feet. The external appearance of the jets is a kind of muddy
basin, from which the fluid oozes. The water of which we have seen a
bottled sample, has a very unpleasant smell and a chemical taste. In
our opinion, however, the latter denoted the presence of iron deposits
rather than sulphurous ones. We understand that Mr Perry is desirous
of, if possible, getting Mr Mackay of the Geological Department to
take a trip out to the scene while he is in the Wairarapa, and so of
obtaining from him an opinion as to what deposits the nature of the
springs indicate, and also if there is any commercial value in the waters
or the mineral. The waters have already been found very useful as a*

preventive of disease in grape vines. It is quite likely that the springs might be found to be curative ones, and Mr Perry is obtaining an analysis of the waters to decide the surmise.

Forty-five years earlier, at Edmonton, South Kentucky, Ezekiel Neal began digging a well on the bank of South Fork Little Barren River. Edmonton has a healthy annual rainfall and despite its name the river usually runs clear and plentiful. So, Ezekiel wasn't looking for fresh water—he was attempting to hit a salt spring.

Salt springs (or 'brine wells') were a good source of income in the United States in the nineteenth century. The collected brine was either sold directly for preserving food or evaporated to extract the salt. Ezekiel knew a well was successfully issuing the valuable fluid from under the river not far away. His hand- and horse-powered drill hit a seam at 180 feet and, according to local legend, the resultant pressure sent water, his auger, and parts of the drill shaft shooting over the top of a nearby sycamore tree.

The water from Ezekiel's bore did contain salt, but not in high concentrations. It was, however, found to contain magnesia, iron, and sulphur—a combination of minerals believed to fix stomach problems and nervous disorders. Word about the discovery got around and cure-seekers began travelling to Edmonton to imbibe the smelly water.

Ezekiel Neal opened his home as accommodation for the new wave of visitors. Other locals cashed in, building boarding houses and hotels close by. Very soon the burgeoning settlement became known as Sulphur Well. In 1854, the Neals sold 186 acres of their land, including the well that is now part of an attractive park owned by the local County and still popular with people convinced of its health benefits.

Meanwhile, across the Atlantic in Yorkshire, England, the Royal Pump Room was being built over the Old Sulphur Well, the most famous of all the 'Harrogate Waters'. The Pump Room offered guests of the town of Harrogate an all-weather facility where they could drink the well's sulphur water—'taking the waters'.

Harrogate became quite the place to be in the eighteenth century, with visitors from all over Europe seeking a cure for whatever ailed them.

Back at Te Ore Ore it seems Mr Perry never followed up the Geological Department's advice, if indeed he ever received any. By 1912, a substantial homestead had replaced the earlier whare and the hill behind had been largely cleared. A book compiled by British explorer Somerset Playne says that the property 'is greatly advantaged by having about 150 acres of native bush dotted about in stock shelter patches, varying from a quarter of an acre to 40 acres in extent.' These patches of bush—still there, some under QEII Covenant—were what attracted Scotsman Neil Petrie to Sulphur Wells in 1967.

*

Neil Petrie first arrived in Aotearoa New Zealand in 1961 in a Mk1 Austin-Healey Bug-Eyed Sprite. His friend Andrew Henderson had set off from Scotland in 1959 at the age of nineteen on what he dubbed 'The World Sprite Expedition', intending to circumnavigate the globe in his tiny white convertible sports car. Henderson's original co-driver bailed out in India so Neil, who was working on a farm in Australia at the time, joined Henderson for the Australasian leg. He also did part of the United States circuit.

During their journey through Aotearoa, the dashing young pair stopped off at a polo match in Rangitikei where Neil met his future wife, Phillippa. After marrying, they lived in England for a few years where they had three of their six children. The couple then returned to Aotearoa and bought Sulphur Wells.

The entrance to the Sulphur Wells homestead turns off a gentle curve in the Te Ore Ore-Bideford Road. White fence railings taper to a cattle-stop. A bend in the tree-lined drive reveals a classic County tractor weathering gracefully under the oaks. A Monet-style bridge crosses a swift-running brown stream as the rustic cream homestead comes into view behind a dark grey stone wall. A large add-on conservatory faces the drive, piled-up furniture visible through the glass. It's wet at the carpark and several cars and utes are scattered around. A fibreglass boat sits on a trailer—it crosses my mind that the boat could come in handy soon.

It's two days after Cyclone Gabrielle has lashed the country, particularly the eastern side, and I'm visiting Neil and Phillippa's son Alexander, known as 'Tundy'. We're sitting at a family-sized wooden table in the homestead's comfy kitchen. There are alterations taking place and builders are screwing plasterboard to timber framing around the back door. A portable halogen lamp is firing shafts of light into the small room we entered through.

A general gloom filters through the foggy kitchen windows as the big storm's tail sends steady rain which pelts the iron roof.

Tundy is in a sunny mood though as he puts an enamel kettle on the gas hob. His farm has so far suffered relatively little damage from Gabrielle. And he's keen to know about my interest in Sulphur Wells.

First, I want to get the question of his name out of the way. 'I was a chubby baby,' he explains, 'And my parents called me Rotundus. My brothers and sisters couldn't say Rotundus so it became Tundy and it stuck.' That was easy enough, so I turned to the story of the healing waters.

'See that lawn out there?' He pointed through the window. 'If it wasn't so wet I'd show you, but in areas of that lawn, and up by the cottage, there's water bubbling out of the earth. It doesn't steam. It doesn't really smell. It's like liquefaction I suppose— fine grey silt. I don't know if Dad was playing tricks, but I vaguely remember him lighting a match and flames flickering above the bubbles.

'The big one on the lawn is like a sponge. I put eleven or twelve tonnes of rocks in it once, I thought I might lose the digger. You can drain the holes but they just move somewhere else. They've got to be spring-related but I haven't come across any elsewhere on the farm. I can't tell you much more, although I have heard that Wairarapa has the potential for gas. Maybe there's not enough for anyone to pursue it.'

Maybe that's what Bennet Perry decided about his bubbling springs back in 1888.

Tundy runs a traditional sheep and beef farm here, with a bit of cereal cropping and occasionally a few deer. As a boy he went away to school, boarding at Huntley School, in Marton, then Whanganui Collegiate School. He remembers holidays at home, the Bideford Horse Sports, and tennis tournaments at the nearby Whangaehu Hall. He's now fifty and has three daughters with his wife, Paula; two are away at university and one is at St Matthew's Collegiate School in Masterton. Paula also has a successful children's clothing business, Merino Kids, based in Greytown.

'The girls all enjoy the land but I'm not sure any will want to take over,' Tundy says. 'And let's face it, farming's getting harder and harder. Not just the physical side—although my body's already breaking down a bit—but all this bureaucracy getting thrown at us. I can see it all getting planted into pine trees. That's the simple easy answer if you wanted to, but it'd be a tragedy, and the last thing I'd do. Don't get me started!'

It appears I already did.

'I mean, look at that beautiful bit of native bush out there. How can that not be considered carbon? There's quite a lot on Sulphur Wells, it was the main attraction when Dad bought it. He would've been better off clearing it all and planting pines. It'd be worth a fortune [in carbon credits]. But all the existing bush, you don't get a cent for it!'

This will be a discussion I have again and again along Route 52. To plant or not to plant. Carbon versus logs. To sell—yes or no? It's always a very circular conversation.

*

I take my leave and Tundy accompanies me back through the construction zone and out the door. Where my car was parked high and dry forty-five minutes ago, it's now almost axle deep in water. A collection of LPG bottles is partially submerged and the garage they're sitting beside has a flooded floor. The stream I crossed on the way in has widened and heightened considerably and now covers part of the lawn, lapping the big sulphur well. An earlier bridge would now be underwater, Tundy tells me when I ask, but this newer one has plenty of clearance. I'm pleased to find he's right. Splashing through the puddles on the drive, past the vintage tractor, I head back out on to the road.

Windscreen wipers swish and clank as I drive back past the Whangaehu Hall where Route 52 heads up the valley to the north. The marae flashes by, rain sheeting in at forty-five degrees. Turning into Masterton-Castlepoint Road, the former Te Ore Ore School—now a distinctive private residence—looks glad of its slightly elevated site. On the corner of Watsons Road, soggy sheep huddle together against a fence.

At the vegetable shop carpark, a sandwich board advertising tomatoes and cucumbers wobbles in the wind. A light shines brightly inside.

The beginning. Or the end?
CASTLEPOINT ROAD, MASTERTON

PLUCK A DUCK

A T LEAST IT DIDN'T GO INTO PINE TREES,' WILLIE James says as we sit talking in the dining room of the Masterton house he shares with his wife, Sharyn.

I've driven to the James's home, down a long tree-lined track on the suburban fringe of town. Through a gap in the trees there's a hint of a driveway to the front door, but I carry on around the back. A tractor sits in a shed, a Toyota ute and European SUV in the parking area.

A doe-eyed golden Labrador is lying in the shade of a concrete porch. She gets to her feet and stretches with a yawn as I crunch to a halt on the gravel. Willie approaches and offers his hand with a firm shake and a broad smile. He's tall, apparently in pretty good shape for seventy-four, with an enviable head of grey hair. He's wearing a checked shirt and baggy cargo shorts.

Willie and Sharyn retired off their Whangaehu Valley farm four years ago now. Their new home, a smartly-renovated villa, has polished wooden floors, elegant dressers, and an ornate barometer hanging on the wall. It sits in an established setting of trees, gardens and lawns. At the front of the house there's evidence of where a former owner, Donald Thompson, had sculptures scattered around—some his own work. His collection included a share in a work by British artist Barbara Hepworth, now held at Aratoi, Wairarapa Museum of Art and History in Masterton. A neatly painted white garden shed takes up a leafy corner under some trees, its symmetrical door and two windows resembling a blank face. I can sense that face has seen many a convivial gathering here, both inside and out. It's a lovely place for a farming couple to retire to—flat, spacious, close to town.

But bright-eyed, forthright Sharyn has been wrestling with it ever since they've been here. 'The garden was very out of shape,' she comments, filling the electric jug. 'It was big, old, and overgrown. It still needs a lot of work.' She says the garden they created from a bare paddock up the Whangaehu Valley is constantly on her mind. 'I can't go back out to the farm. If we're driving past it for any reason, I look the other way. This doesn't feel like our place, not like Wai-iti did.'

*

The James family first settled in 1870 at the very bottom of the Whangaehu Valley, at the southern end of Route 52. Henry and Isabella James had a sizeable holding there which, to this day, is farmed as Whangaehu Station.

Wai-iti Station, (so called because of the natural springs, 'small-waters', all over the farm) is halfway up Whangaehu Valley between Te Ore Ore and Alfredton. It was bought by Willie's grandfather—also Willie—and his brothers in 1920 when they returned from World War One. Willie Senior farmed there for seven years before moving the family to Moata, a small but high-producing block of 400 acres at Upper Plain, just a few kilometres from Masterton, for the purposes of the children's schooling. Willie Senior died in 1944 and his son Alan, Willie's father, took over. Moata, with its grand homestead still occupied, is just a hop, skip and jump from where we're sitting talking.

'There were managers on Wai-iti from 1927 until I went out there in 1970. Mum and Dad never lived there, but I remember going out there with them in the '50s in the Humber, and with Dad in the International to pick up the wool. The road was all metal then. It was twisty and dusty.'

Wai-iti is the bottom end of what was then called 70 Mile Bush, Te Tapere nui o Whātonga. Along with the McKenzies across the road at Te Rangi, and the Petries at Sulphur Wells in Te Ore Ore, Wai-iti has some of the last remnants of the original forest. 'On our block there was a little whare where an old fencer lived. It was made just from ponga logs and had a small fence to hold his draft horses. He used to go out and split tōtara to make the posts. Russian Jack, the swagman, called in occasionally too.'

Willie moved to Wai-iti as a single shepherd under the manager Buster Sutherland. Buster was a bronze medallist for the shooting team in the 1966 Commonwealth Games in Kingston, Jamaica. 'I worked with Buster for three years. He and Marie, and their five children. I lived in the shearers' quarters,

Rural delivery
WHANGAEHU VALLEY

but I ate with them in the house. Buster was passionate about his shooting, every week he'd let off at least fifty rounds into the side of the hill. He also loved his golf, and I tagged along with him every Sunday to play a midday round up at Alfredton. When the Sutherlands eventually left for another farm, I was in Australia. I got the call from the old man telling me I had to come back and run Wai-iti. I was actually just heading off on my OE, but he made it clear saying 'no' was not an option. That's how it was in those days. I was twenty-three.'

*

In the 1970s, Masterton's flagship hostelry was the Empire Hotel on Queen Street. Its plush dining room—starched white linen, polished silver cutlery—was the favoured venue for reunions, farewells, product launches, and anniversaries of local land-owners and business leaders. In 1954, the Empire had hosted the newly crowned Queen Elizabeth II and her husband, Prince Philip, for a night. In 1980, the United Ancient Order of Druids Stonehenge Lodge No. 1 held a centenary dinner there. Rebuilt, tweaked, re-styled and re-purposed over 143 years, the fading, earthquake-risk Empire was eventually laid to rest, demolished in 2018 when Big Save Furniture arrived. (Coincidentally, the original colonial wooden Empire was built in 1875 by James Nicol, a farmer from Whangaehu. The brick replacement, which started life in 1908 in the Italian Renaissance style, was designed by Joshua Charlesworth, architect of the Wellington Town Hall.)

On Friday nights in the 1970s, the Empire came alive when all the local shepherds came to town looking for liquor and love. 'Every year we put on a bachelors' ball,' Willie remembers. 'We invited all the newly arrived teachers and nurses.' On one such occasion, Willie's eyes alighted on a young lady posted to the provinces from Wellington Teachers' College. It wasn't long before they married and Sharyn joined Willie at Whangaehu.

In 1985, Willie and Sharyn bought Wai-iti from the James family estate. 'The farm was 1100 acres[4], too small to be viable really,' Willie says. 'In fact, for twenty years we never drew any money at all from the farm. We had a whopping mortgage, which we were paying twenty-three per cent interest on.' All the losses from the farm were added to the loan, too, so the debt was compounding. At one stage they had an opportunity to buy some more land from the neighbours but didn't have enough equity in Wai-iti to extend the loan. 'It was a debacle we never really recovered from.'

It was still a great lifestyle for raising three boys though, Sharyn says. 'We just got on with it. I went back to teaching full-time in Masterton when our youngest was five. Willie was quite a good cook in those days, he'd have dinner ready when I got home from school. He's not so good now . . .

'The homestead was just a standard old villa, built the wrong way for the sun of course. In the beginning, the phone was on a party line—there were ten on our party. There was no carpet or plasterboard in the house, just the sarking and wallpaper that flapped in the breeze. The valley had only been connected with electricity for fifteen years.

'We renovated the whole place, pulled all the doors off, stripped them down. Moved the kitchen to the other side. Started again really.'

When the Jameses took over Wai-iti, there were a few big old trees around the house but no garden. Possums were rampant and had to be controlled before any significant planting could be done. Eventually Sharyn could put in the roses she wanted. Wire cages were built over a vege patch. A new driveway was bulldozed around to the back of the house. 'Dick Newcombe, the landscaper, came out in his little Morris 1000 van, a trailer on the back loaded with all sorts of trees and shrubs. They were two dollars each. We planted them all at two-metre spacing and put trickle irrigation on the lot. As they grew up, we just took out anything we didn't like. Thirty years later it ended up looking not too bad, the old place.'

A keen duck hunter, Willie built a large pond and maimai with financial help from a few young professional city lads who'd been 'stalking the dams' on the farm for a few years. The scheme was to put in $500 each, get some machinery in, plant the pond out, and gather at season opening weekends for a roast duck feast. 'A lot of people just whip the breast meat off them,' Willie says. 'But I reckon you need a bit of fat. They taste much better roasted in their fat.' The weekends were reciprocated annually by a duck dinner at Dockside Restaurant in Wellington.

More recently, Willie built another pond by damming a dog-leg stream in a gully, but the planting he did was soon decimated by a mob of red deer that had been roaming neighbouring farms. 'But the main dam is really, really pretty,' Sharyn says. It's got beautiful oak trees and crab apples.'

Just a week before we talked, Willie and his old city mates gathered again at the maimai on a still, clear Whangaehu morning. They got two ducks between them for the weekend.

*

The conversation eventually turns to trees, as seemingly every conversation with a Route 52 farmer does. Willie says Alfredton School, further up Whangaehu Road, is doing very well now with children from local shepherds and owners, but 'lots of farms are being sold for forestry around there, so there will be fewer kids in the future'. Trinny the Labrador nuzzles my thigh with a black, wet nose as Willie lets off a bit of pine-tree-steam. The dog has heard it all before, I guess—it's the conversation that just won't go away.

Another consideration for today's farmers is succession. Wai-iti is too small to support a modern family, so the three James boys have ended up elsewhere. Andrew, forty-six, has been on a farm not far away in Mauriceville for the last ten years. Henry, forty-five, is managing four staff on a large station at Omakere, between Waipawa and Pourērere Beach. And Ritchie is a stock buyer for Silver Fern Farms in Taupō.

'It was a hard decision to make,' Sharyn tells me. 'To put one boy on the farm, pay out the others, and draw a living for ourselves—it just wasn't going to happen. But it had to be Willie's decision when to leave. The farm had been in his family for so long. He had to decide when he'd had enough.'

'I figured I'd done pretty well to get to seventy, but my knees were buggered. It was getting to the stage where I couldn't do it physically any more. A nearby farm had been on the market and sold exceptionally well. I thought, do I really need to go through another winter?'

So in 2018, the farm was sold to a syndicate of two neighbours wanting to increase their acreage and improve their own viability. A term of the sale agreement was access to the duck ponds for fifteen years.

Before I leave Willie and Sharyn, I'm given a tour of their new property. It's sheltered and sunny and quiet. They can't get built out because it's zoned green belt. There's room to run a dozen cattle 'to pay the rates'. Attractive little outbuildings dot the garden, waiting to be turned into a B&B or another tool shed. A gorgeous historic barn is begging to be rebuilt to its former glory. A fully-equipped workshop and row of garages house several vintage cars and motorcycles at various stages of restoration. An empty swimming pool also needs attention.

'All my life I've been involved with Young Farmers, Federated Farmers, A&P Association, various car clubs. I've pulled back on all that sort of stuff. I'm happy just fiddling with the vehicles, going down to the Masterton Club for a beer on a Friday.'

The James family owned Wai-iti for one year shy of a century. Despite the early 'debacle', I figure Willie and Sharyn really haven't done too badly.

*

On a whim one autumn morning, not long after I'd spoken with the Jameses, I whistle up our furry fox terrier, Meg, chuck her in the car, and take a spin up the Whangaehu Valley. The narrow road snakes above the river. Copper coloured leaves flutter down from poplars and beeches. Regular signs warning '50kph Temporary' indicate the inevitable dropouts and potholes.

No pines
WAI-ITI, WHANGAEHU

There's lime on the road's edges, boulders holding up banks where they've slipped. I pass the familiar white rural mailboxes, red fire numbers nailed to their flanks.

My visit to their new home had prompted Willie to write me a list of the dozens of farms up the valley. As I drive I see Bagshot, Waratah, Ditton, Maire, and Banavie, along with some familiar Wairarapa family names. Soon on the river side of the road, I come across Te Rangi, the McKenzie farm with the significant 70 Mile Bush remnants.

A little further on, opposite, a quad bike towing a trailer full of freshly split firewood rattles over a cattle stop and pulls onto the road. I slow, and wind down the window to wave. There's a pair of fenceposts cradling a simple tin mailbox. I can't see a name on the gate but the fire number nailed to the post tells me it's Wai-iti.

An unpainted picket fence blends into railings over the cattle stop. A profusion of trees and shrubs—an ancient redwood, some agapanthus, camellias, a native or two—forms a welcoming guard of honour on the narrow driveway. The sun filters through only so far that I can see the first bend, but from what Willie and Sharyn have described I can imagine what's beyond—or should be—and hope it hasn't changed too much in the time they've been gone.

At least I know it hasn't gone into pine trees. Yet.

CHURCH WITH ONE BELL

I HAVE A QUESTION FOR RENOWNED CHURCH ARCHITECT, the late Frederick de Jersey Clere. In his otherwise small but perfectly formed St Aidan's at Alfredton, why on earth is the coffin hatch off-centre?

The pretty little white weatherboard church sits right where it was built in 1901, 100 metres or so off Route 52 on the Castle Hill Road to Tinui. It is surrounded by farm fences and paddocks on three sides and cocooned by a variety of natives and exotics. On its western side a row of oaks lean lovingly towards the building, as though wrapping their arms around it for protection from Alfredton's stiff prevailing winds. A finely wrought iron gate invites entry along the roadside from where the belfry and its decorative bell are clearly visible against the vast Tararua sky.

Heritage-listed St Aidan's was one of the last churches designed by Clere in the architectural partnership he had with

John Sydney Swan. As well as their designs together, on their own accounts both men were prolific around Wellington, and also in various collaborations elsewhere with others. Clere himself was for some time the Diocesan architect for the Anglican church and designed over 100 churches for the Episcopalians around the lower North Island, mostly of wooden construction. Ironically, his best-known church—the Roman Catholic St Mary of the Angels in Boulcott Street, Wellington—is of reinforced concrete, a building system of which he was a keen proponent. He also designed the elegant Wellington Harbour Board Wharf Office Building on the waterfront—now housing stylish apartments. Swan is known for the imposing St Gerard's Church and monastery, also of concrete and brick, which looks down on Oriental Bay. The huge Gothic building can be seen from just about anywhere in the inner city.

In days gone by, a coffin hatch was often installed in houses with upstairs bedrooms. When someone died, it was customary to leave them in an open coffin in the room where they slept, on display to be farewelled by friends and family. Where a house's staircase was very narrow, as they often were, a hatch was built into the upstairs floor through which a coffin could be lowered. The hatch might be disguised with a rug or table until it was required, but the block and tackle hanging from the ceiling usually gave the game away.

The hatch in the porch of St Aidan's is, as far as I can tell, unique. An architectural quirk at least. While there's no need for lowering a coffin at St Aidan's, the tiny entrance porch is entirely unsuitable for carrying a coffin through in to the church and back out again. Apparently, Clere and Swan's

Symmetry spoiled
ST AIDAN'S, ALFREDTON

solution was to incorporate a hatch on the front of the porch. The hatch is hinged at the bottom and opens outwards—a latch either side and a pull-knob in the middle. It looks rather like those cupboards under rural mailboxes where milk crates used to go, or perhaps the door to the food safe in pre-refrigerator, south-facing kitchens. It sits off-kilter under a narrow, perfectly-centred window.

Someone who has seen a few people travel both ways through the St Aidan's coffin hatch is former manager of nearby Te Hoe Station, Neal Hull. Neal was born at Te Hoe in 1959, a year after his parents, Fred and Margaret, took up management of the large farm owned by descendants of prominent Alfredton citizen Cecil Kebbell. You'll find Cecil's name engraved on St Aidan's foundation stone, laid on the opening of the church on 1 November 1901. (The first service was on 30 January 1902, at which his son, Cecil Mark Aidan, known as Bob, was christened.)

After Cecil died in 1938, Te Hoe had several managers in the twenty years before the Hulls took over, when by all accounts it was in pretty bad shape. 'The Kebbells basically just left Mum and Dad to it,' Neal tells me by phone from Pahiatua where he now farms with his wife, Shirley. 'They seemed quite disconnected from it really. We ran the property for thirty years like it was our own.

'They even left quite a lot of their stuff in the house—a leather-topped desk, books, paintings, and other things.' One of the items left behind by the Kebbell descendants was a portrait of Cecil in an ornate gold frame. 'It always hung in the main lounge,' Neal says. Mary's portrait was found in a cupboard.

Mystery mansion
TE HOE, ALFREDTON

The Te Hoe house is a 450 square metre, eight-bedroom concrete homestead. It was completed for Cecil and Mary Kebbell in 1924, replacing their two-storey, fourteen-room wooden home which burned down in 1918. These two events—the loss of one significant house and the completion of its equally significant replacement—made the newspapers of the time and are well documented in various archives. However, neither designer is identified. With the St Aidan's church commission being awarded to such a prominent Wellington architectural firm, and with Cecil Kebbell's involvement in that selection as a member of the planning committee, I'm curious to know if there's a connection.

Consulting my best friend Dr Google I quickly find a phone number for Sam Kebbell, a Wellington architect. Yes, Cecil was his great-grandfather but no, he really doesn't know much about the family history. Sam gives me his father Arthur's number. Arthur tells me he doesn't have a lot of Kebbell history, either, but that he was involved in winding up Cecil's estate and selling Te Hoe in 1990.

Consulting my second-best friend, the National Library of New Zealand, I find a sketch plan drawn by another prominent Wellington architect, William Gray Young. (Gray Young designed the Wellington Railway Station, among many other notable public buildings and private houses.) This plan is for a large two-storey wooden homestead such as the Kebbells lived in before losing it to the fire. It's undated but it can't have been drawn before 1913 when the Kebbells had been settled at Te Hoe for some time, because it's signed 'Wm Gray Young FNZIA'. Gray Young was elected a Fellow of the NZ Institute of Architects in that year.

After several weeks going down various rabbit holes, I deduce with the help of Te Herenga Waka School of Architecture senior lecturer, Dr Robin Skinner, that this sketch must be for a replacement of the original homestead after the 1918 fire. But it is certainly not for the single storey concrete house that was built. For some reason, then, there was a major change of tack. I put the quest aside—for now.

*

Cecil Kebbell and Mary Cameron married in 1896. Mary was the granddaughter of Donald Cameron of Pahaoa, one of Wairarapa's original settlers and runholders. The Te Hoe homestead was always bustling with a large staff and family. The garden was often used for social receptions and community gatherings. Mary herself was busy doing good deeds around the growing village and bringing up their four children—with the help of a governess, of course.

Besides his farm, Cecil's business interests included a scheme to extract coal from a local seam and sell it in Masterton. The idea was to transport coal south via a light line railway. The railway would also carry farm produce along with firewood, a by-product of milling the huge tracts of native bush still standing around this part of Route 52. The rail line was never built. (For this reason also, the planned Alfredton township with 233 sections never eventuated.)

Cecil's community mindedness saw him elected as captain of the local golf and rifle clubs and as a councillor on the Alfredton riding of the Masterton District Council. He chaired the

Domain Board responsible for the recreation ground that still exists opposite the new community centre on the edge of the settlement. He was also an inaugural member of the planning committee for St Aidan's and a significant donor of trees for the church's site. He remained on the church trust as secretary and lay reader until his death.

In 1902 Cecil resigned from the Rifle Club, saying he was 'leaving for the old country soon'. There seems to have been much to-ing and fro-ing between England and Alfredton over the next fourteen years as the children were educated at various European schools, universities, and finishing schools. The social pages of *The Dominion* newspaper record various arrivals and departures, and Mary appears to have lived quite the life—visiting friends and staying in the establishments *du jour* on Lambton Quay. By 1916 they appear to have settled back at Te Hoe not long before disaster struck; a fire razing their stately home.

*

I've driven past the block-walled entrance to the Alfredton Domain several times but until now never opened the gate. *No Dogs* says a sign on the post. Meg the foxie is not with me this time—I've brought retired architect David Kernohan instead. David is the author of *Wairarapa Buildings: Two Centuries of New Zealand Architecture[5]* and I'm hoping he can shed some light on the provenance of Te Hoe homestead. Sheep graze happily under trees along the curved gravel drive. A small carpark neighbours a simple toilet block, a lichen-covered tennis court, and a tiny portacom-style clubroom with a gas barbecue and

Sorry Meg!
DOMAIN GATE, ALFREDTON

tennis net visible through the window. A picnic table invites sitting and eating. The slotted iron box bolted and padlocked to a fence suggests a donation from campers, encouraged by the current Domain Board to make use of these simple remains of the once-thriving recreation ground. I gratefully use the loo—soap supplied—and we head back out the gate to meet Neal Hull at the Alfredton Cemetery.

Neal has good reason to return to Alfredton regularly. Since leaving Te Hoe in 1990 he's been tending to the tiny graveyard, a mere couple of acres sited a little further up the road from St Aidan's church. The late autumn sun is still low in the sky as he stands waiting beside his black ute. The lawn mower strapped to the deck of a caged trailer makes pinging noises as it cools down. We turn up the path to the cemetery, fresh grass clippings glistening with the remains of the morning's dew.

Neal is a fit looking 64-year-old with clipped grey hair. As we walk he picks off names of the friends, neighbours, and family resting quietly, overlooking peaceful forest and farmland. 'Alan and Nancy Algie, the Rollses—old names from the district. Roy Nordlof—he was killed in the sawmill down on 52, an accident. Some Smiths. My godfather, George. Napiers, Irwins—Dave and Jessie, I remember them. My godmother. Hughie Burch—a prominent stockman in the area, he was a good friend of my dad's . . .'

The gravel scrunches under our feet. We reach a family plot spanning 1988–1990. 'The Edmonds family. That's a sad lot. Brian had a heart attack, Rachel got cancer at a very young age, and Jeanine had a car accident just up the way here. All within two years.'

We walk on. 'My great uncle George. My brother and my dad—my older brother that is, Trevor. He was four, died in Masterton Hospital from nephritis just after I was born. It was bloody tough in those days. The doctor just said to Mum one day, 'You'd better go home and make another baby because this one's not going to live.' Mum's still around though, she'll be ninety-two in September. She's got her space waiting on the left there, with Dad on the right. Whether I'll end up in here I don't know—hopefully that's a few years yet.'

Neal's father, Fred, grew up in Alfredton on the family farm, Poplar Grove, and worked around the district for around fifteen years before taking on Te Hoe with Margaret in 1958. During their nearly thirty years there they made significant improvements to the Te Hoe operation, an opinion widely held and documented in the book *Alfredton: The School and The People*.[6]

In 1990, the beneficiaries of the Kebbell estate decided to sell. Fred and Margaret had left three years earlier, allowing Neal to take over in what turned out to be a short-lived management position. Te Hoe has changed hands a few times since. I've made an appointment with the current managers to take a look around Neal's old home, for David and I to try to figure out who designed it. Neal's keen to tag along.

'It's a shit of a house to live in,' Stewart Mitchell says when we pull up at the rear of his home. The remains of an ornate concrete wall head off into the distance beside a driveway. A pair of two-metre-high iron gates lie discarded against a fence. In the background, a huge shed is stacked high with firewood.

Stewart invites us in. Neal looks a bit shocked. The property is in considerably different condition than it was when he had to leave thirty-odd years ago. Time has not treated his old home well. But he agrees with Stewart, the house was very cold. 'Moisture would run down this wallpaper here,' he says excitedly as he recognises the wall coverings still there from his time. 'As kids we'd play in this corridor here but if we brushed the wall, we'd have to change our pyjamas—it was that wet.' He also recognises the alcove in the kitchen where at one point the Hulls decided to put a ranch slider door in an exterior wall. When they went to cut through the concrete, they discovered there were in fact two concrete walls going straight into the ground with a cavity between them, and that the reinforcement was by way of '#8' fencing wire. 'But hey, it's gone through a lot of earthquakes,' Neal says. 'It used to shake like hell but it's still here.'

David and I wander around inside while Neal and Stewart talk septic tanks (there wasn't one when they first arrived, Neal says—the waste just went over the bank). This house isn't what I had visualised either. Apart from a very large living room with a huge but surprisingly plain fireplace, the rooms and corridors are quite poky and dark, not what you'd expect in a grand mansion. The concrete utilised in building the house isn't great quality either, David says, not surprised to learn that the aggregate came from the stream running through the property. He wonders whether anyone actually designed this house, or if it was a DIY job.

Walking around outside, it starts to make more sense architecturally. There's a lovely Palladian symmetry to the main part of the building. The decorative entrance portico has obviously been thought through, as has a large sun porch on the opposite wall. The accommodation wing which runs off at right-angles does so logically and cleanly. The soffits are generous and consistent. And the garden retains its elegance, hinting at generous society garden parties and hide-and-seek games and Easter egg hunts for generations of children. It's a beautiful setting and the property certainly has kerb appeal, but we still have no clues as to who designed it.

Stewart and Neal have a great time comparing notes about the farm—the trout-filled stream, the deer that were captured by helicopter, the hectares of remnant bush up on the hills. Stewart and his wife, Carla, have been here sixteen years and are at the point where they need to make some decisions. Their four kids have all been through the local Alfredton School and then on to college in Pahiatua. The farm is going well. They love the community and don't want to move on. But the century-old house badly needs attention. We all agree they have a quandary on their hands.

Back at home I email some photographs of the house to Robin Skinner. I get a quick reply. 'It has an elegance I associate with Gray Young,' he says. 'But that's not conclusive'. Thinking that Cecil Kebbell decided against another wooden house—perhaps he didn't want to risk a repeat of the fire—and asked Gray Young to design something in concrete, I head back to my research. But there is no record of the house I've just seen anywhere in the National Library's extensive Gray Young archive (I know this because I trawled all 1,036 items). I give up.

Until the next day.

I drive up to Masterton and stand tapping my toes outside the Wairarapa Archive until it opens at 1pm. One last search. Nothing under Gray Young. Nothing I haven't already found under Kebbell or Te Hoe. Nothing under the names of the 'well-known contractors Kerr & Thompson' who I've seen credited with completing the house in 1924. In desperation I ask the archivist to dig out a folder labelled *Research North Wairarapa*. My very last shot.

The folder contains dozens of random newspaper clippings of unconnected events and news items around Mauriceville, Whangaehu, Bideford . . . and a large Wrightson Real Estate notice on page twelve of the *Wairarapa Times-Age*, Saturday 17 February 1990. It's for the upcoming auction of Te Hoe on behalf of the estate of C Kebbell. There's a small black-and-white picture of the house. There's a lot of text with stock rates, pasture and fertiliser details, description of the community and climate, and the following sentence: 'Principal building is a substantial Homestead designed by Heathcote Helmore, built in 1924 and set in attractive grounds which include fine deciduous and English trees.'

'Well, well,' says David Kernohan.

'Terrific!' says Robin Skinner.

'Phew,' I sigh.

Heathcote Helmore was a prominent Canterbury architect who was known for designing grand country houses, including Fernside on the edge of Featherston (coincidentally—or not—also in 1924). Somewhat incongruously he was Aide de Camp for various Governors General between the World Wars, as early as 1917 it seems. He is known to have designed another couple of houses built around Wairarapa.

Helmore was no doubt on the Wellington social circuit, plying his Government House side-hustle organising important engagements and accommodation for visitors such as Eleanor Roosevelt and Lord Mountbatten. There are screeds of records in the National Library, but I'm not going down another twisty warren. Instead, I draw myself an image of Cecil and Mary Kebbell being introduced to Helmore in the dining room of the Midland Hotel, discovering his architectural credentials, and commissioning him to build them a new—concrete—house. I might be miles off the mark, but for now that'll have to do.

*

St Aidan's Anglican Church is one of the very few public structures surviving from Alfredton's pioneering days. When Cecil Kebbell trowelled in the church's foundation stone in 1901, the settlement—originally called Moroa—boasted a hotel, blacksmith, recreation ground, two general stores, a school, town hall, bakery, butcher, saddlery, and a post and telegraph office that, according to an observer at the time, was 'an elegant production of the architect's art'. (The same could very much be said for St Aidan's. Apart from the off-centre coffin hatch.) Several flax mills operated around the village, including one on the Te Hoe property.

I'm standing with Neal Hull at the intersection of Route 52 and Castle Hill Road. It's almost the winter solstice and already the midday sun is threatening to dip behind the hills. A ute swooshes by, trailer rattling. A magpie squawks on a nearby branch. We're on the site of the Alfredton Store. 'As a kid I watched the store burn down,' says Neal. 'And later, the hall, just along the road there. Both electrical fires.'

What's left
MAIN ROAD, ALFREDTON

Nearby, there's a bloke brushing some paint on a house—it used to be the post office. The pub and the blacksmith were over the road, and a boarding house. The school along the road a bit, now with the shiny new hall.

'It was a bit sad in there,' Neal says, referring to our visit to Te Hoe. 'Dad did such a service to the Kebbell family. But we had a good life. Things move on. Mum and Dad retired out of there. It was nice to make the connection with Stewart just now, I might catch up with him again.'

As Neal drives off, I look back up at St Aidan's. I imagine Fred and Margaret with a three-month-old baby in their arms, saying goodbye to his big brother. The small church is over-flowing. There are flowers, hymns, tears. Trevor's little casket is carried down the aisle, into the tiny porch, and gently passed out through the wonky hatch.

THE OUTLOOK FOR TUESDAY

FARMERS THROUGHOUT HUMAN HISTORY HAVE started their days with a cuppa, then pulled on their boots and oilskin and gone out to check the rain gauge. For many, the humblest of instruments would suffice—a glass jar, a clay pot, a tin bowl. Tied to a fence post, wired to a waratah, or just plonked between the parsley and peppermint in the herb garden.

In its simplest form a rain gauge provides an indication of the precipitation fallen in that location since the last time it was emptied (allowing of course for evaporation, and birds and spiders drinking it). Measuring the gauge's contents and keeping regular records allows graziers and horticulturalists to predict soil conditions and how well their grass or crop will grow. Accurate records reveal a pattern over time. This pattern will eventually lead to the ability to forecast what the rainfall is likely to be at some point in the future.

Since the late 1800s both the Meteorological Service of New Zealand (MetService) and the National Institute of Water and Atmospheric Research (NIWA) have kept detailed rainfall records across thousands of Aotearoa farms. Standardised collection and measurement instruments are issued to volunteer farmers around the country who record their results and report them regularly. At one time there were over 2,500 involved; today there are still at least 250.

Someone once responsible for making sure these official instruments maintained their accuracy is former weather communications adviser Cameron Coutts, recently retired from MetService after forty-seven years—the company's longest-serving employee. Back in the 1970s and '80s Cam travelled the length and breadth of Route 52, and beyond, with a micrometer in his pocket. He was checking for any change in the shape of the collection vessel as well as for leaks and obstructions—anything that would render the gauge inaccurate.

Originally from Northland, Cam started at MetService in Wellington in 1974. 'I was hired to go out and look at the weather,' he tells me as we sit at the dining table in his Greytown home. 'I worked at airports and in the main cities, too. I was called an Observer.' There were very few forecasters in those days, he says, and the Observers did all the donkey work, plotting weather maps by hand, using red and black pens. As well as the information they obtained themselves, they used data which was phoned, telegrammed, and radioed in by people from manual weather stations all over the country.

'I remember visiting a farmer at Pōrangahau who not only phoned in daily with his observation on the weather, but also on the sea state.' That volunteer's weather station was replaced some time ago by an automatic one at Cape Turnagain.

When Cam wasn't out and about on Tararua or Central Hawke's Bay farms, or observing wind shear at Palmerston North Airport, he reported for work at the new MetService building in Kelburn. The eye-catching building, completed in 1968, sits on the crest of Salamanca Road—that carriageway that curves its way up from the apex of The Terrace, nudging Kelburn Park and the university, dipping under the cable car track. A narrow access road—now part of Te Araroa Trail—climbs further to the MetService building and leads on to the Carter and Dominion Observatories as it curls into the Wellington Botanic Garden.

The Botanic Garden is twenty-five hectares of native and exotic trees, esoteric plant collections, and seasonal flower displays running between Kelburn and Thorndon. For kids growing up around there in the 1960s, it was the local playground. If my younger brother Chris and I didn't catch a trolleybus to Kelburn Normal School from our home in Tinakori Road, we'd happily walk through 'the gardens'. Several steep gravel paths led to the swings and slides in the hilly clearing at the centre—a regular diversion. Later, our scooters and skateboards plied the sealed walkways. Poking around the bush-flanked stream running down from the bottom of Glen Road, we'd find small koura crawling around the jagged carbon-coloured river stones. From the heights of the Salamanca Tennis Club, slippery slopes plummeted to the Lady Norwood Rose Garden and Begonia House, perfect for the trolleys we built using pram wheels and apple boxes. Many a grass-burned knee or forehead was dressed by our mother after one of us had come a cropper.

55

Around the observatories there were other adventures to be had. From the World War One-era Krupp gun or old Kelburn Scout Hall we'd watch the weather balloons drift skywards as they were launched from the original Meteorological Office building. Later there were pop concerts by The Avengers or Tom Thumb down at The Soundshell, and Summer City festivals in The Dell featuring circus acts, mask theatre, and gamelan orchestras.

*

The new MetService building on Salamanca Road was designed by Wellington architect Bill Alington while he worked at the Ministry of Works. Alington started with MoW as an architectural cadet in 1949 before completing his university studies in Auckland in 1955. He returned very briefly to the MoW—where he designed the stunning, mushroom-like Bulls water tower— before heading overseas for the remainder of the decade to study and work. Re-joining the MoW with a Master of Architecture from the University of Illinois, he created a variety of highly regarded public buildings before going into private practice in 1965. His own family home in nearby Karori, self-built in 1962, is deemed a 'Modernist masterpiece' (a term annoyingly misused by a legion of real estate agents) and is Category 1 listed by Heritage New Zealand Pouhere Taonga.

The MetService building is in the Brutalist design style, characterised by bold forms using rough-cast concrete. Derided by some as, well, brutal, the Brutalist period overlapped the international Modernist movement and has a large following of architecture enthusiasts. (Waipukurau's Civic Theatre building, mentioned elsewhere in this book, is another example.) While not currently listed, Heritage NZ has indicated the building would be seriously considered if an application was made.

The MetService forecasters, observers, and technicians occupied the over-sized storey that sits like a mortarboard hat atop three lower office floors. Dozens of vertical concrete fins set a couple of metres from the panoramic windows were designed to control sunlight coming into the office. A floor and a roof supporting these fins created an informal exterior walkway which harboured some of the building's services. Cam Coutts told me it was possible to get onto what was no more than a ledge, high above the carpark and free of railings or restraints, through the windows. 'I walked around there sometimes. One of my colleagues used to feed a seagull. He'd bring mice in, and the seagull would somehow fly between the fins and land on the window ledge.' It didn't take long before the reinforcing iron inside the wafer-thin fins began to rust, and the fins were removed. 'One of the scientists took them to Eastbourne to build retaining walls.'

In January 2021 a 'request for proposal' was issued on the Government Electronic Tender Service (GETS) for an office upgrade for the MetService building. Since then, the project has been deemed 'no longer feasible with the proposed design' and put on hold 'indefinitely'. Cam says the building, especially the top floor, is not particularly well suited to modern forecasting, and I'm guessing that with everything so connected and automatic these days—no more balloon launching required—the office's top-of-the-world site is not especially important either.

MetService moved out of the earthquake-compromised building in January 2022 and is currently located in the Wellington CBD. The building's offices are advertised for lease. It seems likely the weather gurus won't return to Salamanca Road.

*

In the Wairarapa house I share with my wife, Pip, there's a painting my father Ron did of my mother, Jacquie. The scene is the sitting room of our little family home at 240 Tinakori Road. It's not dated but I'm going to say it was painted around 1960. Mum is sitting in a faded teal armchair wearing a pink top. Her trousered legs are crossed, right over left. She's reading a book. The dining table next to her is covered by a blue cloth on which a china teapot and an enamel jug holding a large bunch of pink and ochre flowers are sitting. The shadows on the tablecloth suggest a sunny day, the light filtering through a gauze net on the window behind. At Mum's left elbow a bookcase supports a large wedge-shaped wooden radio.

I remember the crackle of that radio as it warmed up. The rich, full sound from its eight-inch speaker. The glow of its vacuum tubes. The sweet smell of electronic heat. I recall Chris and I sitting before it on Sunday mornings to listen to 'Little Toot' or 'Diana and the Golden Apples' on 2YA. In the evenings 2YC would play a Brahms symphony maybe, or Miles Davis' 'Kind of Blue'.

The wooden radio met its demise at the same time as our father; it was purely ornamental by then anyway as Dad had embraced the transistor age. The old thing may still have worked but it was full of borer so met an undignified end in the Happy Valley Landfill. It had, though, prompted a lifetime of National and Concert Programme radio listening for me.

One of MetService's roles is providing weather forecasts for Radio New Zealand, now known in this initialism-mad world as RNZ. (I recall the old Marriage Guidance service being rebranded 'MG'. I mean, WTF?) My regular nocturnal traipses to the bathroom often coincide with the 4.05am coastal forecast on RNZ National's All Night programme. Vicki McKay or Peter McIlwaine dutifully announces the interminably lengthy script, almost incomprehensible to a landlubber but great for getting back to sleep. The oft-lamented retired presenter Lloyd Scott somehow made it a bit more playful (as he did with most things), worth sticking with despite it being completely irrelevant unless you were a mariner or considering making—or anxious about—a Cook Strait ferry booking.

What RNZ call the 'short forecasts' are broadcast with the hourly news. Regional forecasts are presented twice every early morning. You can hear the main centre and urban forecasts in the mornings, long-range forecasts at the middle of the day, and the mountain forecast at 4.05pm.

As I've listened to the various forecasts during the day and night over recent years, it's often struck me as odd that the Tararua District—through which a large part of Route 52 runs—is sometimes mentioned, sometimes not. And when it is, it's always like this: 'Wairarapa including the Tararua District' or 'Wairarapa excluding the Tararua District'. Before 2006 it was never mentioned at all, leaving Tararua listeners scratching their heads as to whether they should believe the forecast for their neighbour to the north—Hawke's Bay—or to the south—Wairarapa—or indeed to the west—Manawatū. In 2006, petitioned by frustrated locals, a delegation of Tararua area officials convinced MetService to consider forecasting for Tararua separately.

Tararua District is technically part of the Manawatū-Whanganui region (apparently this is because the Manawatū River headwaters are within the district). However, geographically and climatologically, Tararua is more akin to the Wairarapa region, although the way the Tararua and Ruahine range stoop around the Manawatū Gorge, Tararua is more exposed to weather from the west than the rest of Wairarapa is. Hence some forecasts include Tararua and others don't. 'The Wairarapa forecast doesn't have to mention the Tararua District if it's not significantly different,' Cam tells me. 'In other words, if we think it's going to be fine everywhere it'll just say "Wairarapa, fine".' It's the only district in Aotearoa which is treated like this.

*

Pondering his career in the weather business, Cam Coutts says it held his interest for all the time he spent there, including periods living in the Kermadecs and on the Chatham Islands. He says it was a very social place to work, with good people and little disagreement. It was noisy. It was the young people's workspace, he says. 'Communication around the office was by Lamson pneumatic tube—it was always fun sending the capsules shooting downstairs.'

Cam says he's not a meteorologist as such, he just worked his way through the system. 'I probably could've been a proper forecaster—there were a couple of courses available early on but I wasn't brave enough to have a go at them. Unfortunately, though, the future's not looking too bright. The carbon is definitely having an effect. My generation, we've seen the best of things.'

Pip and I live on an eastern hill outside Carterton where it's known in farming parlance to be 'summer dry'—we can often stand outside, coatless, watching showers and squalls swirl around us, dumping their watery contents on distant hills and nearby flats. But being on top of the peak means we cop all the wind—it can be dead calm in the village while the Hills Hoist is spinning our laundry to tatters.

'Forecasting still relies on local knowledge and you don't get that sitting in an office,' Cam says. From that I initially understand he's referring to the farmers and their rain gauges and his own observations from cities and airports. But as I'm driving out of Greytown towards home, I ponder something else. He also said that forecasters rely on us, as users, to apply our own local knowledge to their work. To adjust their predictions in our minds using our real-world experience. To fill in their gaps, as it were. I think—weather forecasting as philosophy? As collaborative art? As architecture?

When the plastic rain gauges nailed to fence posts on our driveway finally submit to the sun's rays and splinter to the ground, it takes me a year or two to replace them. Other than determining how often I have to mow the lawns, rainfall is no longer of any practical consequence. There's a community stockwater scheme for the paddocks we now lease to the neighbouring (proper) farmers. Our boys are long fledged so it's only a shower and a bath a day in the empty nest. The oaks and laurel hedges can fend for themselves after twenty-odd years. We don't garden. We have lots of roof; the concrete tanks are almost always close to full.

And anyway, as that ubiquitous 'someone' once said, if you want to know what the weather's like, just look out the window.

SOLDIERS IN MONOCHROME

A T THE CENTRE OF THE TINY VILLAGE OF PONGAROA, halfway along Route 52, four roads meet at the point where a stack of three sculpted boulders sits. The boulders are connected by a pattern of intersecting grooves representing the structure of DNA—the basis of all life. Apparently, the sculpture tends to crack in a frost when water in the grooves expands into ice. (Thankfully Pongaroa doesn't get a lot of frosts.)

The sculpture is a memorial to scientist Maurice Wilkins, who in 1962 shared a Nobel Prize for the discovery of DNA's foundation—the double helix. Wilkins was born in Pongaroa in 1916, son of the local doctor. His family moved to nearby Pahiatua, then to Wellington, while Maurice was still an infant, and by the time he was six they were living in England. Wilkins never set foot in Aotearoa again, but his memorial stands at the crossroads as a reminder that little towns like this have unique character. Their own DNA, you might say.

Double helix
WILKINS MEMORIAL, PONGAROA

I come to Pongaroa from the opposite direction. Born in England and having grown up between London and Wellington, I've lived the last two decades in a rambling old house on a dead-end rural road, a few miles from the small Wairarapa township of Carterton. Small places appeal to me. They seem at face value to be altogether less complicated than big cities. They're not, of course; sometimes the nuances of living closely with other people can amplify our differences and make relationships tricky.

Pongaroa (meaning 'tall tree fern') came to be in the late 1800s when a large part of the lower North Island was cleared of its native bush. The huge tracts of dense forest presented a challenge for the teams of mainly Scandinavian loggers with their energy-sapping two-man saws and simple axes. Clearing the bush created pasture for grazing sheep and cattle, while the tall, arrow-straight trees were perfect for building material. For a time a large timber mill was the centrepiece of Pongaroa, processing masses of mataī, tōtara, rimu, and rātā. 40 Mile Bush, as it was then known, was part of the mass of land acquired from the Rangitāne iwi in 1871. Its clearance was the largest in the colonial history of Aotearoa.

When I've passed through Pongaroa over the years it's always felt vacant, as if its residents were avoiding each other. There seemed little reason to turn off the engine except to use the public toilets or buy a limp-looking pie from the corner store, if it was open. This time, however, I'm stopping for a couple of nights, hoping to find out what makes this miniscule, isolated place tick.

I collect instructions from the corner store's efficient new owners and tow my little yellow caravan around to the Pongaroa

Domain. There are a handful of elevated camping sites under some gnarly old macrocarpas. They all back on to attractive farmland and face east over the nearby school and houses. The sites are right in the path of the prevailing northwest wind (Pongaroa is known for being very windy, which is why it doesn't get many frosts). I choose the most sheltered one and leave the caravan to head back to town.

*

The Pongaroa Hotel sits prominently in the middle of the main street and, as in most small towns, it's the social hub. The hotel's signature dish is Mrs Monk's seafood chowder and the kitchen ladles up generous bowls for hungry shearers, farmers, retirees, and a nosey outsider. The Tuesday night conversation is lively. Next to me, local kaumātua Wright Broughton fills a seven-ounce glass from a quart bottle of the local brew. 'I'm just in for one,' he says with a twinkle. Word has got around that a stranger has blown into town to talk about trees. That's not entirely the case, but I'm happy to oblige. 'Huge farms covered in carbon sink,' says Wright. 'It's really becoming an issue out here.'

The New Zealand Emissions Trading Scheme is the Government's main tool for reducing greenhouse gas emissions. Participants in the scheme plant large numbers of trees, predominantly pines, which remove carbon from the atmosphere and store it. This process, called sequestration, earns the participants carbon credits which are sold to industries, including agriculture, to offset their own CO_2 emissions. What's become known as 'carbon farming' is now more popular than traditional forestry due to hugely superior returns. Its rapid escalation is highly contentious and was very noticeable as I drove in to Pongaroa this afternoon.

The consensus among my pub companions seems to be that carbon farming is tempting generational sheep farmers off Pongaroa's good, productive land. Those who have already sold to the foresters claim they had no choice; the wealthy companies will always pay above the odds. If they sold to another cockie the chances are that land would be on-sold for trees anyway, and for a decent profit. Others reckon the widespread planting is spoiling the countryside for the tourists, that the once scenic roads are becoming shady, slippery, gloomy. The ETS is a cancer, they say between spoonfuls of fishy soup.

Back at the campsite, I screw the caravan's parking legs down hard enough to make the night comfortable. No other camper has arrived in my absence so I'm alone, feeling slightly vulnerable under the groaning conifers. As my two-wheeled accommodation shakes and shudders in the wind, I wonder why everyone at the pub assumed I'm here to talk about carbon farming. They know I'm here to write something, but do I look like a raging tree-hugger? Does every stranger ask about the trees? Or is the subject simply top of mind at the moment?

*

Trees can certainly cause trouble. When Pip and I bought our house, Cannon Heath, it had recently arrived in five pieces from Dannevirke and was sitting all alone in the middle of a ten-acre paddock on top of a ridge. No driveway, no electricity,

Could be tidier
UNDER THE TREES, PONGAROA DOMAIN

no water, no close neighbours, no fences—and no trees. When we established the long curvy drive, we artfully grouped turkey oaks on each side, hoping to create interesting vistas of surrounding farmland and distant hills. We foraged common oak seedlings and dotted them around to provide shade and further interest. We formed hedges alongside paths and around lawns and parking areas with hundreds of young cherry laurels ('Ooh, you're brave,' a friend's green-fingered mother said, a remark I recall every time I get the hedge trimmer out). With naive ambition, we planted a small orchard of heritage fruit trees. When it became clear we would soon have a construction site next door, a double row of fast-growing Leyland cypress was employed to provide a bit of privacy.

Back then we had views to all four corners, plus the bits in between. We could see the glistening waters of Lake Wairarapa and the blinking of headlights coming over the Remutaka road. I liked to look at the way the eastern hills have been shaped over millennia by the wind. My favourite view was of the Ruamāhanga River winding down the valley and dipping under the Kokotau Bridge.

Twenty years on our planting, and that of the increasing number of neighbours, has matured. We've lost sight of the river. The lake and the hill road have disappeared, too. The driveway oaks now obscure the gentle slopes of Tiffin Hill as well as the distant, craggy Mount Bruce and lopsided Rangitūmau. The methodically selected orchard trees are now unidentifiable, badly pruned, and rarely harvested. The common oaks have grown all over each other and cast a pall of shade over the barn. The cypresses do their job brilliantly—they're known in the nursery trade as 'neighbour-blockers'—but require specialist annual trimming at considerable expense. They also obscure the last of our midsummer sun, and some of our neighbours' view to the north.

All around us, eager beavers move onto subdivided lots and plant trees. Lots of trees. No doubt they have good intentions as we largely did, but perhaps, like us, not much thought for what impact their planting will have on other people or themselves in the future.

Maybe the carbon farmers around Pongaroa are also well intentioned—after all, we are in the middle of a climate crisis. But all I saw as I drove into the village was vast swathes of dark green. I could feel them sucking the life out of the soil, and now I'm learning that they're sucking the life from the community, too.

*

Wright Broughton and his wife, Anne, have lived in the same unassuming brown-and-white cottage a short walk from the Domain for more than forty years. The house was once the transport office for the trucking firm Wright drove for; where Anne did paperwork and answered phones. Wright was born in Pongaroa; Anne came here when she was five. They married fifty years ago, when he was twenty-nine and she was seventeen. 'All my dad said was, "do you love him?"' Anne recalls.

I'm enjoying tea and wedding anniversary cake with them at their kitchen table. They make an attractive couple and are easy in each other's company. They say they've had good lives in Pongaroa, that the smallness, the sense of community, suits them. Wright is now retired as both a JP and marriage celebrant, but still does the occasional funeral for friends.

Wright is kaitiaki of the land of his hapū here. His responsibility stretches along the coast from the Whareama River, south of Castlepoint, to Poroporo, north—past Cape Turnagain. He grew up around Owāhanga Station, which runs down to the South Pacific Ocean for twenty-three kilometres along this part of the coast. He recalls a happy, carefree childhood being raised by his grandmother and aunt, among nine siblings and generations of family. His memories are of a red whare with sacking bunks, and as much koura as you could eat. There was a school at Owāhanga then, one of around ten in the area when Wright was a 'primmer' in 1947. Anne drives a school bus, as she has for the past forty-odd years, which collects kids from the road to the station, past the station to Akitio, and on into Pongaroa village for their schooling.

Wright's father, Ronald Matai Broughton, arrived at Owāhanga during the Great Depression of the 1930s. He came from Levin to join the gangs of men cutting scrub and mānuka, clearing the land for livestock. (Now, a century later, mānuka has been replanted for honey production.) His mother, Tangimoana Pōtangaroa, was born at Owāhanga on 13 February 1913, six weeks after her father, Hamuera, drowned at the mouth of the river after which the station is named. Tangimoana means 'weeping sea'.

Wright is still intimately connected to Owāhanga Station and its two marae, Pāpāuma and Owāhanga. He's on the management committees and was chairman for a year before realising his inability to speak Māori was a hindrance. 'Mum died when I was twenty,' Wright says. 'I suppose you could say I went a bit wild. I never learned te reo Māori. I couldn't express my ideas to the marae committees the way they wanted me to. It's better now. Those who can speak the language run things well.'

One of the decisions the station's owners have had to make recently is whether or not to join the carbon farming club. Wright says he doesn't have a problem with pines being planted on marginal farmland—areas where stock don't thrive, or which are hard to manage. But he's seen farms where they've been planted all through the wetlands and springs. 'The wetlands are dead once you've planted pine trees through them,' he says. After previous poor returns from trees harvested for logs, Owāhanga now has 140 hectares in pines for carbon credits. For the station's shareholders, the potential payout was too good to resist.

*

Pongaroa grew rapidly before the nineteenth century ended, with the expectation that the planned Masterton-Napier railway would run through it. When the line was cut through Pahiatua instead, Pongaroa suffered an exodus. In 1976 there was further depopulation when it lost its status as administrative centre for Akitio County as the county was assimilated into Dannevirke. (Wright Broughton was a clerk in the Akitio County office when it closed.) At the same time, sinking farm returns and the advent of the four-wheeled motorcycle forced workers (and their horses) away. By 2018 the official population of Pongaroa village was eighty-one.

Considering its apparently dwindling population, the village has maintained surprisingly good infrastructure. So far I have counted one electrician, three joiners, at least three builders, and several farm contractors. Community services include the primary school and its neighbouring early learning centre, the squash and rugby clubs, a craft group, volunteer ambulance and fire stations, a substantial hall and library, and the motorhome camping at the Domain.

The main street accommodates a pub, a seven-day corner store with café and takeaway, a community-owned self-service fuel station, and a very busy farm supplies centre. But all these services are being supported by a declining number of rural dwellers—something that worries Heather and David Monk.

The Monks have been living in the Pongaroa district since the year before the Broughtons were married. The farm they bought became victim in the 1980s to massive interest rates, droughts, a failed business partnership, and the removal of farm subsidies. They now live in a neat, green-roofed house behind the village's community centre, a monument to home maintenance in a street of houses badly in need of a lick of paint.

The Monks operate a farm contracting business and have a council contract to mow the town's grass and look after the public restrooms. David has a large shed full of machinery and is known to be able to fix anything. Heather is the village busy bee, volunteering on every committee, and serving her seafood chowder at the pub. For some time she was the area's sole ambulance officer. They both care deeply for Pongaroa and worry that a visitor in fifty years might find it abandoned. Because of the pines, they say.

'I hear you want to talk about trees,' David says as we meet at their gate. I've actually come to talk to Heather, because every time I ask someone a question about Pongaroa they say, 'Ask Heather Monk.' I'm in town to research a magazine article about Pongaroa and it seems I will get a lot of information from one interview with Heather. Clearly David has got the same memo as the folk in the pub and is keen to talk, too.

While their perfectly behaved grandson entertains himself with toys on the carpet, David explains that everyone in Pongaroa, whether retired in the village or working out on the tractors, is involved in farming one way or another. 'Everything—the pub, the store, the fuel station—is here because of the sheep and cattle,' he says. But the community is shrinking because the carbon farmers, as predominantly absentee owners, aren't involving themselves in it.

On a practical level, the problem is that pine trees don't need as many humans to tend them as animals do. But as both the Broughtons and the Monks see it, there's also a demographic issue. They say the companies buying up the farms are slicing off the homesteads with a couple of manageable acres then selling them to city folk looking for the rural idyll with a paddock for the pony. These people typically keep to themselves, school their kids elsewhere, and don't last long there. Putting her civil defence hat on, Heather Monk worries that the newcomers' lack of community involvement creates a safety issue, too, because they're not easily contactable in an emergency.

I've been hanging around the village doing a lot of listening for a couple of days now, and I've concluded that the Monks' opinion about carbon farming is the prevailing one. Everyone's been eager to talk about it, and no one has offered an opposing view. The forest workers are a nice enough bunch of guys, they all say, but soon Pongaroa will be nothing but bloody pine trees.

*

At the northern edge of Pongaroa village, Urupā Road snakes through remnant native bush up the hill to the cemetery. From among the headstones, the expansive view sets the village firmly in its surroundings, making the settlement look as small as it feels when you're down there. The brooding shadow of the Puketoi Range inland contrasts with an airy light-filled vista towards Owāhanga and the coast. Next to the cemetery, elegant Akaroa Peak stands guard over the district's deceased and, for a century, a quarry near its summit provided material for Pongaroa's life-giving roads—those four branches forming the crossroads where Maurice Wilkins' DNA memorial stands.

Pongaroa is now at a figurative crossroads as well as a physical one. The Broughtons have neighbours they've never met. Heather Monk notes the ageing population: 'It's a retirement village!' The pub owners are looking to move on. There is chatter of new gang presence (it didn't eventuate). And the burgeoning carbon farms, with their off-site corporate owners, creep ever closer.

I won't be around in fifty years to see if the Monks' fears have been realised—that Pongaroa has emptied out. The odd new house is being built and old one renovated. A couple of disused commercial buildings are being rescued, optimistically, for tourist retail. The publicans say there's a growing number of groups stopping for lunch, commonly motoring enthusiasts

Never ending green
INFANT PINES, ROUTE 52

enjoying the curvy Route 52 roads. But it's all pretty small change in the scheme of things, and my short time here has revealed an underlying unease I wasn't expecting.

I'm leaving Pongaroa, heading south from the Domain, past the farm supply store and the pub, the DNA memorial and the fuel station, the former maternity hospital, Dr Wilkins' house, up a long, gentle hill. The road here is open and light. A new cell phone tower glints in the sun.

Soon enough it closes in, becoming twisty and dark. As I drive over them, copper pine needles flick up and waft through slithers of light piercing the branches above. Emerging from the gloom I'm greeted by thousands of small green blobs dotting a lifeless landscape.

Further along, where I recall a road previously surrounded by verdant paddocks dotted with fluffy white sheep, I now drive through a mass of murky dark green. Small stands of natives are menacingly hovered over by sticky, prickly pines. Signs clipped to now-redundant fences warn *Strictly No Hunting!* and *Motion Sensor Cameras Installed!* As far as I can see are trees, thousands of rows of trees. Soldiers in monochrome on the march.

Before my visit to Pongaroa I knew the trees were a problem, but not how much of a problem, or even, really, what the problem was. People's readiness—eagerness—to talk about it lingered in my thoughts on the journey home. What will their village look like in five years? I wondered. Let alone fifty. Will the pub still be open for chowder and beer? Will travellers park up at the Domain, look at the cracked Wilkins memorial, buy a pie and some petrol? Will kids still be bussed in from the coast to go to school? Will there even be a school?

Arriving home, manoeuvring the caravan through the gate, dodging the low-hanging oaks down to the shaded barn, I make a commitment to find out more, to talk, to read. But first I have grass to mow, hedges to trim, rotting fruit to pick up, and trees to prune.

Lots of trees. Seemingly forever.

COLOUR CODE

HEADING NORTH ON ROUTE 52 OUT OF PONGAROA you'll pass the early learning centre—now shut down— to the left, and the community hall with recycling facilities to the right. Kids might splash and chatter in the school swimming pool. Perhaps a police car enters the station, which is hidden up a concrete drive behind a group of twisty cypresses. If you're lucky, a simple white wooden church might show a bit of itself through a couple of wild oaks.

Steer through a gently sweeping bend and a softly colourful sight will reveal itself—four houses almost alone in a linear clump. State houses, each slightly different, and each a pastel hue—powder blue, quiet lilac, two-tone green, an orangey yellow—sitting proudly together, saying 'look at us, aren't we pretty?'

Pretty in pink
STATE HOUSES, PONGAROA

Greeting me under the iron-roofed carport at the side of the lilac house is four-year-old Demi Bassett. She's bright as a button—dark curls falling from her face, inquisitive brown eyes. Demi spends her weekdays here in the care of 'Nanny' Laura Bassett while her dad, Kelvin, works. A shearer, Kelvin lives on River Road near Waione and works around the district. He drops Demi off here every morning at 6am; she's usually still asleep. If she wakes, she'll join the Pongaroa School bus run which Laura drives, collecting children from farms in the Puketoi range. Since the Early Years preschool closed earlier in the year, Demi spends the full day with Laura. Kelvin will collect her when he's finished in the sheds.

Laura comes to the door; she's expecting me but I'm a little early. 'Oh, I was just coming out for a quick smoke,' she giggles. The smell of baking scones wafts from the kitchen as Laura ushers me in, foregoing, for now, her mid-morning roll-up. Demi follows and finds a puzzle to play with on the sitting room carpet. Laura plugs in the jug and checks the scones while I settle at the sunny kitchen table, gazing through gauze curtains to the green house next door.

Laura has lived in this house with her husband Bill for fifty-two years. They met in a woolshed in Akitio—he a shearer, she a young rouseabout. When Laura was eighteen and Bill twenty-two, they married and moved into a local farm cottage. The couple worked the shearing seasons together across both islands for a year or so. Then, expecting their first child, they began renting this Housing Corporation home at 1B Tui Street. In those days the house was blue.

In 1995, through an act of community generosity and during a period when state house renters were being offered the chance, the Bassetts were able to buy what Laura calls their 'forever home'.

*

Laura was born in 1952, two years before this forever home and its three siblings appeared on Tui Street.[i] Coincidentally, Laura grew up as a Tui—Laura Ihaia Tui—but dropped the 'Tui' when at school. 'I'm not sure why I did that,' she says, checking the scones again. 'It was probably because we had to drive past that blasted Tui brewery every day on the way to school.'

The school bus passed the brewery heading to Pahiatua from the cottage Laura spent the first eight years of her life in on family land at Ruawhata, just the other side of Mangatainoka. Her father, Joseph Tui, was a casual farm worker around the district—shearing, fencing, cutting scrub. Towards the end of the family's time there, Laura's mother, Ngarongo Ihaia— known as 'Lovey'—was hospitalised in Masterton. She had tuberculosis. When she was discharged, the Health Department found the family a Housing Corporation home in Wilson Street, Pahiatua. (I took a drive there one day to find around thirty houses in the sunny cul-de-sac pretty much the same as they must have been then—a little time capsule of state care and innocence.)

---

i   Local wisdom is the Tui Street houses were built in 1951,
    but my research says otherwise.

'There were seven of us kids when we moved to Wilson Street,' Laura remembers. 'It was a three-bedroom house. We were so excited to have a flush toilet—it was just a long-drop on the farm.' It was a very busy home. Although some of Laura's total of eleven siblings were 'whāngaied out', other children were sometimes whāngaied in. Grandchildren came and went, too, and Ngarongo was kept on her toes. 'All her days. She always had someone there to look after.'

Laura remembers some big families on Wilson Street, and thinks they were just the second Māori family to move in there. 'It was cool,' she says. 'Everyone mixed in. Us kids would all walk to school together, get out to play on the street, go roaming over the hills—mushrooming, eeling, picking watercress. Swimming under the bridge. All of us.

'Even to this day, if we bump into someone from Wilson Street we always stop and have a chat about it. I've got great memories of growing up there. It was like here when our kids were growing up, with all the nannies—big families. The kids would be in and out of each other's homes, these four houses, just like a big marae.'

Laura's parents paid rent at 25 Wilson Street for the rest of their lives. Ngarongo died in 1989, Joe in 1996.

*

New Zealand's state housing initiative is commonly thought to have begun in 1937 with a house built at 12 Fife Lane, Strathmore, Wellington, the first house in what was called the Miramar Subdivision. The Fife Lane house now has a protection order on it and was re-purchased by the government in the 1980s to put back into the rental stock.

But as early as 1906 there were state-built cottages on Petone foreshore and on the edges of other centres around the country such as at Grey Lynn, Riccarton, and Wakari. The Liberal government at the time passed the 1905 Workers' Dwellings Act (spearheaded by Richard Seddon) to provide affordable rental housing for city workers. Unfortunately, these houses were often in new subdivisions—suburbs—lacking infrastructure, and further from people's jobs than ideal, so the scheme was not a big success. Rent-to-buy and government loan schemes saw most of these early 'state' houses fall into private ownership quite quickly.

During the 1920s, a post-war demand for housing saw rental prices soar and big competition for the existing housing stock. With its own workers struggling to find accommodation, the New Zealand Railways Department formed an architectural branch to embark on a house-building scheme. They created a factory at Frankton in Hamilton to build prefabricated houses which were sited next to railway yards and stations. The idea was to standardise a simple design so they could be built quickly and inexpensively, thus keeping rents down.[ii] An initial run of 400 houses mushroomed to over 1,500 before the scheme was axed in 1929 due to pressure from the private building sector—it was too successful. Many of these small cottage-style houses are still around, a century later, grouped together in little settlements in Ngaio, Ōtāhuhu, Taumarunui, Newmarket, Ohakune.

---

ii   Interestingly, the head of the branch was architect George Troup, responsible for the rather flamboyant Dunedin Railway Station.

In 1935, the first Labour government was elected and quickly initiated the largest housing construction scheme in the nation's history. They bought hundreds of acres of suburban land around the country and contracted private tradesmen to build houses designed by their Department of Housing Construction and intended for renting by working people unable to buy. Prime Minister Michael Joseph Savage opened the 12 Fife Lane house with much fanfare and publicity.

Although the architectural community at the time decried the houses' designs (there was a variety of them) as rather too conservative, they were similar to what was generally being built in the private sector. In fact, in the very early stages of the scheme, distinguished Wellington architect William Gray Young was one of those invited to work with the government architect in the design of the prototype state houses. According to Wellington architect and onetime Mayor Sir Michael Fowler, Gray Young's contribution was responsible for their high standard of design. (Thirty years earlier, a 20-year-old Gray Young had been well-placed in a competition for the Petone working-men's cottages mentioned above, and four were built to his designs.)[7]

The houses were known to be well-built from solid native timber and were often situated in what became desirable locations where there was sun and views and proximity to town (think the Ōrākei Basin in Auckland or Hayes Paddock in Hamilton). They were sometimes built in crescents backing on to a central park or reserve (like the Fife Terrace house, or Savage Crescent in Palmerston North), or as separate little townships (Naenae in the Hutt Valley). The man responsible for much of the siting of these houses, Reginald Hammond, was the first New Zealander to complete a professional town planning qualification. Along with the department's chief architect Gordon Wilson, and director Arthur Tyndall, Hammond was a key part of the implementation of the state housing scheme.

From Fife Lane in 1937 there was really just a window of a dozen years for the scheme to run its course—the term of the first Labour government. But during that period a rather incredible 30,000 houses were built for working families throughout Aotearoa. Why is it so hard to do something similar now?

In 1949, a bristly National broom (the Party formed in 1936 by a merger of the United and Reform parties) swept through what had become the Public Works Department, and then the Ministry of Works. The new government favoured home ownership, and its new Group Building scheme, combined with State Advances government loans, meant housing developments by owner-occupiers were popping up all over the place. Design, too, started to change quite radically with the influence of the émigré architects escaping Europe and bringing their Modernist ideas with them. Many of these émigrés, like the highly regarded Austrian Ernst Plischke, worked in both private practice and for the government. They were responsible, either directly or by osmosis, for some of the most coveted buildings in our architectural history.

Since the 1950s, the construction and sale of state houses has fluctuated considerably depending on which of the major political parties has been in power. In general, National governments have encouraged tenants to purchase state houses, while Labour governments have discouraged or prohibited sales in order to conserve rental stocks. These trends were especially marked in the 1990s when the sale of state houses soared under National, until a new Labour-led government placed a moratorium on further sales in 1999.[8]

*

Many New Zealanders maintain a genuine fondness for the golden Labour-era 'staties'. Jill Ramsden, in her stylish limited-edition photographic homage, *State Houses—A Roadside View*[9] says of her Naenae childhood: 'I didn't grow up in one, but our street was right in the heart of this new housing boom and street after street of sturdy boxes growing like topsy are what I remember.'

Jill's house was just down the road from the semi-detached 'statie' in which her parents started their married life. 'It's still there,' she says. 'Families were proud to call them home. Scorched earth for a garden but big (often quarter-acre) sections to grow the veges, space to run, to race the bike around the house and park up the car for the Sunday wash . . . hanging over the fence with the neighbours . . . the weekly deliveries, the meat van, the milkman and the bread being delivered door to door. Community spirit thrived back then.'

Jill says Naenae represented the burgeoning post-war egalitarian Aotearoa, with professionals and blue-collar workers rubbing shoulders and sharing each other's skill sets. 'A great example of this was our uncle who was a bricky. He helped build our house as well as the Naenae cinema. He was popular!'

'Staties' are now sought-after as a building block on which to create a modern family home. In areas where they're not protected, all manner of architectural beauty and hideousness have been wrought on the simple little charmers, but generally the changes lean towards the reverential side of things. Bill McKay, Andrea Stevens and Simon Devitt's handsome book *Beyond the State*[10] delves into fifteen of these houses and their occupants in great detail, complete with original plans and design numbers where they've been able to find them. It's a fascinating read.

*

At 1B Tui Street, though, not much has changed since Bill and Laura bought it in 1995 for $15,000 during the National government sell-off. Bill had a nasty road accident that year which kept him in hospital for a long time. I don't pry for details, but it must've been bad because the community, in a pre-internet version of Givealittle, raised enough money for them to put down a deposit.

The tea has brewed (milky gumboot for me, Earl Grey for Laura), and she brings a plate of generously buttered scones and jam to the table (you won't find any margarine in this house). The kitchen table we're sitting at encroaches slightly into the lounge area, which it wouldn't have been able to do had the wall not been removed to make room for a growing family. The white Marley guttering I can see through the window used to be tin. And a freestanding pantry sits where some built-in cupboards were. 'I'm too short to reach the original top ones.'

Apart from that, the carport, and the flush toilet (installed when they finally got hooked up to the town sewage—the kids grew up with a chemical can in the back shed), the biggest change to the house is the colour: 'Milton', #C289 from the Dulux 'Colours of New Zealand' range. 'My son was living down in Milton,' Laura explains. 'The other kids said, "Ooh, why'd you paint it that colour?" I said, "because he lives in Milton!" But now it needs re-painting, they're nowhere to be found.'

As well-built as these houses are, they still require maintenance. A while back, the wooden windows in the back bedroom needed refurbishing and refitting—they'd moved a little over time. 'It's not easy finding someone locally to do that sort of work. The first chap I approached said, "You need aluminium". I said, "I don't want aluminium, I want my wooden ones!" She eventually found someone to do the job. 'I was so happy. Now I want to get the double-hung windows in the lounge done, but the tradesman's retired. As for that aluminium, no thank you.'

The other three houses in the block—1A, 1C, and 1D (blue, green and yellow respectively)—look pretty original from the outside, too. Jack Herbert and Shona Te Huki have been at 1D for twenty-seven years. Jack is a farm worker, while Shona travels the pot-holed and pine-strewn road to Dannevirke daily, where she works at the Alliance meat processing plant as a labourer.

At 1A and 1C, farmers and shearing contractors David and Rebecca Buick use the houses ('quarters' in farming speak) for putting up their seasonal and other workers. The Buicks have owned them since 2015, bought from private owners who'd made some updates to the interior, but nothing structural. 'They've got great bones,' Dave told me on the phone a few days after coming third in the Golden Shears open final in Masterton. (Dave might well say the same of himself, having suffered a near-deadly crushing accident on his farm just a couple of years ago.

He says he was very lucky to survive, let alone get back to competitive shearing.)

The Buicks have made simple improvements—interior painting, carpeting, and upgrading the bathrooms and water pressure. One house is fully furnished and equipped, Dave says; the guys just have to walk in with their personal items and food. The other is set up more as a long-term family home for senior staff. 'Having the houses give us options for our business. We regularly have around twenty workers and struggled to find accommodation for them when we started.'

Which is exactly why the four houses were built in the first place.

In the late 1940s, the Akitio County, as it was then, was having trouble attracting workers due to the area's isolation and lack of accommodation. As early as 1945 the county clerk was pestering local member of parliament and future prime minister Keith Holyoake, who was in turn lobbying the Minister of Works, saying there was 'an urgent need' for State rentals. Correspondence from the time outlines the County's immediate requirement for a grader driver, a bridge carpenter, bridge hands, a storeman, and a quarryman. There was regular pushback from the Government, continually declining the request on the basis they hadn't received any applications from potential renters. (At one point, the clerk rather pithily responded that the reason for that was there were no workers to apply!)

The County eventually got the four Pongaroa houses—plus one on Coast Road for the Rabbit Board—but it took until 1954 for them to be built. The project came back to bite them somewhat when the ten-year 'head lease' they thought they had, which would allow them to ensure the tenants were always their own employees, was never formalised. On several occasions workers quit their county jobs but stayed on in the houses (their rental agreement was with State Advances, not the County), causing damage and running up bills. The County's offer to guarantee the tenancies and rental for ten years to get the project signed off soon looked like a rather poor decision.

*

'Koro's home,' Laura tells Demi as she hears Bill's car pull up outside. The little girl drops the building puzzle she's nearly completed and runs to greet her grandfather. 'I wonder if he'll come in?' She's warned me that Bill is a man of few words, but he does come in briefly to make cuppas for himself and his boss, Lewis. They've been fencing up the range, he tells me. 'Wasn't so nice up there first thing,' he says. 'Bit of a cool wind.' His laconic delivery is very Crumpian, I think, as he repairs to the carport where Demi is entertaining Lewis. 'He does better with a beer in his hand,' Laura says.

But Bill returns a bit later and I manage to extract from him the fact he fenced at Owāhanga Station for twenty-five years on and off, that he's shorn sheep in most of the sheds in the district—Moanaroa, Akitio, Maraīnanga, Ware Ware, Te Tumu . . . before he heads back out to sharpen a chainsaw. 'He loves his fencing,' Laura says. 'He was determined to continue shearing after his accident, and he did for a while, but for some time he's just been fencing. He's seventy-six now, so half days suit him. The rest of the time he's just here, getting in my way.'

Why would you move?
BILL & LAURA, PONGAROA

Bill grew up not far along the road, in Weber. Apart from some island-hopping for the shearing seasons, he's not ventured a great distance at all, like Laura. I ask her if they've ever thought of moving? 'A few times, when the kids were growing up and a few places came up for sale around here. But nah, we always ended up just staying in this house.

'It's got noisy around here now, though. The road . . . all the trucks. Then everyone discovered Route 52 so on a Sunday it gets busier with the motorbikes and car clubs. For years it was a secret, we always used to say it was a secret—it was nice and quiet. Within the shearing industry, though, like when we were working down south, everyone knew where Pongaroa was.'

*

It's approaching lunchtime and I need to drop some books off in Mākurī so I take my leave, saying goodbye to perfectly-behaved Demi and hospitable Laura, and to gently-spoken Bill in the carport as he expertly files the chain on the Stihl. A car is slowly driving off from next door, driver's window down. It's the mother of a chap who works for the Buicks—he's staying in one of their houses, the green one. She's setting off back to New Plymouth from where she came yesterday to check on him—he had a road accident a couple of days ago. 'His car's still stuck down a bank,' she says. 'I spent seven hours in A&E last night.' I tell her to drive carefully.

Her son is sitting outside, looking very uncomfortable. 'I swerved for a goat—I didn't want to ding my ute. But I'll drive straight over it if I see another one.' We talk about the time he'll

93

need off work and about the house he's staying in, and the little cluster it belongs to. 'They're neat, eh. I love the way they don't need numbers on the letterboxes—they're colour-coded.'

AT AKITIO

Consider this barbarian coast,
Traveller, you who have lost
Lover or friend. It has never made
Anything out of anything.
Drink at these bitter springs.

So goes the opening verse of James K. Baxter's poem, *At Akitio*.

In 1957 Baxter travelled to the seaside settlement, thirty-odd twisty kilometres off Route 52 from Pongaroa, on an Education Department writing commission. His report *Akitio: A Country School and its Community* painted a rosy picture, but Baxter appears not to have fully enjoyed his stay—the poem he wrote there is full of dark images, referring to the 'barbarian' coast and to disease, drownings, and having 'never made anything out of anything'.

Akitio actually makes plenty from not much. It's a hard-to-get-to, driftwood-strewn stretch of sand toeing the northern boundary of Wairarapa. Although it plays second fiddle to the more fashionable beach playgrounds of Castlepoint and Riversdale to the south, Akitio rejoices in its remoteness.

Rugged landscape, resourceful people. They're close, brought together by family and circumstance. 'We're all related along the coast—at least, as far as a horse can go in a day,' says Fiona Ramsden from Ware Ware Station, a few kilometres inland from Akitio on the Coast Road to Pongaroa. (Ware ware means 'lost' or 'forgotten'.) With the help of a stock manager and a general farmhand, Fiona runs the 1214 hectare sheep and beef farm she grew up on. After a big-city career in fashion and interior design, Fiona returned to Ware Ware in 2012, aged 36, to take over from her parents Dan and Barbara. 'I love making things, and textiles and design. But I wanted to come and do this. I wanted to come back to land and hills and community.'

I get to Fiona's place via a long tree-lined farm road snaking in parallel with the Owāhanga River. An informal entrance through substantial garden planting reveals the farmhouse where a pot of tea and the aroma of home baking await me in the kitchen. Fiona has collected a pile of photographs and papers relating to Akitio School and its hall. A major fundraising drive for the hall is taking place soon, and brochures for the event are piled on the table next to a plate of oven-warm savoury muffins.

The major event for the fundraiser is a walk/run over neighbouring Maraīnanga Station. Fiona is expecting that some participants and supporters will stay at her rustic-but-stylish Coast Road Backpackers' accommodation. 'I started the

Wormwood
AKITIO BEACH

backpackers' lodge in 2013. It used to be the shearers' quarters in the days when gangs stayed on the farm for a week. Now they travel to us daily, so the building was sitting unused. The single man's cottage was empty too—it's now a double with kitchen and bathroom.'

Fiona's brother, Hugh, manages the other Ramsden property, Moanaroa—'long seashore'—with its eleven kilometres of coastline. The station features a substantial Victorian homestead where their parents, Dan and Barbara, lived after Ware Ware until they retired to town in 2022. 'Rather than downsize from Ware Ware, they upscaled to Moanaroa,' Fiona says. 'They just loved the land.' Together, the Ramsden siblings farm the two stations plus a finishing property near Pongaroa. In recent times they've made a concerted effort to further increase the quality of their already well-regarded wool clip.

The Aotearoa wool industry has been in the doldrums for decades. Prices for strong wool are so low many farmers shear at a loss—often tens of thousands of dollars—purely for their animals' welfare. A move to less woolly and self-shedding breeds is gaining momentum. There's been a lot of head scratching going on about how wool can be revived as a viable product but mostly any ideas have come to nothing. Industry representatives say it's reached the point where something has to give.

But the Ramsdens believe there's a future in the strong crossbred wool they grow. Going against the general tide of pessimism, their faith is based somewhat on investment in wool by Aotearoa's biggest furniture retailer, Big Save Furniture. The company has been using a product called Seaqual in its production for some time. Seaqual is a material made from discarded plastics harvested from the ocean and can be used to create all manner of fibre products. Their furniture manufactured using Seaqual became popular with customers, many asking for it by name. When their national buyer Daniel Norman heard about the plight of the sheep farmer he wondered what his company could do to support them, as well. 'We thought, we must be able to use wool in our furniture, we just have to figure out how.' They've done that, and now use woollen textiles for cushion and bed coverings, and the raw product as stuffing for pillows and cushions.

Big Save Furniture owners, the McKimm family, also own the grand Akitio homestead which was subdivided from its namesake station some time ago. They've recently bought four farms in the area totalling 3,000 hectares—farms which could easily have gone into pines but which the McKimms have pledged will stay as 'enhanced sheep and beef farms, with a focus on New Zealand strong wool and our positive ecological footprint'.[11] Like everywhere else on Route 52, pines are an issue around Akitio—Ware Ware Station is now surrounded by them, to Fiona Ramsden's disgust.

*

*This gullied mounded earth, tonned
With silence, and the sun's gaze
On a choir of breakers, has outgrown
The pain of love. Drink,
Traveller, at these pure springs.*

While farming is the mainstay of present-day Akitio, it wasn't always so. For decades, hardy commercial fishers risked life and limb launching their boats through Baxter's 'choir of breakers' to gather crayfish, cod, and tarakihi. According to Akitio Boating Club stalwart Di Fergus there were traditionally six or seven 'commercials' here, but in recent times there's been a drift to Castlepoint where launching conditions are more reliable, so that only one commercial operator remains.

Di ran the Boating Club bar for fourteen years. The Club's more than 300 members live mainly in Dannevirke and Palmerston North; many have baches on the beach or overlooking it. The handful of locals who keep the Club going over winter swells to a sizeable throng in summer. Fishing competitions attract the crowds, too. 'Fish Akitio' regularly receives fifty boat entries and many more anglers who try their luck in the land-based section. Separate competitive events are organised for the ladies and kids.

I'm at the Boating Club on a Friday night, and a dozen people—around half the permanent beach population—are in the bar discussing the sharing of weekend labour and equipment. There is always work to be done where boats and coastal baches are involved, often heavy work requiring noisy machinery and more than one pair of hands. 'Permanents' might also keep the grass down for the weekenders, or clear the launching ramp of logs and other debris deposited by regular heavy swells.

There's no freedom camping permitted at Akitio, but at the privately-owned camping ground next to the Boating Club a 'seafront site' means exactly that. It wasn't busy when I arrived with my caravan so I had the pick of the unpowered sites right

Absolute waterfront
CAMPING GROUND, AKITIO

on the water's edge. No other Route 52 campground affords campers such a direct connection to the sand and sea.

As well as catering for those of us 'just passing through', the campground provides facilities and services for a couple of dozen fixed cabins and caravans. I am just getting settled when the owners of a nearby cabin arrive on their quad bike with a glistening, bright-eyed, blue moki. They slice off a generous fillet that later sizzles on the trusty little charcoal barbecue I've set among dark brown kelp and sea-worn stones at the high tide mark.

∗

> *Squirearch, straight-backed rider, built*
> *An ethos of the leisured life,*
> *Lawn, antlered hall and billiard room,*
> *Glass candelabra brought from Paris . . .*

Farming at Akitio is no life of aristocratic leisure. It's steep land, summer dry, winter wild. Farmers here tend black and white mobs, but not the Friesians popular for their milk and farmed on the flatter, wetter pastures further inland. Here the meaty black Angus cattle and sturdy white Romney sheep are the main source of income, over a century since the timber mill closed.

Cecil and Matt Radford own 1052 hectare Maraīnanga Station ('plentiful whitebait'). Wairarapa-raised Cecil has significant family history here—her grandmother was born in the station's colonial homestead—and the couple bought Maraīnanga back into the family in 2016. For eight years previously they'd farmed at Waihi Falls, an hour north up Route 52. Matt is a self-described Southern man, hailing from rural Wānaka. After owning a café and bar in Wānaka township, the couple farmed and ran other businesses in Canterbury before moving to Akitio. 'I'm gradually working my way north,' Matt jokes. 'We sold a small, flat farm to buy a big, steep one.'

The powder-blue two-storey Maraīnanga villa is unmissable as you cross the river bridge entering the northern end of Akitio settlement. Along with the native tōtara and rimu, which used to grow like weeds all around here, the house unusually contains some kauri; barged, Matt says, from Northland. The interior panelling and decorative mouldings look identical to what's in my family's very similar (but half the size) house, built around the same time in Dannevirke and relocated to rural Wairarapa.

As I climb the ornate wooden staircase with the Radfords, I suggest the timber for our house and theirs probably came from the same mill—most likely right here at Akitio—and that the same Dannevirke joiner created the mouldings for both. An exciting discovery. William and Alice Hartgill, who built our house, had some ownership of the Akitio timber mill. The mill went broke and closed in 1903 after a storm swept all the year's logs out to sea. William had a somewhat mysterious wealth but was otherwise a model citizen of Dannevirke. He died in the influenza epidemic of 1918, aged fifty-four.

Over a cuppa in the farmhouse family kitchen, the Radfords describe their vision for the Maraīnanga property. In a bid to diversify their income stream and for a bit of social variety, they have turned to agritourism. The substantial shearers' quarters provide stylish holiday accommodation, sleeping nineteen. The river is on the boundary and the beach a short walk away.

There are paddocks for ponies, an acre of flat grass for the kids, and marked farm tracks for the energetic. 'Bring your horse, bikes or shoes,' they say.

With their children away at boarding school during the week, the couple work together across the farm, homestead, and accommodation. There's also track maintenance to take care of. They provide much of their own produce when they cater, along with the bounty of the land or sea when someone's been hunting or fishing. They're busy but I'm not hearing any complaints. 'We love it out here, that's why we live here. We want others to enjoy it with us.'

Isolation is in the mind, they say. 'We find you have to be a good sort to want to come all the way out here. It's definitely a new discovery.'

*

Enjoying his own isolation at Akitio is retired master stockman Lloyd Newland. Lloyd has spent his entire life living and working on the properties around here. He lives with his wife, Denise, opposite Maraīnanga's grand entrance in River Cottage, formerly the head shepherd's house.

Lloyd looks worn out from many decades of physical farm work. He hates quad bikes—he's always walked everywhere or saddled up a horse. I'm sitting with him at the cottage's kitchen table and notice his hands; fingers bent, stiff-looking. 'They're buggered,' he says. 'The hearing's not great either.'

Lloyd's life began on a 400-acre settlement farm—'Korora', at Kaituna, between Pongaroa and Waione. His father, like many soldiers, had returned from World War Two 'unsettled'. 'Dad buggered off when I was ten,' Lloyd says. 'There were eight of us kids. My sister Marie was a year older than me. Being the oldest boy I had to run the place. I think that shaped me.'

The Newland family was informally adopted by Pongaroa Church minister, Reverend Keith Elliott. Elliot was a war hero, awarded the Victoria Cross for displaying 'great personal courage and leadership' in the first battle of El Alamein. 'Mr Elliot stepped in, passed on his own Pahiatua farm to his brother, and became a trustee for our family. With his and neighbours' help, we built Korora up to 2,000 acres.'

While he was at Pongaroa, Reverend Elliot was responsible for building a new church at the tiny nearby village, Mākurī. In the *Dictionary of New Zealand Biography,* Peter J. Lineham recalls: 'His idiosyncratic style of ministry included blunt remarks, pre-emptory decisions, and very practical aid—such as milking the cows of sick parishioners. His approach to fundraising was also practical: using a trailer, he collected rags, dags, and beer bottles from around the parish.'[12]

Lloyd left school at fifteen and started working lambing beats around the neighbourhood. 'Then Mr Elliot took me to a farm over in Rātā, near Hunterville. He said, "You can learn some different things here, just remember you are the equal of any man." I milked cows and did sheep work for a year.' Returning to Akitio, Lloyd went to Wakawahine Station—bought by William Hartgill in 1908—where, with his own horse and dogs, his shepherding career started in earnest. At eighteen, he went to Maraīnanga. 'Jack Thom was managing it, Mum's cousin, big fella, abrupt.' Then a Lands & Survey farm, Branscombe.

'I was there for quite a while but didn't like it much, there was a slack attitude because it was government owned.' After four years in the single men's quarters at Mangahuia, he ended up the manager.

At Korora, Lloyd's brother had taken over and bought a bit more land. 'I went back there briefly, then ran Maraīnanga where I got snagged up with Denise. We went back home for two years, and to Wairākau where I was head shepherd. Then Michael Kight offered me the manager's job at Akitio Station so I rode my horse over there. Denise followed with all our stuff and we spent fourteen years in the house up on the hill.' That stint was followed by ten years next door at Taumata, then Glencoe until Lloyd was sixty-nine when they retired here to River Cottage.

During all this time, through a multitude of living arrangements, Lloyd and Denise raised two boys, Clint and Brad. They both attended Akitio School, the one James K. Baxter was sent to write about. 'They were big strong buggers,' Lloyd says. 'They had to be because sometimes I needed some help. When they finished at Akitio I said, "Right, we're gonna wean these buggers properly," so we sent them to New Plymouth Boys' High. From the sea on this side of the island to the sea on the other side.' Lloyd financed their schooling by running a few cattle on the stations he worked on. 'I thought it was better to do that than shift out of the area as a lot of families do.'

As Lloyd reminisces at the kitchen table he remembers Wattie Kingston, the occupant of the little stucco cottage which still stands on the point opposite the Boating Club. Wattie drove bullock carts carrying wool destined for a coastal steamer anchored offshore. He pictures the boarding house along the beach which accommodated all manner of people, including workers from the timber mill next door. The distinctive board-and-batten hardwood house and its rambling, colourful garden was occupied for sixty years by George and Muriel Cowan. George's family had owned the house since the 1930s. Sadly, everything burned down in 2019 and Muriel died two years later.

Lloyd also recalls Ferry Reserve at the river mouth, not far from this cottage, where, until the wooden bridge was built, people camped while waiting to be floated to the other side. He can still feel the excitement of running heavy stock over the bridge to be loaded out from Akitio Station's yards. There were raucous dances after the Aohanga horse sports and a colourful New Year's Eve ball at the landing shed next to Wattie the bullocky's cottage.

The landing shed—a building for many purposes and harbouring myriad memories—was dismantled in the early 1990s. A new hall was built behind the school with free farmers' labour and a few subcontractors funded from a lotteries grant. Lloyd contributed to the fundraising by mustering feral goats and selling them to the freezing works. 'Once we did it by plane. Ed Kight flew it; we chased the goats up onto the ridges. We got 300 goats in that mob. That started the ball rolling, then we got smaller lots of fifty or twenty over the years.'

When the school closed in 2014 its roll was four children, including the teaching principal's own two.

These days, Lloyd's concern is the proliferation of forestry around Akitio. 'Stock numbers on the farms have collapsed,' he says. 'Beautiful mobs of sheep and lovely black cows going to the works. To plant pine trees. Jeez! People used to come through Akitio because there's a lane that goes right through to Herbertville. Horse trekkers, farmers from up the way, drivers . . . And they all commented on our beautiful stock, beautiful land, how we'd turned it around from what was rough, rugged country. Their comments would bring tears to my eyes.'

'It's called progress,' I suggest.

'Yeah, progress alright. Jeez!'

Lloyd still walks the surrounding hills fixing things, pitching in with mustering, offering his lifetime's experience where it's appreciated. 'I'm pretty well known around here. Even the new people get to know me pretty quick. I go walking, help myself over fences. Quite often if I see something going on I'll stop to help, you can always stand in the right place or open a gate, that sort of thing. I stand up the hill and look around. I know the country because I've mustered it all, down to Owāhanga and further, way down the coast. I've been here, done that all over the place.

'It's surprising what you find walking around—a dripping trough, a sheep stuck in a fence. It's only a matter of doing a little thing and fixing it. And when you get back you can sit down and think, at least I saved that sheep, saved some water.'

> *Think what you were born for. Drink,*
> *Child, at the springs of sleep.* [13]

*

As I drove out of Akitio I stopped briefly at the disestablished school, now kept an eye on by the community as best they can.

I wanted to think about James Baxter's time here, his poem so full of despondency, his report about the school and the community so eloquently written, his being a teacher himself (he graduated from Wellington Teachers' College in 1952).

In 1972, a few months before I began my own teacher training, also at Wellington, Baxter died in Auckland, in a stranger's house, after a heart attack. He was forty-six. My first posting was to a small Bay of Plenty town, at a country school. I was a fish out of water; a bearded, long-haired, young white bloke in a predominantly Māori world. I was greeted with a deep suspicion I never really shook off.

I lived with my golden retriever, Redda, in a Fibrolite cottage, past the dog pound behind the paper mill. We were surrounded by pumice, native bush, and hissing steam vents. The toilet was in an iron shed outside—a black twenty-litre bucket with a sturdy lid and some blue chemicals thrown in. Bathing was done in the thermal pool nearby; there were makeshift timber seats, a natural dirt floor, the acrid smell of sulphur permeating the air.

I sometimes cooked in the wooden boxes built by the mill workers around the steam vents—half a chicken or a few sausages and some orange and green veges tied up in an oven bag. Scratchy rats piled Redda's Tux biscuits up outside the hole they'd chewed in the Pinex wall by the open fireplace. Clouds of angry wasps randomly erupted from a grapevine curled around the eaves.

Just as Baxter found when he moved to the Whanganui River settlement of Jerusalem in 1969, the culture clash was visceral. But Baxter learned a lot, and so did I—no doubt more than I taught the kids. Kawerau was remote to me in all senses of the word. As physically distant as Jerusalem. As hard to grasp as a darting dragonfly.

As indefinable as the Akitio coastline in a stormy, hazy dusk.

Fishing at river mouth, a woman
Uses the sea-drilled stone her mother used
For sinker, as big kahawai come,
As tides press upward to time's source.

COCONUT GROVE

ON THE SURFACE, PŌRANGAHAU IS A CLASSIC Aotearoa coastal village. Its entrance is flanked by the elegantly carved Rongomaraeroa marae and the Kaiwhītikitiki urupā, its wire fence adorned with roses and frangipani. Across the river bridge, a turn-of-the-century timber hotel stands prominent. Opposite, a blindingly blue Tip Top dairy serves ice cream, fish'n'chips, and mail. The corner garage has a car on one hoist, a tractor on the other, and a quad bike waiting its turn.

Past the fire station the wharenui-like war memorial hall lies waiting, too, for the next community fundraiser or ANZAC service. Around the corner a classic colonial church sits behind a white picket fence. There's salt in the air and tūī in the trees.

This is about as Kiwi as it gets.

*

Pinned petals
URUPĀ, PŌRANGAHAU

According to the 2018 census, seventy per cent of Pōrangahau's population of 141 identify as Māori. But say hello to a local and you're almost as likely to be greeted with 'kia orana', or even 'buon giorno', as you are with 'kia ora'.

Every small town has a busy bee and Kim Steffert, or Ropiha, is Pōrangahau's. When I meet Kim, she's farewelling someone in the middle of the road. She looks a bit uncomfortable but greets me warmly. 'Come in and have a cuppa,' she says, turning gingerly to lead me past a large sign on the grass in front of her house.

The sign reads *Te Ahurangi Services*. It says *Closed* but I hear the snip-snip of scissors as we enter a sun-filled room stacked with business brochures. A hairdresser is with a customer in the corner, cutting and chatting. Kim shuffles through a door to an open plan kitchen and lounge, puts teabags in two mugs, arranges six biscuits on a plate, and motions me towards a pair of comfy chairs either side of a round occasional table.

'I've had cancer three times,' Kim says as she settles herself in her chair. 'I lost my large bowel. Then I had a car accident. Then a house fire. I'm lucky to be alive! And my Mum moved in because she was sick with cancer, too. I looked after her for two years. She died not long ago.'

Te Ahurangi means a link between heaven and earth, Kim tells me, sipping her tea. 'Basically, I connect people with others and with community services. I just set this up at home here. I do it for free. My friend gave me money for computers and I put Wi-Fi in for the young people, to help them learn. I call it the Kōrero Hub. Different organisations come and use it. I was on that *ASB Good as Gold* programme on *Seven Sharp*.

They blessed me with $10,000—that helped me survive for a little bit. Actually, it helped me save my house! It was leaky, rotten. My motto is: Love is the key, so have a cuppa tea. People tell me important stuff over a cuppa.'

Kim was brought up in Wanstead, twenty-five kilometres away. Her children were both born in Australia. They moved to Pōrangahau in 1998 when the children were three and six. Her mother was already living here. 'At that time people were leaving this place in droves, but I wanted to bring my kids up here. I wanted them to know where home is. We always call Pōrangahau home even if we don't live here, because this is our marae.'

Kim's mother was Marina Sciascia. The Sciascia name is almost synonymous with Pōrangahau. 'It's a bit of a story,' Kim tells me. 'A story within a story really.'

The story goes roughly like this.

Nicola Sciascia was born in 1840 at Trani, a historic fishing port in Southern Italy. Nicola spent his early life as a merchant seaman and was thought to have arrived in Wellington around 1873. He worked in the maritime pilot service around the Wellington and Manawatū coasts. In Foxton he met Riria McGregor, granddaughter of a Māori chief. They married in 1882 and moved around the country as Nicola got work in various lighthouses. His last job was at Portland Island off Māhia where he was the principal keeper. He died there at age fifty-eight when he was gored by a bull. The couple had eleven children and today there are more than 5,000 descendants from that union.[14] [15]

'Riria's brother, Hokowhitu McGregor, was a master carver,' Kim continues. 'He was asked to come here and carve

Kiwiana
PŌRANGAHAU VILLAGE

the wharenui at the marae. When he came, he brought some nieces and nephews who were Sciascias. They married into the families here.

'Most people in Pōrangahau have a Sciascia connection. We're all related. My Mum, Marina, is Sciascia. My Dad's mother is Sciascia. So I have it on both sides.'

Kim is Ngāti Kere. 'Kere is the son of a chief, Pōrangahau,' she tells me. 'We all descend from him.' I wonder about the translation of Pōrangahau. '"Mad wind?"' Kim suggests. 'Or "researching in the night"? Because pō is night, and rangahau is researching. If you Google it, it'll say "mad wind", but I like "researching in the night" better.'

Kim reckons Pōrangahau is paradise. 'It's a beautiful place to live. It's safe because we all know each other. There's hardly any unemployed, maybe none. There are lots of new people moving into town, houses are selling like hot cakes. It grows in the summer with seasonal jobs and holiday people. There's a shortage of houses at the moment but because it's where our marae is, everyone comes home anyway.'

As our conversation winds down, I carry two empty mugs and a plate with four biscuits back to the kitchen and leave Kim to do more connecting. I have an appointment with her cousin.

*

It's only a short walk to The Duke Hotel where Ahuriri and Angela Houkamau are proprietors, but I've left Meg the foxie in the car outside the hall, so I drive there. The high midday sun makes it hard to find shade but there's a patch under a hedge on the roadside opposite the dairy. I sneak in as close to the hedge as I can, and walk around the corner to the pub.

The Duke is a large off-white weatherboard building with dark red double-hung sash windows. A wooden veranda runs across the second storey, its balusters, friezes and post brackets revealing contrasting construction eras. A token plywood ramp with curled up corners provides rudimentary wheelchair access. The signage is bilingual—*Wharekai/Café & Restaurant; Pāpara Kāuta/Bar.*

A wheelchair sits on the deck and Angela is at a table nearby. Ahuriri emerges from inside, walking with the aid of crutches after an accident thirty years ago left him with permanent spinal injuries. Angela leaves to make coffee—three flat whites in takeaway cups.

The Houkamaus have owned the pub since 2019 when it was called Duke of Edinburgh Hotel. 'We weren't very fond of that name,' Ahuriri says. 'But we didn't want to go mad and change it too much so we called it The Duke.' They'd actually looked at the property ten years earlier when it was on the market, and they bought it for the same price someone had paid back then. 'We noticed property prices going crazy so we looked at it not just as a pub but as real estate. It was damn cheap. Seven acres of land as well.

'That's how we thought about it at the time—as an investment. But I've fallen in love with the place. With the people.'

Ahuriri grew up mainly around Waipukurau and Pourērere Beach. His parents moved away from Pōrangahau just before he was born. 'Why did they move away? A little bit to do with work but mainly to do with broken hearts. Two of my brothers died tragically, one from a tractor accident just outside our home, and a few months later one of our brothers died from sickness. He was just a baby. My mother couldn't live here anymore so we moved to Taradale, Napier, then Eskdale. My father was a farm labourer. He did sheep work, fencing work. We just moved around like that.

'But we always came back here. It was always home.'

Ahuriri feels his home has changed a lot. 'Ever since the shearing industry went into decline, people have moved away. There was a time you had to be careful crossing the road there were so many shearing vans driving through. Good days; everyone had money, there was no unemployment. It's vastly different now.

'This place has been struggling for many years, a lack of employment. At one stage the real estate prices were quite low and people from out of town were buying up land, especially places at the beach. Now the rates have gone up, making it hard for local people to survive down there. They're continually moving out.'

Hospitality is at the core of te ao Māori. It's bound up in the word manaakitanga—giving and receiving respect and upholding each other's mana when meeting in formal situations. So although the Houkamaus had no formal hospitality experience when they bought the pub, they feel it comes naturally.

'It's something that's been ingrained into us all our lives,' Ahuriri says. 'Growing up on marae, it's the all-day-every-day thing—looking after people. The only difference now is money's involved. But either way, the be-all and end-all is looking after the comfort of people, so we try to maintain those values. Is it appreciated? Well, I hope so.'

Thanking the Houkamaus for their hospitality, I gather up the coffee cups and deposit them in the bin outside the blue dairy. Resisting the urge to buy fish'n'chips for a late lunch, I head for Te Paerahi Beach.

*

'The Beach' is little more than a five-minute drive but it feels a world away. While there is a smattering of new houses scattered around Pōrangahau village, Te Paerahi Beach has rows of them. Well-kept residences dot the hill above the golden sand, and smart holiday homes encircle the camping area where I plan to park up tonight with the caravan. While the village has its century-old pub, marae, church, and hall, the beach welcomes me with the architecturally designed Country Club at the core of a manicured golf course.

The free camping area across the dunes from the beach has recently been mown, revealing how uneven it is. But for now I have the pick of the sites so I steer away from the clutch of gnarly old pines and choose a flattish spot with a glimpse of water through the marram grass. A fancy white campervan rolls in a few minutes later. The middle-aged couple tell me they're from Woodville and have a business servicing scales. Why do I find that such a quaint notion? I take Meg for a run along the beach where she finds a large hairy canine friend to play with in the surf. Back at the 'van I settle in for some phone calls.

Earlier while I was talking to Kim Steffert, I mentioned I was keen to speak to a roading engineer. Without pause Kim pushed a couple of buttons on her sizeable mobile phone and David

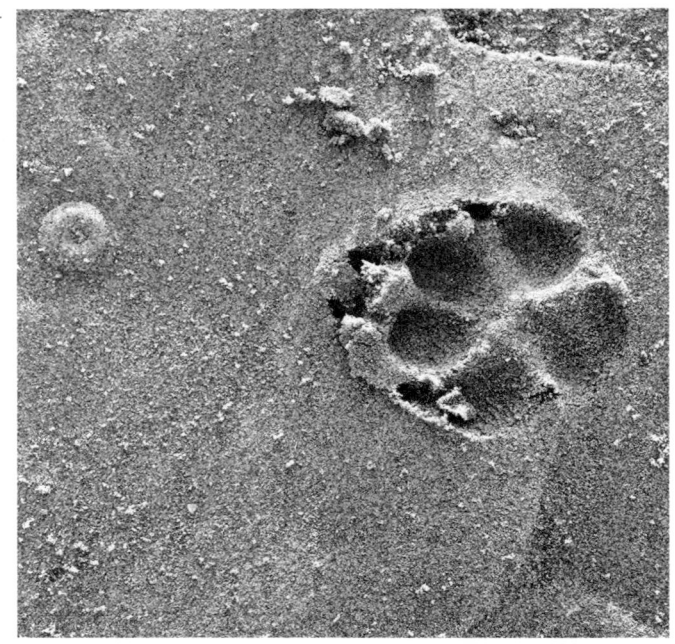

Planted paw
TE PAERAHI BEACH

Aupapa appeared on its screen, a couple of ring binders tucked under one arm. He was in Palmerston North, rushing between meetings, so we agreed to catch up another time. Another connection made at Te Ahurangi Services.

We spoke by phone a couple of weeks later, discussing the terrible state of Route 52 and the politics thereof. As that conversation was winding up, David asked me if I knew that Pōrangahau once had the largest Cook Island population in Aotearoa. I confessed I did not, and wondered how that could be.

*

A night's accommodation at five-star Wallingford Homestead, fifteen minutes up the road from Pōrangahau, will set you back several hundred dollars. During World War Two you just needed to turn up for work at Wallingford and a bed in its 'Raro Wing' was yours for as long as you wanted it.

Between 1853–2017 Wallingford was the home and farm of several generations of the Ormond family. The Ormonds tended to have very large families—the fourth generation produced fifty-two first cousins—and large families require large houses. At one stage Wallingford extended to 12,000 square feet. Likewise, large farms require manpower, and when the local men were away fighting in the trenches–or worse, never returned— it was necessary to buy in some labour.

From 1941, a wave of Cook Islanders started arriving in Central Hawke's Bay. Women took jobs as housekeepers, cooks, land girls. Men were mostly farm workers, gardeners, labourers. Wallingford was one of the first to take workers from Rarotonga and other islands, even building an addition to the house—the Raro Wing. Islanders were attracted to other properties around Pōrangahau too. So it was for the family of David Aupapa.

In post-war Wellington, the Majestic Cabaret, Empress Ballroom, and Adelphi Theatre were the places to be on a Friday or Saturday night. Besuited young men bobbed and jitterbugged with young ladies in polka dot dresses as the dance bands plucked and honked. Others stood waiting to fill their dance cards, trying to make eye contact with a potential partner through the haze of cigarette smoke. There was constant movement to and from the Gents or Ladies to swig from smuggled hipflasks. Popular, but more chaste, functions were held at the YMCA and the Ngāti Pōneke Young Māori Club.[16]

David Aupapa's parents, Simona and Vaine, met at one of these Wellington dances. Unknowingly, they were from neighbouring Rarotonga villages. The attractive youngsters bonded over a desire for better life opportunities than their native island offered. After their first daughter was born in Wellington, the family moved north to Ōtāne where Simona found work on a farm as a gardener.

'Dad didn't know anything about stock work,' David tells me, his voice honeyed from a lifetime side hustle as a musician. 'But the farm's head shepherd, Gordon Burnside, was a master. "I studied the bugger hard," Dad told me.'

By the late 1950s, the Aupapas had five girls and Simona had developed into a skilled stockman. Picturesque Papakihau Station, sixty-five kilometres away from Ōtāne on the seaward edge of Pōrangahau, was looking for a head shepherd. Simona got the job and the family moved to what had become the epicentre of the Cook Island population in Central Hawke's Bay. David was born here in 1963.

'We've always been known as the Coconut Grove families,' David says. 'Coconut Grove was what people called my uncle Harry Strickland's home. He lived right where the public river access was. Being a social man, people would often call in for a beer if they were passing by.

'On Friday nights there would be a big crowd and the beer would really flow. The Cook Island population all turned up, as well as farmers, fencing contractors, shearers, whoever. Our neighbour Duncan MacIntyre would be there for a quiet one.[iii] The guitars and ukeleles would come out and the aunties would be dancing the hula. Everyone was singing. It was the families' way of reconnecting to the island life they'd left behind.'

Papakihau Station, with its ten-bedroom homestead, has expansive views over the fertile Pōrangahau River flats to the South Pacific Ocean. The station was managed at that time by Paul and Dorothy Hunter, fourth generation Pōrangahau farmers. The original 53,000-acre Pōrangahau Station was established by Sir George Hunter in 1854. Papakihau—meaning 'slapped by the wind'—is the result of splitting the farm between two brothers three generations later. It is now run by sixth generation Hunter brothers Scott and Lochie whose father, Robert, grew up here when Harry Strickland and the Aupapas were working here.

---

iii Duncan McIntyre was Minister of Lands, Forests, Māori Affairs and Island Territories around this time. He was also Deputy Prime Minister between 1981 and 1984. He died at Waipukurau on 8 June 2001, Ngāti Kahungunu held him in such high regard for his conduct as Māori Affairs Minister that his body was at the Pōrangahau Marae for one night before the funeral. Source: Wikipedia.

'They were great people,' Robert recalls. 'They were a part of our family. Dad really enjoyed having them around.' Robert says between Papakihau, Wallingford, and Rangitoto—another Hunter family station—they employed many of the Cook Islanders who swarmed into the district.

When David Aupapa was seven, the family decided to move to Hastings. In the years following, they went back to Papakihau regularly. 'The Hunter family has always been part of our lives,' David says. 'I have photos of Mum and Dad at their children's weddings. They came to my wedding and to Dad's eightieth birthday. Mum was always up at the main house helping Dorothy with the boys and the single shepherds, and where Mum went, we went. I have more memories of that home than I do of our own.

'A while ago I plucked up the courage to ring Rob Hunter. I said, "You know that old house we lived in up the hill, would you mind if I planted a tree up there for my kids to have something to come back to?" I told him it's the only place that's ever made any sense to me.

'He said, "David, you were born here, you've been coming back all your life and you've always looked after the place when you're here. We've been waiting for you to put something up there." I went, "Really?" So, in 2015, I moved a converted shipping container onto the land. It's my run-to place; totally off-grid. Somewhere to catch up on sleep, write some songs.'

David has a music label called Coconut Grove Music. 'It's my way of honouring the memory of those days and the land and the people,' he says. 'Y'know, I come out here to Pōrangahau and there's family everywhere. Mum and Dad left all theirs behind in

Raro. My father never saw his own father again after he came to New Zealand. He was seventeen.'

One of the songs David has written in his container home has a section that goes like this:

There's only one place where it feels to be in bliss
A million stars around, sent down with heaven's kiss
Here on ancient land with silence that abounds
To be oneness on this holiest of grounds
Papakihau, this is home
Papakihau, I am home
Papakihau, my beginning, my middle, and my end.

*

The sky at Te Paerahi Beach is lit with those same million stars when I'm woken before dawn by a restless Meg. She is impatient to get out on the grassy dunes, having dreamed of chasing bunnies half the night—I could hear her muffled yelping in her sleep.

Down at the southern end I can see the man with the large dog Meg played with yesterday. From the north a horse comes trotting towards us, legs a perfect criss-cross. Its helmeted rider guides it along the wavy tide line. They create a striking silhouette as the sun breaks the horizon.

A woman emerges from the dunes like a ghost in the half-light, her schnauzer and Jack Russell running free while a boisterous black Labrador strains on its leash. Meg and the Jack Russell instantly recognise each other as cousins and begin the Terrier Tutū, a dance known only to them.

Hazy horsey
TE PAERAHI BEACH

'You're camping, eh?' says the woman. I reply that yes, I've had a lovely night here thank you. And isn't this the greatest beach for dogs? 'I live just across from the campground,' she says. 'I'm glad you've enjoyed it.' They move on.

The sun is gradually highlighting the distant headlands as it rises. A vehicle races down the line of froth in the shallows, its headlights piercing the mist. When it gets closer, I see it's a small farm vehicle. Two men are sitting side by side. As it passes, Meg takes off after it. It's going too fast for her to catch and after a few seconds she veers off back to me. The vehicle spins hard and follows her, stopping dead at my feet.

The driver eyeballs me for several very long seconds. 'Your dog chases me again I'll shoot him,' he says, and speeds off, sand spraying from spinning wheels.

WHEEL OF EXPERIENCE

O NE SULTRY WAIRARAPA NIGHT IN 2012, THE LAST straw finally bent until it snapped.

'Lounge' was a short-lived bar and music venue situated in what had been Carterton's movie house, the Regent. On this night, instead of popcorn being scooped into cardboard buckets, doses of buttery chardonnay were being drizzled into oversized glasses. A curvy coffee machine hissed at the counter, its bespoke copper construction bouncing glints from the spotlights above. Plates of colourful tapas-style food appeared from the kitchen through a single, windowless door.

An eclectic array of tables, couches and chairs provided seating for maybe seventy-five people. We were there to enjoy the combined voices of three of the finest young country music singers in the land—Tami Neilson, Jackie Bristow, and Lauren Thomson. Except that some of those who'd handed over their twenty bucks to listen were more intent on making the noise themselves. Especially the group of six 40-somethings at the table directly between us and the small, raised stage. Shouting at each other over the band. Non-stop. All. Through. The. Show.

This was becoming a bit of an issue, not just at Lounge but at venues everywhere. The artists—and the rest of the audience—deserve more respect, I muttered to myself as I regularly gave the rowdy group the evil eye. Later, Tami told me she could hear them while she was singing—they were mostly talking about what she was wearing. But what they were discussing was immaterial—my mind was already made up. No more live music in bars for me, I'd put on my own shows. Listening shows. In my own lounge.

*

The inaugural Cannon Heath House Concert featured a young Kiwi-American singer-songwriter, Jess Chambers. I'd seen the diminutive, sweet-voiced Jess treated similarly a few weeks before the Lounge show, at a sparsely attended divey bar in Wellington where she was opening for Auckland singer/song-writer—and now Green Party MP—Steve Abel. (As it happens, Steve would play a memorable gig at Cannon Heath a few years later.) Jess eventually lost her patience with the talkers, but I thought her music was good and deserved a better hearing. After the Lounge episode, I contacted her.

The idea was simple—put a few extra chairs in the sitting room, make up the guest bedroom, email an invitation to friends and neighbours, rustle up some cheese and crackers, and enjoy peace and quiet from the audience while Jess and her boyfriend/guitarist Peter Hill entertained us uninterrupted. 'What a great

Tiny Ruins
CANNON HEATH HOUSE CONCERT

idea!' everyone said, and they turned up in number. 'That was wonderful!' they said afterwards in texts and emails. 'That was more work than I expected,' Pip said, and I agreed.

Within weeks, Jess' friend Mel Parsons contacted me, so we rinsed and repeated. Same result. Then an email arrived from Donna Dean—could she please have a spot here. Another sell-out. They were the first of thirty-six-and-counting concerts.

A few shows in, we became aware that someone was doing the same thing in Hawke's Bay. We discovered it was stonemason and local cultural identity Jamie Macphail who, it turned out, we'd already met while holidaying at Mangakurī Beach where his family has a bach. We began sharing artists, creating a little 'circuit'. It was the beginning of a long association with Jamie's 'Sitting Room Sessions' during which we've hosted a who's who of the folky/poppy/countryish type musicians we like to listen to.

During the long tail of COVID, Jamie developed a series of tours he called the Small Hall Sessions. The tours utilise a network of village halls he's chosen around the Hawke's Bay region. As with his Sitting Room Sessions, the performances are usually by well-known artists—think Marlon Williams, Tami Neilson, Barry Saunders—who do a run of four or five consecutive nights in different halls.

Creative, driven, and extremely well connected, Jamie is smallish in stature but extra-large in presence. If it's not his smoky radio voice you notice first, it'll be the bustle and hustle as he races from one task or appointment to the next. 'My vision for Small Hall Sessions is to bring live music to communities who don't often see it,' Jamie tells me. 'I love the quirky and characterful community halls dotted around this countryside.

Many of them are only used for the odd wedding or AGM. I hit upon the idea of making more use of them by gathering up the local communities and putting on these concerts.'

*

It's rare for Pip to join me on a caravan trip, but we have good reason to go to Pōrangahau together to see one of Jamie's Small Hall Sessions. So, on a sunny February morning we hook up the old Vagabond, put Meg in her bright red car carrier, and hit Route 52 towards the promise of some quality entertainment.

We make the rookie mistake of approaching the village via Dannevirke, something, we find out later, the locals would never contemplate (they're happy to take the long route via Waipukurau). It's a tortuous section of road. While the elevated views would once have been magnificent, now it's all pines and a mess of muddy logging tracks strewn with piles of tree slash and countless orange road cones. The old gold caravan is not at all happy, and nor am I, both of us cursing and groaning and shuddering as we hit pothole after corrugation after rockpile.

We limp into Pōrangahau, the caravan's trailer wiring draping from behind a rear panel, which has lost all its rivets from the shaky drive. The Duke offers free motorhome parking and I find Ahuriri sitting in the dimly lit bar. 'Park wherever you like,' he offers, so we choose a pretty spot behind the hotel under a heavily laden apple tree (another error we discover later when the wind gets up). We appear to be alone, it's quiet enough, and we're not bothered by the biggest pig I've ever seen, loafing in the adjacent paddock.

*

A short walk takes us to the Pōrangahau War Memorial Hall, venue for tonight's performance. Because it's Friday the audience is sparse. Earlier Ahuriri at The Duke told me there's competition on Fridays from karaoke at his pub, and from dinner and dance at the Country Club. He'd put a poster up for Jamie, but he didn't hold out much hope of a crowd.

The hall's entrance is warm and welcoming, featuring a permanent ANZAC display by Wellington photographer Sal Criscillo. Young tour staff are busy behind a flamboyant portable bar designed like a circus sideshow. The concert set resembles a goldminer's hut and has been erected on the floor rather than on the elevated stage, avoiding a gulf between performers and audience in this not-so-small hall. An assortment of stringed instruments is propped up around the set, including the oft-maligned banjo. A trombone sits ominously upright on the floor. Jamie and his crew have found some period clothing of their own to add character to the event. The lighting designer has done her best to create an intimate atmosphere among the fifteen or so people gathered.

'Wheel of Experience' is a piece of musical theatre from Auckland quite unlike anything the locals, or for that matter I, have, ahem, experienced. Three actors and musicians wearing dungarees held up by braces, dented bowler hats, and sturdy boots, perform songs they've written about old New Zealand characters, murders, and shipwrecks. They portray an assortment of rogues and vagabonds, sailors and sealers. They play, sing, and

Boots & Braces
SMALL HALL SESSION, PŌRANGAHAU

talk their way through stories of New Zealand's settlement, and the trials and tribulations of those times. Unfamiliar stories are brought to life via vibrant, unforgettable characters. The show has prompted respected music reviewer Nick Bollinger to write, with typically thoughtful observation, 'Neither musical nor theatrical experiences come any more astonishing than the Wheel of Experience. You hear about good performers bringing songs to life, but in this case the songs seem to have given birth to the performers.' Despite the meagre crowd the show is at full volume, and the stories the ensemble describes as 'struggle, triumph, and iniquity from another time' are well received.[17]

The next time Small Hall Sessions comes to Pōrangahau, oft-awarded soul singer-songwriter Hollie Smith fills the Memorial Hall with an eager crowd. 'Hollie's show was the most emotionally charged performance yet,' Jamie told me later. 'Every tour is full of magic moments, but that one was special. To the point where a group of local wahine waited until everyone else had left, and then honoured Hollie with a personal waiata. That moment will live with me for the rest of my life.'

*

'Small Hall Sessions are an ode to our affair with the rural heart of NZ. These are the out-of-the-way places . . . their architecture and essence is heady with community pride, celebration, and connection,' says their website. The sessions now number into the hundreds and have utilised forty-one halls. Jamie's relentless positivity and enthusiasm have helped forge ongoing relationships with the cream of Aotearoa's musical talent—Julia Deans, Delaney Davidson, Reb Fountain—as well as a reputation that attracts international artists like Steve Gunn, The Handsome Family, and Mary Coughlan.

Though the COVID years might've made life a bit bumpy, Jamie seems to have come out the other side as bubbly and energetic as ever. His latest bunch of troubadours are moving around Hawke's Bay as I write, with golden-voiced Nadia Reid's classy trio playing halls in Poukawa, Te Awanga, Bayview, Puketapu, and Maraekākaho. I have no idea how he keeps it up.

Meanwhile our concerts have taken a break while I cover similar geographical ground, collecting stories of my own. 'No shows for 2023,' I told Pip. Truth is, they seem to take a month out of me, whoever and whatever the show. The original concept of putting out a few chairs and a plate of bikkies was all very well in theory, but it doesn't really work that way. Because of that, I think it's fair to say, Pip's humour through the first few set-ups was tested somewhat (although, being a bit house proud, she never shirked from the work). But as the years have passed and she's had more input into who we book (Tiny Ruins was her inspired suggestion), she's likely to say 'yes' before I get a chance to say 'no'. Which is how we recently ended up having Aotearoa music taonga Don McGlashan swinging by Cannon Heath, playing to sixty people and also, at the band's insistence, to Meg.

There's no way I could've said 'no' to that one. So, for the thirty-seventh time we enjoyed a couple of hours of beautiful music, in the company of friends and neighbours, uninterrupted by cameras or chatterers, in our very own Lounge.

HOWZAT?!

THE CORNER OF DANNEVIRKE'S GUY STREET AND Hartgill Crescent looks a little tidier than it did twenty-five years ago when Cannon Heath, which sat here since the turn of the twentieth century, was removed in the dead of night. Known then as the Tweedie Flats, having been divided some decades previously, the substantial house was then chain sawed into five sections, leaving the site a tangle of severed wires and fractured plumbing. An old laundry room and cutesy garden shed were left orphaned, unruly foliage lapping at their roofs. The pieces of house were then transported one by one through 187 kilometres of darkness to rural Wairarapa where, once reunited, they became my young family's home.

The grand eighteen-room house originally set on seventeen acres on the fringe of Dannevirke's township was built for

prominent entrepreneur and businessman William Henry
Hartgill. It was named after Cannon Heath Down, an area of
rolling green hills and valleys in Hampshire, England, where
William's wife Alice was raised. Cannon Heath Down borders
picture-perfect Watership Down, the real-life setting for
Richard Adams' dark and some say allegorical tale of a group
of rabbits meeting sticky ends as their warren gets destroyed.

Although built in late Victorian times, Cannon Heath has a
distinct 'arts & crafts' tinge. It's been added to and reconfigured
several times over the years, including by Pip and me, but retains
the decorative panelling and timber nooks and bays which give
it its character. We've reduced the eight open fireplaces to
three, one of which has a surround that for reasons unknown
to us features a sculpted brass figure of the Greek god Mars,
framed prominently above the mantel. On either side of Mars
are little stained glass-fronted cupboards, seemingly sized for
whisky bottles and cigar boxes. If you grope around the side of
the fireplace you might find the keyhole which unlocks a secret
vertical space designed to hide who-knows-what (I suspect more
bottles, perhaps the host's best).

Cannon Heath is built almost exclusively from native
timbers: rimu and tōtara from the vast area of bush felled
by Scandinavians, mostly Danes, and others who settled
Dannevirke from 1872. But the room with the fancy fire
surround is different. It was once the 'morning room', but it's
where I now listen to music in the setting evening sun. It's lined
with oak—a nod to the Hartgills' homeland I suppose. Or was
it to show off? Imported timber was expensive and this was the
room opened to the local citizens for Sunday parish breakfast

gatherings and garden parties, when bonneted guests spread on to generous verandas through door-sized sash windows and Sweet Adeline spilled from the phonograph.

Back then the room looked east over a curved drive passing through rhododendrons, azaleas, and maples to meet a scented rose bed of myriad colours. Adjacent were twin tennis courts, their startling white markings and net edging sharp against clipped green grass. Now, sometimes with those sash widows open, I gaze west from the room over valleyed dairy land to the Tararua Range, winter snow-capped, summer hazy, while Joni Mitchell or Luther Vandross sing from a digital audio streamer.

Apart from my music room's oak panels, the timber for Cannon Heath most likely came from Akitio, the nearby coastal settlement where William Hartgill had a short-lived interest in a timber mill. The grand homestead of Maraīnanga Station at Akito shares many of Cannon Heath's details, particularly the rich rimu ceiling battens and intricately moulded wall panelling. Maraīnanga was built around the same time as Cannon Heath, a scant few years before the mill closed.

William Hartgill was a renaissance man. As well as being the timber mill owner he was a thespian, a horse racing judge, stock agent, sportsman, choirmaster and oil explorer. He was also captain of the Dannevirke Cricket Club and member of the Dannevirke High School Board of Governors. In the minutes from a 1907 School Board meeting discussing the development of the school's new sports grounds, it is noted: 'The thanks of the Board are due to Mr Jas. Armstrong, who has borne the expense of laying the ground down. Also to Mr W H Hartgill for providing the special grasses for the cricket pitch.'[18]

My family's connection with Dannevirke is tenuous but tangible. Of course, it's Cannon Heath, on which we've sporadically spent time and money nurturing it back from the three Tweedie flats to a stupidly large family home. It isn't, and will never be, finished (at least by us), but the piecemeal restoration has given our two sons, Oliver and Lucien, the opportunity to practice playing cricket, a game they were always good at and still enjoy.

Over the years the boys would have ding-dong one-on-one battles. Grassy areas roughly mown to random lengths demonstrated variable bounce. A wind-dependent choice of verandas provided unpredictable ball movement if pitched on a gap in the decking. And when the rain came, a couple of bare-floored, glassless hallways afforded experience in skiddy low light conditions. (The halls' unpainted timber panelling fended off knocks from ball or bat with ease, bouncing back as it had over the decades despite large families and disregardful tenants.)

Our relationship with Dannevirke was cemented by a silver-plated cup which will be sitting right now in the glass-fronted trophy cabinet of either Wairarapa College or Dannevirke High School. The occasional exchange cricket match between the two schools became an annual fixture during the boys' time at Wairarapa College when they both played for the First XI team (although, being five years apart, never together). Before the younger Lucien's last match, Pip and I decided to donate a cup for the fixture. The handled vessel we had inscribed with *The William and Alice Hartgill Memorial Cup* was awarded to Wairarapa on that occasion, and now travels back and forth between the victors.

A house for all occasions
HARTGILLS, CANNON HEATH

*

I recently parked the caravan at Dannevirke Holiday Park for a couple of nights, intent on settling a couple of small details about William Hartgill. Firstly, I wanted to confirm when he had a stake in the Akitio timber mill and that the dates lined up with when Cannon Heath and Marainanga were built. Secondly, I needed to know when he acquired Wakawahine Station, farmed by his son Jack, which only recently passed out of the family.

It's a stonkingly hot January afternoon when I seek refuge in the airconditioned comfort of the Dannevirke Library. Librarian Pamela leads me past the Adult Fiction and Young Readers sections to a locked door by the staff kitchen. She punches a few buttons on a keypad and twists the handle to reveal the tiny Local History Room. Steel cabinets heave with faded photographs and copies of newspaper pages. Wooden shelves labour under the weight of scores of books of all shapes and sizes. A microfiche machine sits on a beige Formica desk. Everything is reachable without moving an inch.

After a flick through the photos and papers I turn to the shelves and quickly find *The Main Road*, by Toby Humphries.[19] Humphries grew up at Akitio and describes how 'W H Hartgill and others started the Akitio Sawmilling Company' and says that 'over 40 men were employed to fell the trees on the Huiarau block of Akitio Station which was covered in heavy bush'. Close by, there's a book by the prolific Akitio writer and resident Muriel Cowan, *26 Akitio Men from the Last Century*.[20] Cowan confirms that Wakawahine was carved off Akitio Station in 1908 and sold to Hartgill. My curiosity is sated within half an hour, and I make notes of a few bonus facts for possible future use.

Back in the car I decide to make a quick pilgrimage to the suburban corner where Cannon Heath once stood. Turning into Hartgill Crescent and pausing briefly I can envisage the gravel driveway snaking through maples and azaleas now gone, and the house sitting proudly overlooking the roses and the tennis courts down to the village. In my mind I hear the breakfasting parishioners chattering on the veranda, Alice Hartgill playing the piano, and squealing children racing around the lawn. Horses with buggies come and go, clip clop, the occupants dressed in their Sunday best.

Parking under the only shady tree on the street, I get out for a snoop. Where Cannon Heath's elegant grounds once were, mismatched dwellings lie behind fences that shout *GO AWAY*. The driveway that led to the Tweedie Flats passes a couple of remaining trees on the shrinking plot and terminates at a matching pair of cheaply built dwellings plonked on an unadorned section. 'A great way to start your investment portfolio' reads the online sales blurb I find later. Several neighbouring houses are on the market, too, including a portfolio of three spread out along the street: 'For The Astute Investor,' the listing claims.

Later I speak to a real estate agent. I'm curious to know who designed a house she has on her books, a stylish 1970s place a few doors down on Guy Street. It's on a generous, leafy site that must have been part of the original Cannon Heath acreage. I came across it months ago on Trade Me and am wondering why such a beautiful architectural house with a seemingly reasonable asking price still has her sign hammered into the front lawn. 'It's partly the market,' the agent explains. 'And partly where it is.'

Back around Hartgill Crescent children's bikes lie jumbled on bare lawns in front of unloved houses. A wheel-less car sits on a quadrangle of red jack-stands. A trio of pre-school kids play in the middle of the road. The sun beats relentlessly down. People go about their daily lives.

*

William Hartgill's innings ended in Dannevirke on the 19th of November 1918. He was 54, a victim of the global influenza epidemic. On the same date in 2018 we held a memorial dinner for him in the cluttered and rarely used formal dining room at Cannon Heath. A small gathering of appropriately attired friends was treated to dishes taken from the first- and second-class menus of the Titanic, chosen to reflect the period and the Hartgills' social status. We toasted William with sparkling wine and Canapés à l'Amiral, then enjoyed Chicken Lyonnaise, Minted Green Pea Timbales, Château Potatoes, and Wine Jelly with Nectarines. [21]

ONE MORE CIRCLE

ON A GOOD DAY CAPE TURNAGAIN IS A PLEASANT forty-five-minute stroll along golden sand from the beach settlement of Herbertville. On such a day the Cape's outcrop is a beacon—the sun glinting off bleached fossil-encrusted boulders and seals frolicking in sparkling pools, their wakes effervescent. On a bad day the skies are like charcoal and the wind blows so hard it threatens to rip human flesh. It's taken me three attempts to walk to Cape Turnagain—good days seem hard to find.

In 1769, while navigating HMS *Endeavour* down the North Island's east coast, Captain James Cook struck trouble. Cook and the ninety-four other souls on board were sailing south from their first Aotearoa landfall in Poverty Bay. They had just passed the wide mouth of Pōrangahau River when a huge storm stopped them dead in the water.

Although they were within sight of a large misty headland, there was no guarantee of safe anchor. So they turned around and sailed back past their first touch of this new land—the place they named Young Nick's Head. The HMS *Endeavour* continued north, around East Cape, through Mercury Bay, and up to the Bay of Islands where the party spent two weeks. Eventually the expedition rounded the top of the North Island and headed south again.

After successfully charting the long and wild western coast, Cook pulled his ship into a sheltered cove at the head of Queen Charlotte Sound. A climb to a high point on nearby Arapawa Island afforded the sailor a view back north from where they'd come and he spotted the narrow strait which now bears his name.[22] Sailing through this strait and rounding Cape Palliser, the HMS *Endeavour* headed north again up to Castlepoint where they sheltered in scallop-shaped Deliverance Cove then passed the mouth of a muddy river spilling into blustery Akitio bay.

Soon they came upon the headland where they were forced to turn around three months earlier. Realising they'd completed a circumnavigation and that what they'd sailed around was an island (some of Cook's colleagues thought it was part of a bigger land mass), the crew turned away again, this time south. The captain fetched his trusty quill and at this position on his map made an inscription—*Cape Turnagain*.

*

In 1998, Barry Saunders wrote the song 'Cape Turnagain' for his band, The Warratahs. Saunders sings of gathering up his thoughts and his things and heading out for the Cape to see the eastern sky. There's a man walking back from the Cape, he tells us. And 'Just one more circle, three sixty degrees, 'til I'm standing out on Cape Turnagain.'

The song is typical of Saunders' use of the Aotearoa landscape in his compositions but is distinctive for his inclusion of a poem, *Naming the Gods,* by his friend Sam Hunt. Hunt narrates the poem over the song's instrumental second section.

On first listen the poem seems out of place—it appears to be about experiencing an earthquake in Taranaki, for a start. But when Hunt was performing the poem in Auckland in March 2010, he introduced it like this: 'Here's a love poem. Is it a love poem? I don't know what it is. It's a poem about feeling the ground under your feet.'[23]

Feeling the ground under your feet while it's shaking. Grabbing your stuff and going to stand on a Hawke's Bay headland. A man coming back from the headland. A circle, 360 degrees. I want to make sense of all this, so I visit Barry one winter's day in his cosy Greytown cottage and ask him to explain.

'I wrote the song after I'd done a tour with Sam,' Barry tells me, stoking the log burner we're sitting before. 'I got the feeling while we were playing at a winery in Martinborough. We were on a balcony looking east. I was in the process of moving to Greytown from Wellington which was a hugely unsettling time for me. Sam was on the move north, too, leaving his famous boat shed in Mana. It just seemed like everything was changing and turning at that time, going in circles.'

Barry has never been to Cape Turnagain. 'I'd just seen it on the map and liked the name,' he says. 'I do that sometimes;

include places, put myself in the land somewhere. It could be to do with a name, or just a feeling.'

The link between the name, 'Cape Turnagain', and the subject of his song—the change of direction in his life—is reasonably explicit. But it surprises me that the 'three sixty degrees' lyric doesn't actually refer to the HMS *Endeavour*'s circumnavigation—the reason Cook turned the ship around again when he'd completed it. 'Not really, no. The song is purely an 'inner' thing. Sometimes you do that with songs, use a name or phrase simply because it has good imagery to it.'

*

Herbertville is a ten-kilometre dead-end detour off Route 52. Like many of the villages along the coast, it was settled in the nineteenth century as a port of sorts to service inland towns. The settlement was first known as Waihi, after the river which ends its journey here. Trading ships were able to beach on the smooth sand of the outgoing tide. They took on wool and timber and offloaded provisions for the station owners and workers, the hotel, the blacksmith, and a handful of shops. Then they'd float the ship on the next high tide. Or bullock teams would haul dreys along the beach to the Cape taking goods to and from small boats known as 'lighters', which would be rowed out to waiting ships anchored beyond the breakers. These days trade and transport is all by road, and recreational fishers and divers launch their small craft through a tricky channel at one end of the beach.

I first came to Herbertville late one afternoon in January 2017, towing my first caravan, the cute little gold one. On that

Camping at the cape
SEAVIEW ROAD, HERBERTVILLE

occasion, I ventured through and beyond the settlement itself in search of a place to camp for the night. I drove past the empty Beach Haven Inn and the deserted camping ground, along a narrow road flanked by a lolly-jar assortment of baches, to a farm track hugging the coast. After a few minutes and a couple of cattle stops, I found an informal selection of grassy spots right on the water. The parking is free here, granted by the two sheep stations, Burnview and Pipi Bank, whose land falls gracefully to the beach from battered cliffs behind ornate colonial homesteads.

From the spot I chose, two fishers were visible at the south end of the beach, flicking the tips of their rods towards the strengthening surf. A couple of dog walkers passed by, their retriever's fur matching the sand and coastal grasses creating a brief summery picture before the clouds began to gather. Soon a white campervan pulled into a nearby spot, headlights on, windscreen wipers swishing off the dusty drizzle. I tied down anything that might blow away, closed the roof vent, turned on the house battery and LPG bottle, and settled in for one of those nights that give Herbertville its breezy reputation.

Sleep was fitful but I was rewarded with a sun that rose magenta and majestic into a peaceful new day. I was due home that morning so at 7.30am I retraced my tracks to Route 52, turned south, and buckled in for the bumps, twists and turns that lead, eventually, to Masterton and beyond.

I visited Herbertville again in July 2020, arriving in mid-afternoon sunshine with an accompanying midwinter gale. Figuring the free beachfront site I parked at on my last trip would be pretty uncomfortable, I turned in to the Herbertville

Campground. The camp is situated on the muddy, slow-flowing Waihi River, a good distance from the beach. After checking in and creeping a couple of circuits around vacant sites and unoccupied cabins I chose a spot which appeared to have the most shelter—between a two-metre fence and a large caravan and awning. I plugged into the camp's power and switched on the electric heater. I then donned a well-worn woollen peacoat and stepped out to survey my neighbourhood.

Just through the campground gate I came across Masterton-based photographer Pete Nikolaison leaning into the stiff northerly trying to take a shot of the pub across the road. Pete was in the area to shoot a rugby match featuring the local Puketoi team and was taking a side-trip to Herbertville to snap images for a Coastal Wairarapa travel guide he was publishing. After a few pleasantries in the whipping wind we adjourned to the pub, now named the Herbertville Inn. The place was completely empty, so we pulled up a couple of stools to a leaner by the simmering log burner. Pete retrieved a mock-up of his new book from a satchel and spread it out on the sticky table for me to peruse while he went to find the publican.

The Nikolaison name is well known in Wairarapa. Pete's father, George, set up a photography studio above the Woolworths department store in Masterton in the early 1950s. He expanded the studio into retail shops on Queen Street, which Pete and his two sisters all worked in over the years. Pete's own career began at the local newspaper in 1975 and for many years he's run his own photography, picture framing, and publishing business from a character corner store in suburban Masterton. You'll find Pete at any number of events around the Wairarapa with a discreet camera bag over his shoulder, quietly blending into the scene, looking for the next frame.

The humble, low-slung Herbertville Inn bears little resemblance to the ornate, wooden two storey Herbertville Hotel built by settler Joseph Herbert in 1884. Herbert's simpler, rougher Bush Inn had been established in 1861 where the campground is now. It provided basic accommodation for the various tradesmen, transport providers and traders who were coming and going in the bustling little village. When the Bush Inn was declined a liquor licence Herbert remedied the situation by building the elegant hotel. The hotel burned down in 1904, was rebuilt that same year, but was razed again in the late 1940s.

Current campground manager John Sedcole says at one stage the camping facilities were owned by the pub. 'We do pretty well to keep two pubs going, to be honest,' he says, referring to the Inn and the hotel at nearby Wimbledon. 'The Inn does very well in summer. It has a captive market with the campers and the bach owners. Wimbledon gets the travelling public who don't come down here so much.' John says he and a few other locals tend to gravitate to Wimbledon where they have farming and golfing friends.

As well as Pete Nikolaison's regular photographic roster of calendars, school photos, and local photojournalism, he has published several books about Wairarapa, including one with his father, showcasing old Wairarapa buildings. I was pleased later to see Pete's shot of the inn where we were now sitting was included in his finished coastal travel guide.

Pete had to drive back to Masterton, darkness was setting in, and I could feel the incessant gale shaking the pub so after a second beer we thanked the publican and left the still empty bar. Back at the campground the caravan remained attached to the towbar and I left it that way for added weight against the wind. I tied down everything I could while the trees on the riverbank behind me hissed and moaned.

As the 'van rocked and rolled I heated up a ready-made supermarket pasta on the gas hob and poured a plastic glass of rough red to go with it. There are a few favourite books I keep in little nooks in the caravan and a bit of rustling around revealed Peter Hessler's *Country Driving*. Hessler is American but has lived for extended periods in Egypt and various parts of China. *Country Driving* is a collection of pieces written over a ten year period in China, and is perfect for dipping into when on the road. I spent an hour or so re-reading a chapter about life in a little village by the crumbling Great Wall where Hessler had rented a house. Then after making sure lamps or water bottles weren't going to fall off a bench or table I took to my bunk.

The wind screeched all night. Glasses and cutlery rattled in the pressed-tin cupboards. The neighbouring caravan's awning flapped and slapped. Sleep was hard to find as the 'van shook and bumped and banged. I stepped outside a couple of times to make sure we were still where we parked. It looked like there was no-one in the neighbouring caravan and I gave thought to ripping its awning down to stop the racket; instead I did the neighbourly thing and tightened the guy ropes. It was freezing cold and pitch dark and I could hear the surf pounding in the distance and steel ropes clanking in the kids' playground over the fence. I wondered if my poor little 'van had ever suffered through such a tempest before.

The morning dawned gloomy and wild, matching my mood. I was planning to spend the day walking out to the Cape, snooping around the village and staying another night. But it was just too nasty, so I headed home. Progress was at a snail's pace as we creaked and swayed past Wimbledon and Weber. I thought about stopping at Pongaroa or Alfredton but they were getting hammered, too. Swirling pine needles and stabbing rain squalls made visibility difficult. The fuel economy gauge was bent hard to the right as I wrestled the little 'van through the storm. By the time I emerged at Te Ore Ore, I was starting to take a distinct dislike to Route 52.

*

Two years later, with the new, slightly bigger caravan, I decide to give Herbertville another chance. Just one more circle, as the songwriter Barry Saunders said. Determined to get to Cape Turnagain, I plan this visit by weather forecast.

Google Maps suggests accessing Herbertville from Dannevirke, through Weber (such as it is), to the Wimbledon turnoff. I know from recent experience that this road is caravan-damagingly bad, so I turn off State Highway 2 at Eketāhuna, heading for Alfredton and Pongaroa. What I've forgotten, though, is that you still have to go through Weber and that section of the road to Wimbledon is the worst. It's a painful drive, at times I'm slowing to a crawl to navigate potholes and subsidence caused by both logging trucks and biblical quantities of rain during 2022. There is also the appalling mess left by the loggers. Where once the panorama of native bush and rolling

Tortured boughs
BACHES, HERBERTVILLE

farmland partially compensated for the discomfort of the road's twists and bumps, the view now is an endless, monotonous green.

But I've timed my visit well, and a perfect spring afternoon greets me as Meg and I roll into the campground. I find John Sedcole with a bright orange chain saw at a riverside site, lopping woody growth from hedges that provide privacy and some protection from the wind. It's been wet here, like everywhere else this past winter, so John points me to a site which offers firm footing. After several vain attempts at avoiding mud and puddles I wriggle the caravan into place, wondering what the overall-clad chap opposite thinks as he nails new roofing iron to the permanent awning of an old house bus, a skinny cigarette hanging from his lips.

On opening up the 'van I find the fridge door has slipped its safety catch and swung open, spilling food and drink all over the floor. Worse, the table which folds out in three panels from the chest of drawers has collapsed, its leg ripped from the outer panel, tipping the chest over with it. The whole assemblage looks like a game of pick-up sticks. On the carpet, socks and computer cables mingle with beer cans and garlic hummus. Route 52's road surface has struck again.

I clean up and make a temporary fix for the broken table. The sun is retreating behind the western hills as my DIY neighbour ceases hammering and lights yet another fag. I have a loose arrangement to talk to the publican, Ian, so I wander over the road to the inn. An older couple sit at a picnic table under the veranda smoking and drinking beer. A pile of muddy boots sits beside a closed wooden door. Smoke puffs from a stainless-steel chimney and hangs suspended in the still evening air. A blackboard announces the Tuesday night jackpot pool competition—$5 entry, winner takes all.

There's already a good gathering in the brightly lit bar. Framed local photos hang on burnt orange walls and wooden dining tables are set on busily patterned yellow and red carpet. Men from a forestry crew have settled at leaners with quart bottles of DB Export or Tui; the few women drink bourbon and cola dispensed from a tap. One of the crew, Joseph, introduces himself and tells me they're planting pines out on Weber Road. He's from Pōrangahau, just over the hill. Ian recognises me as the out-of-place one in this group and we talk as he serves shepherds from nearby Tautane Station who've arrived for a steak or burger and the pool competition.

The pub is on the market, Ian tells me as he flips the cap off my Panhead beer. He and his partner, Michelle, have battled their way through the COVID restrictions and survived, but Michelle now wants to move back to Wellington where she has family and where they lived before moving here. Ian's not bothered either way, he says, but he's happy enough here. He scribbles a couple of names and phone numbers on a business card; contacts he thinks I should talk to about Herbertville. I order the beef burger and start making some phone calls just as the foresters crank up the music. The pool balls click and spin as Ian plays referee. My burger arrives; I go looking for cutlery.

I'm invited to join the pool competition but I'm not intending to stay. The chips are cold and there's a couple of soggy circular purple things in my burger which I eventually deduce are battered onion rings stained by the obligatory beetroot. In between his pool shots, Joseph and I discuss the

157

music. It's classic Kiwi roots, he says. We agree that the singer from Katchafire has a lovely voice and I tell him my favourite song is 'Rainbow', from their 2007 album, *Slow Burning*. He nods in recognition.

Back at the caravan I make some more phone calls, setting up interviews for the next few days. It's still early but I'm tired. I take Meg for a torch-lit toilet stop in a nearby paddock and prepare to turn in. It's starry and quiet apart from light surf in the distance and the emphysemic hacking from my DIY neighbour.

*

At 9am, 85-year-old Spencer 'Top' Gollan greets me at the top of what is, by some distance, the longest driveway in Herbertville. The views from the parking area are a cliché; overlooking the village and everything from the Cape to Akitio. Top's wife, Jan, emerges from their orange and yellow house, the largest and loftiest in the village. They're both dressed for town.

During small talk in the sun, I mention I made the mistake of travelling the Weber to Wimbledon road to get here and the damage it caused inside my caravan. I find myself saying, 'And don't get me started on those bloody pine trees.' The words emerge from my mouth just as the corner of my eye registers the *Wimbledon Forestry Limited* signage on the shiny red ute I've just parked alongside. 'We started the forestry industry around here,' Top says.

Extracting my foot from my mouth, I attempt to cover my faux pas by asking where his name, Top, comes from. 'I have no idea,' Top says. 'My parents must've had a row or something.

Dad never wanted me called Spencer. Only about three people in the world call me that. 'Top' emerged from somewhere, God knows where.'

And talk about bloody pine trees we did.

On Top and Jan's boundary, not too many steps from where we're sitting in their cosy, electrically heated barbecue area, is the tiny Wainui cemetery. The site contains the remains of early settlers dating from 1859 and is remarkable not so much for the familiar local names—Herbert, Franklin, Hales, or for their occupations—fencer, postmistress, farm servant, tailor, but for the number of children listed. Thirteen of the twenty-seven people interred here were aged between five minutes and nine years when they perished. On the other hand, Mary Anne Excell, who died in 1912, made it to the ripe old age of ninety-one.

These higgledy-piggledy burial plots are inaccessible from the road and were, until very recently, invisible to the Gollans. Their neighbours' pine plantation grew right up to the Gollans' boundary, obscuring what remains of the headstones. In fact, before the trees were harvested, their entire house was shaded from the winter sun by 11am.

Top Gollan grew up in Wimbledon on Route 52 where the turnoff to Herbertville is. The family farm opposite the Wimbledon Tavern was less than 500 acres, on which the Gollans farmed around 500 sheep. That was enough for a family to live on in those days during the war years, Top says.

Through the 1980s, during the National Government's 'Think Big' economic strategy, the farm ballooned tenfold to 5000 acres. The family began planting a pine forest for timber, essentially pioneering silviculture in the region. They've just milled a couple of hundred acres and their son, Jamie, who now runs the farm, is keen to plant more.

'Bloody trees,' Top says. 'We get no carbon credits off them. Or off the ones we replant. It's a bloody rigmarole.' But the returns are big, he says before Jan reminds him about the increasing costs. 'It's eighty cents a tree to plant now,' she says. 'When we started it was three.'

We talk some more as the morning warms up. Their foxie sniffs around my car where Meg is snoozing. It's hard to steer the conversation away from pines. It's the topic on everyone's lips and I'm hearing the same thing up and down Route 52. Perfectly good sheep farms being sold to forestry. Populations dwindling, schools closing. Absentee owners of the remaining houses, or they're just left empty. Decades worth of investment in farm infrastructure becoming redundant.

'It's all written off—fences, houses, woolsheds, yards, everything,' Top says. 'One forestry company bought up nine farms around Ti Tree Point and took 600 steel gates to a clearing sale. They've planted trees right through the cattle yards.'

'A couple of farms around us in Wimbledon sold recently,' says Jan. 'They're going into pines too'.

'It's absolutely criminal,' they chime in unison.

I take my leave to let Jan and Top get to town, to Dannevirke. The road doesn't bother them too much, they say. They know every pothole. After two failed attempts, I'm itching to get to Cape Turnagain.

*

The only thing Meg loves more than a beach walk is chasing rabbits, and on this walk she scores the double. As we head to the Cape she roams high and low, nose down through windswept dunes and cliff-hugging vegetation. She's two-and-a-half years old now and more inclined to go a bit off-piste, disappearing for increasing amounts of time. She tests my nerves even more than usual as she shrinks to a tiny dot in the distance. I get the occasional glimpse of her bushy white tail, like a toetoe frond peeking through gaps in the gold and green brush.

For all Meg's endeavours she fails to return with a bunny. But her lengthy absences allow me to ponder the conversation I've just had with the Gollans, and similar—identical—chats I've had with others. To consider the irony, the inconsistency, the dilemmas that come with farming and forestry in the 2020s. In a pub in Pongaroa, at a picnic table in Pōrangahau, in a farmhouse kitchen at Akitio or a café in Waipukurau, everyone says the pine trees are killing Route 52. Yet that same 'everyone' is growing them, selling land for them, or otherwise profiting from them by supplying, feeding, or accommodating the crews who plant them. As Top Gollan mused (an unprompted observation after I'd switched my recorder off), 'The whole world is upside down at the moment, isn't it. It's a shambles. Absolute shambles.'

It's a train of thought too dark for the beauty of the day so as I walk, I busy myself taking photos of seashells and driftwood. Meg reappears from a chase, tousled and panting, just as we reach the tip of the Cape. We both get a fright as one of the dark grey 'rocks' suddenly animates—the seal flaps off to the water to join its frolicking family and Meg growls under her breath.

Toetoe tail
WALKING TO CAPE TURNAGAIN

As we turn back, I take a quick selfie and message it to my friend Barry Saunders, adding the caption: *Man walking back from Cape Turnagain.*

Our return provides yet more opportunity for Meg to roam without reward and for me to take in the expansive view of the coast, trying to ignore the regular dark green swathes blotting the landscape. Rediscovering our starting point, we turn off the beach and flop into the car, content to have completed our own 360 degrees to Cape Turnagain. Back at the campsite Meg collapses in a heap in the shade while I attend to some house-keeping and maintenance. That night we both sleep extra well in still air beneath a star-studded sky.

*

After I've packed up in the morning, Meg and I walk along a sunny Seaview Road. Sheep are grazing the greener-than-green golf course. A tūī screeches to a landing in a pōhutukawa. Gentle surf swooshes in the distance. A muddy quad bike passes, an allsorts collection of dogs on its rattly trailer.

A small schnauzer pads towards us. As Meg performs the traditional circular bottom-sniffing greeting with her new friend, its wheelchair-bound owner appears on his deck calling, 'Mavis, we've got some company!' Propelling himself with impressive speed up the steep driveway, the man appears next to me on the footpath.

The man is David Power and this is his holiday home. A former Mackenzie Country farmer, he's retired with his wife, Mariann, to Lyttelton. Herbertville seems a strange place to have

163

a holiday home if you live in Lyttelton, I suggest. He explains that their daughter and her partner lease nearby Tautane Station and their only grandchild is there. He's about to get in his farm vehicle and visit them.

I tell David I'm working on a writing project and I'm here to walk to the Cape; that a friend of mine wrote a song about it. His eyes light up. 'The Warratahs song? It has the best intro I know of,' he says. He describes the piano introduction in detail then recites lines from Sam Hunt's poem and suggests its theme: 'Don't mess with the earthquake God.'

David says he's running late. With a crisp wrist flick on the chair's grey rubber wheels, he spins and glides back down the drive. As he reaches his vehicle he looks back over his shoulder, an afterthought forming. 'I met a man out walking, just now, today,' he calls. 'Said he'd come back from Cape Turnagain.'

HIDE AND SEEK

ON 5 JULY, 2009 THE *HERALD ON SUNDAY* REPORTED a bombshell: the most celebrated prison escaper in New Zealand history, George Wilder, was playing golf for the Cape Turnagain Golf Club and believed to be living and working in Herbertville. The reporter was warned by clubmates that Wilder was a private man, very unlikely to tell his story. 'He doesn't like attention or media and you'll find that no one is going to help you,' one said.[24] But someone had already told the reporter a juicy detail: that he was a regular at tournaments and had gained a respectable handicap of 17.4.

No-one in Herbertville would have been surprised to read the *Herald*'s story—by my reckoning, he'd been living around Route 52, hiding in plain sight, being sheltered by his friends and neighbours for at least twenty years. The question was, who squealed?

*

A friend told me recently that, as a child in Stratford, Taranaki, she had a pet guinea pig—called George Wilder. The subject came up when I asked if she remembered Wilder from his exploits in the 1960s; probably every New Zealander over fifty still does. And the reason for my question was that while I've been writing this book, several people have said to me, 'You know George Wilder lives on Route 52, don't you?'

My friend's fluffy rodent was named after Wilder because he was her family's hero. Wilder, a seemingly non-violent, low-level Auckland criminal (converting Jaguar cars, burgling shops, and cracking safes were his thing) had escaped from New Plymouth's Victorian-era stone prison in May 1962. He simply climbed a ten-metre wall and disappeared into the lush Taranaki back-country. When he was finally apprehended, eight weeks later, he was sent to Mt Eden Prison in Auckland with some time added to his lag.

Within months he'd escaped from Mt Eden, too. Along with three fellow inmates, he used the time-honoured—clichéd—'bedsheet' method. This time Wilder was at large for six months (his accomplices only lasted days), while his reputation as a loveable rogue grew with every possible sighting and thwarted capture. 'We delighted in his exploits,' my friend says. 'My mother in particular. She loved the fact he was so anti-establishment. He was like our Ned Kelly.'

As the media coverage of daring flights and close shaves with his pursuers ramped up, Wilder's 'folk hero' status blossomed. The central North Island seemed to be his favoured patch—

he knew the Taupō area particularly well, having once lived at the lakeside village of Tokaanu. He was reported to have broken into (or simply walked into unlocked) holiday houses, helped himself to food and drink and a bed, leaving 'thank you' notes when he moved on. Apparently, people left food out for him in places they thought he might be. Sometimes, as he was returned to prison there were supporters waiting to see him arrive. When he was found at Whakamaru, just north of Taupō after the first escape (ironically, *whakamaru* means to safeguard, give shelter) it was reported he hadn't eaten for a couple of days; dozens of offers of home cooked meals came in to the nearby Mangakino police Station. Lifesize images of him featured on floats in a Christchurch university capping procession.

On top of all this, a song was written about him. Recorded by the popular Howard Morrison Quartet, *The Wild(er) New Zealand Boy* was based on an old Australian song, *The Wild Colonial Boy*, which told the story of a young Irishman who was shipped to the penal colony and caused a bit of trouble. Despite the quartet's kiwi version being banned from public radio, it was a massive hit in 1964.

After six months on the run, Wilder was eventually found, asleep, in a hut at Rangitaiki, off the Napier-Taupō Road. Rifles were lying around the hut—he'd been shooting game and wood pigeons to eat—and this discovery somewhat tainted his non-violent image, despite the arresting police officers stating that he was little threat (perhaps this part wasn't reported).

Wilder escaped for a third time, in 1964 from Mt Eden with two others—a fellow safe-cracker, and 'Bassett Road murderer' John Gillies. A smuggled shotgun and hostages were involved, but it only lasted a few hours before they surrendered. However, Wilder's association with a dangerous, gun-toting criminal such as Gillies added to his fading reputation, not helped either by his presence during a riot causing considerable damage to Mt Eden prison.

Wilder was paroled in 1970 but found 'going straight' a challenge. During the only interview he's ever given—that year, to the *Sunday Times*—he professed a deep dislike of prison and a determination to stay out of it. 'I can't stand being cooped up,' he said. 'I couldn't see a future being locked up.' But old habits die hard—he was found in possession of stolen rifles and recalled to jail, this time to maximum-security Pāremoremo.

He was finally released from there in 1973.

*

Around 1980, *The New Zealand Listener* journalist Karl du Fresne tracked Wilder down to a rural address south of Taupō off State Highway 1. Du Fresne and his photographer found no-one home at the house, which he recalls being down a long, rutted farm track, but they decided to wait to see if someone returned. Indeed, shortly a car (an old Vauxhall Velox, du Fresne recalls) rumbled up the drive, Wilder driving, a woman in the passenger seat, children in the back. After a brief, amiable conversation during which Wilder declined the request for an interview or photograph, the media pair left.

Du Fresne wrote the story, being careful not to divulge too much of Wilder's whereabouts. His piece prompted a mailed response, however, in the form of two small pages in neat, childlike handwriting, which the journalist is sure came from Wilder. 'At last someone understands my not wanting to be written about,' du Fresne remembers the letter beginning, before the tone turned a bit menacing.

Another writer I contacted had a similar experience after contacting Wilder by mail. It clearly spooked him to the point he didn't want to talk about it. 'I've moved on,' he told me firmly. Neither he nor du Fresne kept the letters for any length of time. Neither was signed. But it all felt a bit, let's say, heavy.

In 1997, actor/director Tim Balme wrote a short play informed heavily by Wilder's exploits. Toured around the country as *The Ballad of Jimmy Costello,* the production was originally intended to be a biography— *The Ballad of George Wilder*—but written in 'based on' style after Wilder communicated his displeasure.

Interviewed for the RNZ podcast *Black Sheep* in 2021[25], Balme explained he tracked down the former fugitive to get his approval. 'He was living in a remote part of the Wairarapa. He didn't tell me directly—it was a very clear message sent by some friends of his. In no way was it a hostile thing, but they made it clear I wasn't welcome.'

George was not happy about any of this attention. He wanted to be left alone, to quietly disappear. And he eventually found just the place to do it.

*

During the lengthiest of his fugitive freedoms, George Wilder is thought to have holed up for some time in a bach at Waihaha, on the western shores of Lake Taupō. This has been verified by

George's sister, according to travel writer Bruce Ansley in his book, *Wild Journeys*.[26] Ansley spends a sizeable chapter of his book theorising about Wilder's exploits, sifting wheat from chaff, speculating about his motivations, challenging widely held 'truths' and some of the more outlandish claims. He's gathered some wonderful detail of his own, with eloquent descriptions of the territory Wilder covered in his runs.

Waihāhā was also the home for some time of writer, poet, and public relations exponent Antonios Papaspiropoulos. In 2015 Papaspiropoulos published a book of poetry, *Poems from the George Wilder Cottage*, which, in a playful press release at the time, he claimed to have 'stolen' from Wilder.[27] The story goes the poet gained access to the Waihāhā cottage thought to have been the one Wilder holed up in, and essentially absorbed Wilder's time there. 'I was on the run, too,' he said in the media kit. 'From life. I needed a break from the rat-race so I withdrew to this picturesque place and lay low for a while. I took some time to steal some thoughts away.' The result became a poetry cycle interspersed with real life anecdotes from people who 'ran in' to Wilder during his years on the run.

*

As far as I know, George Wilder is no relation to the Wilders we'll meet in a couple of chapters, although a tiny bit of mystery surrounds them too.

George's story has been in the back of my mind all the while I've been writing this book, but by the time I thought I'd finished, I'd decided to put it away. Not so much in the too-hard basket, but out of respect for the man's wish to be left alone. And anyway, I had no solid evidence that what people were telling me was true (to be fair, I hadn't looked very hard).

The reason I picked it up again was two-fold. Firstly, a *Midweek Mediawatch* episode I'd heard on RNZ National[28], and then a follow up conversation with Wellington journalist, author and historian, Redmer Yska, who convinced me I'd never forgive myself if I didn't write it. ('The man is in *your* landscape,' Yska said.)

On Mediawatch, presenter Hayden Donnell was lambasting his own employer—RNZ—for a headline someone had written on a web story by Jimmy Ellingham about the Cyclone Gabrielle cleanup in Tararua. 'Cyclone Cleanup Still Underway in Town You've Never Heard Of', the headline roared.

'What an assumption,' Donnell said. 'To think that people have not heard of Herbertville.' He then added, to laughs from *RNZ Nights* host Emile Donovan, 'And in my case that assumption is absolutely correct.' Donovan confessed he'd never heard of Herbertville either, and the pair continued some good-natured banter for a couple of minutes before getting onto more pressing media issues. When I went to look for Ellingham's story, the headline had been changed.

That conversation might have been music to George Wilder's ears had it taken place fifty years ago, when he was finally released from jail. Wilder was looking to hide somewhere, to get away from his infamy, sick of being on the run from both the law and nosey people. And what better place than one no-one has heard of?

✳

Let's return to the golf club. John Sedcole, whom we met in the previous chapter, is club captain. I rang him to see if he'd talk. He was happy to confirm he'd played golf with George. A lot. 'He was a stalwart of the club, a good member.' He also confirmed that Wilder and his family had lived and worked on a nearby farm for many years, and that he didn't talk much about the past. He 'took good care of himself' and was a regular in the club bar and local tavern. His tipple was rum. His friends and associates around the district had his back, deflecting enquiries, discouraging approaches, as the *Herald* reporter found.

Sedcole also told me Wilder had moved away from Herbertville a while back and, as far as he knew, was still alive. Beyond that, he either didn't know or wasn't saying. I had the feeling he was still protecting his old friend, and fair play for that.

There's tons of stuff out there if you go digging. But, with only the two exceptions relayed to me personally and mentioned earlier, I can't find any evidence of violence or hostility on the part of George Wilder. Press photos show him handcuffed to policemen, grinning from ear to ear, even looking directly into the camera, apparently enjoying his notoriety. Later behaviour presented him as a man just wanting to be left alone after spending—on and off—a decade in jail. He'd done his time, worked really hard to go straight, and had the intellectual and social resources to 'disappear' himself, and did so for decades.

I have no idea where he is now, and I don't really want to know. So that's where I'll leave it.

Except to report on my friend's guinea pig.

Coastal strokeplay
HERBERTVILLE

One day, the fluffy George Wilder escaped through a tunnel under his garden hutch and vanished. Who dug the tunnel is a matter of conjecture—the family dog? A neighbour's cat? George himself? And what happened to him after gaining his freedom? Perhaps he provided a snack for the dog, the cat, or even a pet magpie. Maybe he got run over by a milk tanker. Or it could be he simply went bush and lived out his days in undisturbed solitude.

THE COOKS TOOTH GANG

WHANGAEHU LOCAL ROBERT MCLEAN ONCE SAID
something that stopped me in my tracks. I'd only
known him for five minutes when he made a statement that's
as profound as it is obvious. In fact, I'm rather annoyed I didn't
think of it myself.

I meet 70-year-old Rob at his home on Cooks Tooth Road,
about fifteen kilometres from the Pōrangahau turnoff on Route
52. The road is named for a tooth-shaped limestone outcrop on a
former McLean family farm, Mount Pleasant, apparently noted
by James Cook as he turned around again at Cape Turnagain. I've
been warned that the already-fragile road has taken a hammering from Cyclone Gabrielle; this soon becomes clear as I climb
steadily, slimy mud replacing metal chip under dripping trees.
Temporary bends have been extended over the road's drop-off,
while cranes and diggers attend to the slipping earth uphill.

Irish mist
SUMMIT, COOKS TOOTH ROAD

The grey-green inland landscape goes on, higher and seemingly forever, angry clouds whipping by outside the car window. It's like driving across the Wicklow Mountains. At the summit, Cooks Tooth Road ends and splits in two—the perfectly named Ireland Road along the ridge to the right, Whangaehu Road turning down to the beach on the left. A forested driveway to the left is signed at the gate—*Moananui* ('big sea')—and I turn in. A few metres of crunchy gravel reveals a panoramic Pacific Ocean. A little further, swallowing the view, is a wooden house. Nearby, a cottage and whare.

I haven't actually come to talk to Rob; rather, his sister Jean and her family. I've clearly not been very attentive when setting up this interview—it turns out Jean and Richard Kibblewhite, whose children were at Wairarapa College with mine, are staying here with Rob while their own house down at the beach is being renovated. All I really knew was that the Kibblewhites had bought land out here several years ago and are now running one of their commercial fishing boats from the beach. And that their daughter Ellen—the vivacious schoolgirl who shrieked advice from the boundary as her brothers and my sons batted or bowled or fielded—had at some point skippered the boat. Which is what this story was going to be all about.

Until Rob tells me about the telegraph wire that used to run through Whangaehu.

'It came down the Pōrangahau valley to around where the Scotts are now at the Longest Place Name. Then it went up what we call the fingerpost, along the ridge to Bell's Gate, down Doctor's Gully, and into Herbertville.'

Rob is talking about the telegraph wire that ran from Auckland to Wellington via Tauranga, Taupō, and Napier. It was finished in 1872, before a decent inland road was built, when the area was still largely impenetrable bush. (When it reached Wellington, it was connected to the wire that, remarkably, had been running under Cook Strait since 1866.) 'So, the wire followed the track that people were already using to get up the coast—riding, bringing stock, timber, people, food . . . along with the sea, it was like the first highway through here. The original Route 52, you could say.'

The original Route 52. Why have I never thought of that?

*

When I arrive at Moananui, a display board is waiting for me. It's at least three metres long and spread out across two coffee tables in the living room. The display is surrounded by couches and armchairs on which two small terriers are snoozing (they don't move an inch or make a sound the whole time I'm here). A string of balloons suggests a recent party.

The board consists of photos, newspaper clippings, notes about the McLean family and their farms, and photos relating to the St Hill family from Whangaehu Station. They're all carefully pinned and glued and taped to backing card. Rob constructed it in 1997 while doing a polytech art course in Masterton.

The board's title trumpets *Whangaehu Coastal Park*. It's a concept Rob conceived after he left school and moved to Auckland. 'When I was eighteen, nineteen, we'd go out to the great coastal parks up there, spend the weekends swimming. I had the dream at the time that somewhere along the line we'd have our own historical park developed out here.'

Rob's fifty-year-old, 6,000-acre, grand park plan never eventuated, but that hasn't stopped him thinking about it, nor working towards a kind of mini version—developing a bush reserve on land his family gifted to the Crown in 1973.

Rob has always been the family historian. He's happy to talk about his display, the reserve or the cliff walk he's developed, or anything at all to do with the McLean family. Dates and details tumble from his mouth—stories of hunting trips as kids, the return of birds, the family's love of foxies for possum control (this bit particularly interests me), the movement between two family houses, his mother's Māori ancestry, the bentonite mining near Finlay's Reef, the design and construction of the house we're sitting in now. But particularly the possums.

*

For some reason I've always pictured Whangaehu Beach as one of those idyllic seaside settlements you see in house and garden magazines. You know—all pizza ovens, clipped lawns, picnics in the sand, kids on boogie boards, striped umbrellas. Until now, I've never been game enough to find out—on the map the road to get there looks pretty challenging and I haven't been willing to haul the caravan over it, even if there was a campground, which there's not.

The road to the beach is indeed twisty, no-exit, unsealed. It's on the northern side of Cape Turnagain, where Herbertville lies to the south, with only Arataura and Tautane Stations separating them. It's pretty, for sure—a small crescent bay with golden sand, a reef at one end, a river estuary in the middle.

A typical east coast beach in miniature. But it's remote, exposed, devoid of facilities and has a sting in its tail—a sting that thirty-year-old Ellen Baxter knows all about.

Ellen's parents, the Kibblewhites, run boats in several parts of Aotearoa. They dive for pāua, pot crays, net fish. It's a family affair—Ellen, her brothers, Sam and Jackson, and Jean's brothers, Rob and Bowen McLean, have all been involved off and on over the years, particularly with the boat they launch from Whangaehu Beach.

Their hunting ground is the Pacific Ocean, and this part of it can be tricky—just ask James Cook. Jean knows there's no safe harbour along the coast between Napier and Wellington, so when Ellen found herself out in a bit of a storm one day, Jean had every right to be concerned.

It was a gnarly westerly; double the windspeed the forecast had predicted. Then 27-year-old Ellen and her crew had tried several times to pick up the float on the end of their first net of the day, but a two-metre swell was making a bobbing cork out of *Splashzone II*—the four-tonne catamaran. There's a time limit for clearing set nets and Ellen was right up against it. Not wanting to let her father, employer, and mentor Richard down, she held the vessel as steady as she could while the crew attempted to retrieve the net's floats, waving and stabbing boathooks in vain. Eventually a large wave did its best to tip them over and she told her crew, 'Nah, let's get home.

'The steam home . . . I kept my head up and remained calm for the crew, but I was nervous. It was the worst sea I'd been in while at the helm. I knew we'd be fine, I trusted my boat, but it was a bit scary.

On a calmer evening
WHANGAEHU BEACH

'When it's rough offshore like that we don't worry about floating the boat onto the trailer, we just run it straight onto the sand and winch it on. It's an adrenaline rush, flying through the air between waves. You have to go fast—there's no going slow or you'll nose-dive.'

With Uncle Rob on the beach, his tractor idling impatiently, Ellen successfully landed *Splashzone II* on the sand, foam breaking over the stern. The whining winch cable hauled them onto the trailer, they could begin unloading their reduced catch, and Jean could finally relax.

*

Ellen left Wairarapa College at seventeen and did her first fishing season with Richard on the family cray boat at Whangaehu. Then she decided to do an electrical apprenticeship in Masterton. 'It was hard work,' she says. 'But I enjoyed the problem-solving; figuring out why a commercial oven or dishwasher wasn't working, fixing it under pressure.'

Having completed her papers and wanting to have some fun, Ellen looked to Mount Ruapehu. 'I applied for a lift operator job, but when they discovered I was an electrician they asked me to join the maintenance team. I wasn't that keen but the money was better, so I did it for two years. Then I went back working for Dad, and got my skipper's ticket.'

But fishing—and the electrical trade—very nearly lost Ellen to the world of dance. From the age of three, Ellen studied ballet, tap, jazz, contemporary, hip-hop . . . you name it, Ellen danced it. Competitions, shows, classes—any excuse.

At sixteen, there was a chance she'd train at the venerable Beijing Dance Academy, even visiting China with Rob to check it out with another uncle, Hamish, who was living there. But the huge city was a bit overwhelming for a girl from Masterton, despite her outgoing nature. At twenty-two she gave China another crack, but before she could settle in, her father tempted her home.

'Dad was fishing out of New Plymouth and needed a first mate. He said it was now or never because these positions don't come up often. It was hard. Long hours, no life. Then I ran the boat back here at Whangaehu with my uncle Bowen—he was my deckhand, which was pretty cool. But I was ready to get out of fishing, there wasn't much of an opportunity to have a life outside it. I was starting to think settling down and children, so as a way out I went to university and did a business degree.'

I'm thinking Ellen could even do further training—as a life coach. Here she is now with baby Katherine—'My life'—on her knee, wedding photos on the mantlepiece, while husband Andrew is off culling deer and hares on commercial forestry blocks. Looks pretty good to me.

*

The Kibblewhite/McLean family has chosen to run their fishing business from Whangaehu Beach for reasons that go way back.

In 1874, the brand new immigrant ship *Dunedin* sailed its ninety-eight-day maiden voyage from London to Lyttleton. On board the fully rigged iron vessel was thirty-one-year-old

Donald McLean. Donald hailed from North Uist, a small island in Scotland's Outer Hebrides. After graduating from the University of Glasgow as an engineer, he worked in construction for a short time before deciding to emigrate to Aotearoa. (A few years later, the *Dunedin* was converted for refrigeration and, in 1882, made the first successful meat shipment to England.)

After landing in Lyttleton and working in Christchurch for a few years, Donald made his way to Wellington. There he started a building company, McLean & Archibald, which built wharves and hotels all over the country. The company subsequently became McLean & Todd (the Todd name looms large in Aotearoa commerce to this day).

In 1881, Donald married Mary-Ann Dutch, a widow originally from Dundee with four children. Together they had a further six, including James (Jim) in 1888 and Alexander (Alex) in 1891. After attending Wellington College, Jim became a builder at his father's firm, while Alex moved to Wairarapa as a farm cadet.

On 7 November 1916, *The Dominion* newspaper in Wellington published a story headlined 'Brothers in Arms—The Remarkable Experience of Donald McLean's Two Sons'. The lengthy piece told of the brothers leaving for war together and serving at Gallipoli before heading for France. Then, 'After being in action several times, both were wounded the same day (both shot in the left breast), both found shelter in the same clearing station, were placed alongside one another at the hospital in Rouen, and at present are together at the Brockenhurst Military Hospital in England.' [29]

Before this misfortune, Jim and Alex had had a busy time with the Fifth Reinforcement, serving in Samoa and Egypt. In January 1917 they sailed home to Aotearoa on the hospital ship *SS Marama*, stopping in Durban for three days of luxury in the Fern Villa Hotel.

The last chapter in a 2021 memoir of the inseparable brothers' exploits—commissioned by Jean Kibblewhite, written by Fiona Craig, and titled *Shot at the Somme*—is worth reproducing here in full.

Back in New Zealand, some World War 1 survivors found themselves at the outer fringes of civilian life. Their true mates were those they had shared miles of muddy trenches with and depended on for their lives. Certainly this was the case for the inseparable Macs.

By divine decree, the McLean brothers were allotted neighbouring sheep farms in Southern Hawke's Bay through New Zealand's land ballot scheme initiated through the Discharged Soldiers Settlement Act 1915.

Alex acquired his 910-acre farm on Cooks Tooth Road, near Pōrangahau, in 1917. Jim drew the neighbouring farm on Whangaehu's Cooks Tooth Road [actually, it was 434 acres of coastal land on Whangaehu Road] in May 1918. To cap it off, the McLean brothers were joined by their friend and former soldier mate, Vincie Windle, when he too acquired a ballot farm in Whangaehu. The three young veterans worked and lived in close proximity for many years. They had each landed themselves hundreds of acres of prime farmland when fleece and meat were fetching premium prices at home and in Europe. Once again, the McLean brothers pooled their skills and helped each other develop their respective properties and maximise their assets.

When another soldier pal, Wilf Northcote, moved to Whangaehu,
he got work as station cook on one of the district's earliest sheep farms
[this was Whangaehu Station]. The arrival of Mac MacCutcheon,
shortly after, completed the muster of close friends. Serving at
the Somme, on the same machine gun, Jim, Alex, Wilf and Mac
had been tight. At Whangaehu they continued to be. That Mac
MacCutcheon had lost an arm during their time in France only served
to strengthen their bond. In his years of being gardener, carpenter,
cowman and general handiman at Whangaehu, Mac proved an asset
to the small community that came to depend on him; Jim's sons and
grandchildren included.

The McLean brothers spent a few years developing the land before
settling into their respective marriages. Alex wed Catherine Sebley of
Pōrangahau and Jim took up with Ethel Courtenay Bowen of Napier
who was a family friend of the Sebleys. Jim and Ethel married in
1922 and while away on their honeymoon, Jim's father Donald—
then aged 71—extended Jim's house. Jim and Ethel's first child,
Courtenay, was born in July 1925. A brother, Donald, arrived three
years later. The tight bond that developed between the boys—and the
farming partnership they established in the 1950s—would indicate
history does indeed repeat.[30]

The two settlement blocks stayed with the brothers until they
sold Mount Pleasant (the one with the Cooks Tooth outcrop
on it) when they split the partnership in 1989. The seventeen-
acre Moananui block was bought by Jean and Rob's parents,
Courtenay and Gwitha, from a soldier friend in 1942. They built
their family home here in 1958; the one we're talking in now.
And the coastal block, with the two-storey homestead that

Brothers in Arms
DISPLAY BOARD DETAIL, MOANANUI

Donald occupied, was bought from the McLean family estate by Jean and Richard Kibblewhite when they still lived in Masterton (by the time you read this, they'll be settled back at their renovated homestead).

Which brings us back to where I'm sitting with Jim McLean's grandchildren, Jean and Rob, and great-grandchildren, Ellen and Sam—who's been doing boat work down at the beach and has just dropped in for lunch.

*

This is a listing on the Central Hawke's Bay District Council website:

> *McLeans' Bush (Pōrangahau). Located off Whangaehu Road some 16km south of Pōrangahau. This 27-hectare reserve was gifted to the Crown by the McLean family in 1973 and is an important remnant of pre-European coastal forest, of which there are few examples left in Hawkes Bay. There are no tracks within the reserve, but a stile at the signposted layby indicates the access point to the reserve.* [31]

We're having lunch in the kitchen of the house Jean and Rob grew up in, where they've both lived at various times in their lives. The house, built by their father in 1958 and designed by family friend Barry Sweet, has been updated but still retains that classic mid-century feel, an array of windows framing the beach, the Cape, the Pacific. As we tuck into ham sandwiches and other meaty goodies, Rob tells the story of the reserve.

'It's 1945, Dad is back from the war and he's living down at the bottom house. The rabbiter Scotty Mills arrives. Dad asks Scotty what's been eating the buds off the fruit trees. Scotty says, "It's the Australian possum!" So Scotty gives Dad a fox terrier, saying, "Here we go Courtenay, this'll keep the possums out of your orchard". Well, for the next fifty years Dad was forever keeping possums out of somewhere.'

Courtenay McLean was always interested in native birds. He was surrounded by them while growing up here on his parents' farm. In fact, there were brown kiwi running about when Courtenay was a kid during the '20s, Rob says. 'There are photos of them around the hut by the homestead.'

Despite Scotty's terrier gift, the possums increased, and the birds started to disappear as fast as the budding fruit. 'Dad saw that. When we were teenagers in the '50s and '60s, he'd send us out possum hunting. We were the Cooks Tooth Gang. On the weekends he'd pack us off to the Cape with knives and three foxies. Once, we went to Owāhanga Station. Later, when we were allowed rifles, we'd go as far as Castlepoint—that took us four days: walking, shooting, camping, walking, shooting, camping . . .

'Then Dad got me a job looking after the gannets on Cape Kidnappers. Ron Fisher was the head ranger. I asked him if he was interested in making a reserve from some of our bush. He said I had to ask Dad and Uncle Donald, who were farming together. I was so shy, and they were quite imposing people. The bush was on Dad's deed—Mount Pleasant; Donald had the coast deed. So, I had to ask Dad. He said okay, and in 1975 we got it fenced and donated it to Lands & Survey, which is now DOC. But they don't do anything to it.'

In 1990, a couple of local farms, including neighbouring Tautane, tested positive for bovine tuberculosis, Rob says. It was being spread by possums. The government was obliged to act, setting up trapping and poisoning schemes. 'They got thousands. We had our own poisoning programmes on the farms, too. And in 1993 a pair of bellbirds turned up. They nested by the house.'

Ellen chips in. 'When Jackson and Sam and I were young, we visited Grandma here in the holidays. We'd do arts and crafts with her, then we could walk around the reserve with all our foxies. We'd shoot 100 possums in an afternoon. It was unreal how many were around. Now you'd hardly see one in there.'

'There are now seventy rat bait stations in the reserve, too,' Rob says. 'They were financed by Forest & Bird. And sure enough, back came the birds. They know they're safe here. I trap feral cats, too, maybe fifty a year. The last few years there have been birds everywhere.'

'When the flax is out down at the beach you can have 100 tūī there,' Ellen adds. 'And around here there are flocks of twenty wood pigeons.'

Rob was barely out of his teens when he had the idea for this reserve. So, like his father, he's spent fifty years getting rid of possums.

I finish my sandwich and wander over to Rob's display board to take some snaps. One of the photos is of the sign for the McLeans Bush Scenic Reserve. It's a stout wooden construction, letters routed into two pine planks next to a barbed wire fence at the top of a cliff. A typewritten caption states:

McLeans Bush:
Established 1975—66 acres
Regrowth slow until 1989. Good remnant of coastal forest
DOC bait stations for rats and possums
Huge increase in native birds—Bellbird, Tūī, Kererū

*

There's an unformed, or 'paper' road running from Whangaehu Beach to Route 52, close to The Longest Place Name. This is the track known as the fingerpost or 'the clay road', along which the old telegraph wire ran. I discover it has an official name— Fingerpost Road.

The Kibblewhites and McLeans have a plan for Fingerpost Road. They're worried about the increase in heavy traffic in the area, especially in twenty or thirty years when the massive new pine plantations on neighbouring stations will be harvested. 'When we were kids,' Rob says, 'Dad had a hay paddock down by The Longest Place Name. We'd cart hay up the fingerpost; it saved going right up to Pōrangahau and back around.' They think having the road properly formed and creating that direct link would mitigate the strain on the delicate Cooks Tooth Road, which is already getting a lot of forestry use. 'If we can get Fingerpost Road up and running again, it could take the pressure off,' Ellen says. 'The trucks could drive the loop or just use Fingerpost. It'd be an option anyway.'

Rob says he's tried to broker deals between local farmers and new landowners in an attempt to keep some of the land in use for sheep and beef, but to no avail. The family is resigned to being surrounded by pines, and to having them hauled out in huge numbers at some stage. But Rob's on the case, making submissions to forestry company audits, trying to get his beloved Fingerpost Road converted to a fully formed and maintained road. He says in the last four years there have been five blocks of pines trucked down Cooks Tooth Road and that there's plenty more to come.

On 24 August 2023, Robert McLean was asked to turn up at CHB Municipal Theatre in Waipawa where he was presented with a Central Hawke's Bay Community Award for 'services to pest control and the conservation of biodiversity'. Mayor Alex Walker said, 'These awards mark our outstanding citizens, most of whom fly under the radar and do not seek praise for their tireless work. They are the quiet achievers of our district.'

It seems to me Rob is happy to make as much noise as is required to get things done. He's a master submitter, both in writing and in person, to councils and conservation boards. Possums are on the rise again and with the ongoing issue of rats, stoats, and feral cats, he'll need all his skills and contacts to get the message out there that funding for his activities is dwindling. That without volunteers, his bird-filled scenic reserve will soon be at risk. And, with the help of his display board and the publicity he drums up, there's still time to get Whangaehu Coastal Park up and running.

And most importantly, by reinstating Fingerpost Road, part of what he calls 'the original Route 52' might spring back to life.

THE LONGEST PLACE NAME
IN THE WORLD

IN 1948, THE RECENTLY ESTABLISHED NEW ZEALAND
National Publicity Studios sent their photographer Edward
Christensen on an assignment to Southern Hawke's Bay. A few
kilometres off what was then State Highway 52, in an area known
as Mangaorapa, he photographed a typical rural landscape such
as might be used by the Studios to fulfil their remit—to create
publicity material conveying a positive image of New Zealand.

Christensen's monochrome images are not particularly
remarkable, but he must've had a grand old time collecting
them. He covered royal tours, tourist activity at hot spots like
Rotorua and Taupō, political figures and dignitaries in panelled
offices, picnics on launches moored at remote islands, lifts at
busy ski fields, musters on high country stations, and beach
resorts with kids splashing in the gentle surf. He even scored

a trip to the Cook Islands with Lord Freyberg. Edward had the dream gig.

For sure, a few mundane tasks got in the way—seconded to the Health Department for photos of potential dangers in the modern 1950s electric kitchen, say. Or snaps of Customs Department employees checking incoming parcels at the post office. But his oeuvre primarily consisted of the apparently idyllic colonial life—happy, prosperous citizens, and smiling Māori nurses, farm labourers, and factory workers.

Christensen's rural landscape we're concerned with here is of a young man on horseback with an older man standing, sleeves rolled up, felt-hatted, wooden walking stick in hand. There are dogs and sheep, #8 wire fences, cabbage trees, rolling hills (one looks a bit slippy), and an Automobile Association (AA) sign prominent in the foreground (this version of their logo looks oddly like a couple close-dancing). It's hard to tell if the sign is genuinely part of the landscape or put there for effect—'art department', in other words. It's pointing to an unseen feature somewhere unspecific in the distance. It simply says TAUMATAWHAKA-TANGUHANGAKOAUAU-ATMATEAPOKAI-WHENUAKITANATAHU.[32]

It's also unclear exactly where this sign is pointing us to, but from Archives New Zealand's description it refers to a nearby hill with what was claimed to be the longest place name in the world. The trouble is, nearly half the name's letters are missing.

I found another photograph, an AA sign again, this one taken by a British visitor in 1988. It's in colour, a vivid AA yellow, screwed to white posts (one is broken) under a pine tree against a barbed wire fence. In italics it proclaims:

'*Reputedly known as the longest place name in the world*', and over five tall lines with eighty-five letters and no hyphens says: TAUMATAWHAKATANGIHANGAKOAUAUOTAMA TEATURIPUKAKAPIKIMAUNGAHORONUKUPOK AIWHENUAKITANATAHU. Below that, with an arrow pointing vaguely into the countryside, it says: 'The place where Tamatea, the man with the big knees, who slid, climbed and swallowed mountains, known as Landeater, played his flute to his loved one.'

Another photograph, of almost the same sign, black-and-white this time, shows a cardigan-clad male (a teacher perhaps?) pointing while seven children of mixed age pose in a neat line (a rural school class?). It's earlier, maybe 1960s—the pine trees are young, the fonts are dated, and the kids look exactly like I did in primary school. Photographer: J Waddington, also of the National Publicity Studios.

But, for a long time, there's been a problem. The people, the tangata whenua on whose land the hill with the long name sits, where Tamatea played his flute, say they were never consulted about these signs. And had they been, they would've pointed out that the signs were referring to a view over land at Mangaorapa, some distance from Tamatea's hill.

*

Around 2005, after some pressure from local hapū, the Central Hawke's Bay District Council erected a new 'longest place name' sign closer to the hill's actual location. It was put on a gravel layby on the Wimbledon Road section of Route 52, just south of the

195

Right name, wrong place
FORMER COUNCIL SIGNAGE

Pōrangahau turnoff. The sign—black type on a white background with an explanatory 'interpretation board' above it—had a backdrop of native plantings merging into verdant farmland sweeping up to a bush-covered peak. It displayed the full eighty-five letters in one string and was almost as long as the logging trucks that had started flying by with increasing regularity.

In fact, it was hard to drive past the impressively stretched sign without pulling over to see what it was all about—and many people did. Some made special trips to look at it. Thousands of Kodachrome slides, iPhone selfies, and wide-angle videos of the sign were happily recorded and scattered across the globe.

But the place to which the long name actually refers—Tamatea the land eater's hill, known to locals simply as 'Taumata'—was not the peak behind this sign either.

Along the road a small distance lives the Scott whānau. They are tangata whenua of the land which features Taumata. In December 2022 they decided they'd had enough of watching from their veranda as hundreds of people a year were being misled by a misplaced sign. A sign they felt misrepresented their venerated tipuna, Tamatea, the man who swallowed mountains.

After asking the Council to move the sign and getting no joy, the Scotts took matters into their own hands and made their own. They erected it a short walk from their whare in a sizeable layby on their own land. They also created a welcoming picnic table and a new interpretation board. There's an invitation to park your campervan here, or call the family for more information. In the middle distance behind the sign, looking over the panoramic Pōrangahau valley out to the Pacific Ocean, sits Taumata.

In May 2023, after waiting five months for the Council to remove their now-redundant sign, the family dismantled it themselves.

*

I'm sitting in Ross Scott's 'man cave' with his daughter Peggy Scott and cousin Tungāne Kani. It's a freezing cold June morning—I had to scrape ice off the windscreen when I left the Waipawa campground at 8.30am. Ross's room is a corrugated iron, concrete-floored extension but the log burner is roaring and the atmosphere is toasty warm. Deer antlers hang above the door. Frypans are suspended over the fire where a teapot sits warming. Raincoats and camo fleeces are hooked up around the unlined walls, and boots create neat lines on either side of the brick hearth. A line-up of paraffin lamps sits atop the CD rack. There's the excited chatter of a young girl wafting through the door from the main house.

Peggy's daughter, Pareawa, delivers me a steaming Railways-style mug of milky tea. The Scotts have generously offered to drive me up to the Taumata summit, but the endless wet weather has put the kibosh on that; the track is too slippery today. So we talk here, at the whare where Ross spent a lot of his childhood, where Peggy was raised, where four Scott generations now live.

'I grew up in this area, out on Te Paerahi Beach,' Ross tells me. 'We were the only constant family there for a while. My father bought this place with his first wife, Merehera Tipene Matua. As kids, in the 1950s, 60s, we rode over here from the coast, a horse each, taking shortcuts through the rivers, over the hills.

Taumata pointer
MAN CAVE, WIMBLEDON ROAD

We raced each other, jumped fences to get here. We'd go to work breaking the farm in for nine or ten hours, then sleep in a little bach out the back. It was the only house between here and Wimbledon that had hot water. Everyone used to come and have baths and showers here.'

Ross reminisces about the people on this road, Wimbledon Road. 'The Forrests, the Warrens, Willises, all of that history down that way. Hales, Speedies, Morgans. A lot of good publicans at the Wimbledon, like Old Dutchie. He's retired across the road now—given himself tangata whenua status! The best people were around here.

'We were told by our old people that our ancestor Tamatea is a very important person, and not to let him be denigrated in any way. And so, as kids, that was our journey. And it still is, although we have obstacles we need to climb over.'

I'm thinking back to earlier in the year when the Scotts hit the headlines after the Council apparently refused to move their sign to what the whānau considered a more appropriate place. I ask Peggy to start from the beginning.

'For years, Dad and my uncles have wanted to have some kind of control over how our taonga, Taumata, is publicised and commercialised,' she says. 'The Council thought it would be a great idea to stick a sign up, to gain some sort of attention. There was no conversation with any of the hapū or anything.'

Ross chips in. 'The sign was in front of the hill which had the trig station. I think Pākehā just locked onto something that was important to them, and that was the trig. They just guessed, and they guessed wrong. They imagined dollars flying out car windows as people went to see the sign. I spoke to some of the aunties, and they said yes, that's wrong. So I went to the Council and said I'd like it moved over to here.'

The flute-playing Tamatea is a significant tipuna of Ngāti Kahungunu and Ngāti Kere, the dominant hapū around Pōrangahau. Tamatea Ure Haea originated from Te Waka Tapu o Tākitimu, which is considered by some to be one of the most tapu waka that voyaged to Aotearoa. Also known as Tamatea Pōkai Whenua and Tamatea Pōkai Moana (Tamatea the Explorer of the Land, and Tamatea the Explorer of Oceans), he was one of the greatest explorers in the history of Aotearoa. The names associated with Tamatea and his journeys are found across the length and breadth of Aotearoa.

'I went to Hanmer Springs once,' Ross says. 'I found out that Tamatea discovered those springs. He was freezing to death and he prayed for heat. There are a lot of inspiring things in Māori history, in this, our history.'

*

The Scotts have set up a company—Landeater Limited—through which they tell their story, the history of Tamatea, and Taumata—with the longest place name in the world. They have an active Facebook group and a comprehensive website. Their stated aim is to 'Reclaim and Restore' their taonga.

Their website states: 'For many decades the romantic notion was held that Tamatea played his flute to a lover, and this was promoted in pictures and on the sign posts. However, today this account is less accepted with local hapū actively being involved with the new interpretation board and signage.

'Whilst passing through the inland district of Pōrangahau, Tamatea encountered the Ngāti Hine (Hinetewai) people and had to fight them to get past. In the battle known as Matanui, his brother was killed. Tamatea was grieved at the loss that he stayed for some time at that place and each morning he would sit on the knoll to play a lament on his Kōuau. Hence the name indicating the hill on which Tamatea the chief of great physical stature and renown played a lament on his flute to the memory of his brother.'[33]

The track up the Taumata hill can be taken by 4WD or bike, or many, many footsteps. There is currently no self-drive option but the family is happy to take visitors up. The view from the top is spectacular, 360 degrees across farms and headlands and beaches and villages and out across the Pacific Ocean. With the help of a core group of locals they have created a mown, fenced grassy area. There's shelter growing, an enclosed wraparound wooden seat, and a circular fire pit. A large pou—a carved figure of Tamatea—stands guard. And of course a sign declares the longest place name, on five lines, no spaces, no hyphens.

'You get a view from up on Taumata which you don't get from the road,' Tūngane says. 'Our people can go up there and they can say 'Wow, that's our land, that's our whenua.'

'At the moment we're creating a more comfortable space for our manuhiri (guests). We've created a mārama, a site like a star dome where we can teach ourselves about our Māori calendar, and the way out tīpuna divided up the months and the seasons for us to live more in harmony with our environment. Mārama is like the cycles of the moon, each phase has a name and each month has a name and indicates what work needs doing.

'We have a lovely dark sky; there's no light pollution. It's a beautiful venue for us to meet, hui, and light our fire of occupation.'

Ross sees a bigger picture, too. He's convinced there's a business opportunity for the wider whānau. 'If we get the support that many other New Zealanders do, I think we'll have one of the biggest resorts this side of the island. I think we can compete with places like Taupō and Rotorua. We have lots of places here that've never been touched, between Pōrangahau and Whakataki, to Featherston, Wellington. We can share our income, our education, our tikanga with our iwi along the way. All it takes is a lot of help from people like the Council. Not directing us—that's different. Just listening to us. And one of the reasons I speak like that is our tipuna has a lot more to offer our Māori people than he does Pākehā'.

Ross says it's interesting that since they've put up their own sign and greeted visitors from all over the world, he's found they don't want to talk about the physical hill or place name as much as what it means to them personally. 'They want to cure something, I suppose. Fix something up inside themselves. Find out how we got to where we are; how we fixed ourselves.'

Peggy says they've had a lot of people in their parking area since they opened it. 'Some days it's packed, other days there's nothing. Some people sit there for hours just chilling, having kai, which I love because we want people to come and feel safe and relaxed, to learn something.'

*

Tuna tables turned
EELS, THE LONGEST PLACE NAME

Before I leave, Peggy wants to show me the new steps she's built down to the stream below the house. She's very proud of her steps. She learned from 'cousin YouTube'. I put my boots on and a jacket, although I hardly need it; I'm warm through from the fire and the tea and the generous conversation.

The stream has taken a bit of a hammering from the cyclone. There's a lot of debris piled up—clearing that is on today's list of tasks while Pareawa is at home ('She missed the school bus . . .'). As Peggy calls and splashes the water's surface with her hands, Ross whistles. Peggy's youngest daughter, pretty, wavy-haired Cecelia, is at Tūnganu's feet. She's excited. There's a pīwakawaka hopping and fluttering around. The stream babbles. Soon, a dozen slithery black tuna come weaving towards us. Big fat things. Smaller ones come, too. They know there is food in the offing—the family has been harvesting feral goats to feed both themselves and the tuna. Peggy and Cecelia feed the creatures from their hands, stroking them and picking them up. I decline an offer to do the same.

Traditionally, these tuna would be food for humans, but the tables have turned. 'What we've noticed since we've fully committed to what Dad and others have been talking about for years, is that our tuna have come back. I think they've aways been there but they show themselves a lot more now. We found koura in the streams up in the ngahere. There are lizards, skinks, wētā.

'We've also connected with a lot of awesome people. It all seems to be just falling into place. We take all this as sign that we're doing the right thing.'

I bid them goodbye and head off. They say, 'Make sure you come back'.

PUKKA CHUKKAS

THE BRASS BELL HANGING IN THE CLUBHOUSE CHIMES and with a crack! the third chukka is under way. A white ball fizzes over the cut grass, followed by a stampede of horses, their riders' voices echoing around the vast green valley. A second 'crack!' 'Outside!' a player calls, and another turns to collect the pass, galloping back past halfway. A swing and a miss, a quick turn, but an opponent arrives, shouldering the rider on the grey mare off the ball.

The players all spin, their mounts breathing hard as they race downfield. A blue-helmeted horseman riding a dark bay gelding swings his mallet in a giant arc, connects perfectly, and whacks the ball between the posts for the third score of the match.

Parked around the black timber clubrooms of the Wanstead Polo Club are half a dozen trucks with horses—or ponies, in polo parlance—tethered to twine loops, waiting their turn to have fun. Player Tim Coddington, sixty-seven, and his 55-year-old nephew Simon, the club's president, have shared a truck for their ponies. Today Tim has brought three, and Simon two. Nineteen-year-old groom, Charlee Spotswood, is preparing Tim's favourite, a chestnut thoroughbred called Puzzles, for the last, fourth, chukka.

'Tim's ponies have had very good schooling,' Charlee tells me as she adjusts the blanket under Puzzles' saddle. 'They really know what they're doing out there.' Charlee's plaited ponytail falls halfway down the back of her checked shirt, mirroring all the ponies with their folded and braided tails, which are wrapped to prevent them getting caught in the players' mallets. Their manes, too, are shaved—or 'hogged'—for the same reason. 'Racing thoroughbreds have speed, but you also want something that's sane, that's not going to throw you off. Outcast, who Tim's riding now, and Deputy here, they're purpose-bred polo ponies.'

After spending last season working for another Wanstead player, Lucas Simcox, Charlee has recently begun looking after Tim's horses on his Waipukurau property, Mount Vernon. Tim has recently restored the substantial heritage villa and extensive grounds to a classy standard, funded by his work in the international film industry. It's a lovely spot to work, Charlee says. Originally from Eskdale, north of Napier, she's returned from a stint as a polo groom in Auckland. She seems glad to be back, to be working with the country people and horses. 'It's pretty cool around here.', she says.

On the other side of the horse truck's black ramp, Simon Coddington's wife Charlotte prepares one of his borrowed ponies for the final seven-and-a-half minutes of today's play.

Charlotte is from England and met Simon when he was there playing and teaching and managing a polo yard. 'I turned up for a lesson one day, and, nek minnit . . . ,' she says. The couple has a lifestyle block not far from the club and they both work in sales, he for a livestock trucking company and she in real estate.

The third chukka ends, and the players trot back to base puffing and perspiring along with their horses. Simon decides to take one of Tim's rested ponies for the last chukka. 'The two I've got aren't really fit enough yet.' Charlee makes some saddle adjustments and walks the pony around to a small ladder where Simon is dismounting. He swings his leg over the new pony. 'I've had two hip replacements,' he says. 'And anyway, the day you use a mounting block is the day you should retire.'

Tim uses the block to get on Puzzles. 'I think this is my last season, too,' he says as the two players head back out into battle. The bell tolls. The grooms begin washing and cooling the retired ponies.

*

The Wanstead Polo Club's home is at Lake Station, a multi-generational sheep and beef farm a few kilometres off Route 52. A large club sign sits prominently at the farm's entrance. The gate and fencing are noticeably brand new, courtesy, once again, of the cyclone. Tyre tracks veer off the drive and onto the grass towards a small gathering of cars and people in the distance.

Driving towards the gathering, I follow the wooden boundary boards. A pair of black-and-white-striped goalposts reveal the polo field. A classic red tractor sits under some trees, waiting to be called back into mowing service. Several old wooden buildings are dotted around—the cook house, shearers' quarters—and a newer concrete toilet block. Others have been lost to fires over the years. Around a black shed-like building a few utes and quads are parked, their bonnets warm.

The clubrooms are unlike anything you're lkely to come across at Clevedon, say, or certainly at Cowdray Park or Santa Barbara. The Wanstead Club is more like a covered sheepyard—open sides, iron roof, wooden picnic tables scattered around. A small kitchen is open, but the adjoining bar is closed up with a black shutter. I find Andy Barrett as he's organising some volunteers with sponsors' signs and crates of beer. His fox terrier, Pipi, trails him and immediately finds something interesting—a nest of chirping chicks—inside a wine-barrel table. It's the afternoon before the opening polo game, and two days before another game which coincides with a major fundraising event for nearby Flemington School where Andy has two children.

Andy didn't even play polo until relatively recently, preferring other horse sports, and rugby. But he inherited the club when he and wife Hayley took over the farm from his parents in 2006. Lake Station was originally around 28,000 acres, one of several very large blocks in the area, like Arlington and Wallingford. Andy and Hayley now farm 700 hectares of the Station's 'home block', the rest having been carved off over the last century for various family members and rehab farms. 'So, it's still in the family to a certain degree,' he says. The farm is now fully a trading operation, Andy says. 'Cattle over summer, sheep in the winter. We buy them, fatten them up, sell them. Keep it simple.'

The Barretts also run a native tree business, Kākano Nurseries, in partnership with their neighbours Ben and Jo Percival. Andy says they noticed local farmers undertaking riparian or restoration planting were using seedlings from suppliers in totally different soil types and climates, and that often they weren't doing so well. Seedlings sourced from nearby farms and QEII blocks have a much better tolerance to Hawke's Bay's hot, dry summers and winter frosts, he says.

Before the polo club emerged in 1958, the area down here on the farm flats was a racecourse, where Andy's great-grandfather trained horses to race nationally. 'They were pretty successful,' Andy says. 'We have cups and ribbons and banners from all around the country.' The paddocks around the clubhouse are still referred to by the function they had back then—Birdcage, Saddlers, and so on. 'In the 1950s, a polo player from Hawke's Bay convinced Dad and his friends to evolve it. Of course the local farmers all had farm hacks they used daily. They trained them up for polo, basically by swinging sticks in front of their eyes.'

Andy's father John made the land available to mow for the summer, and the Barretts' good friend and neighbour James Dearden used his farm's machinery to convert the racecourse into a polo ground. 'We have the same arrangement now. We farm this area over the winter, then the boards go up in October and it's used by the polo club through to about March.' A polo community soon grew up around the club with names like Barrett, Coddington, Simcox, McDonald, Dearden, Reisima, Wilder, Hunter, and Bellerby still regulars over a beer in the club bar.

'Polo is a huge commitment,' Andy says. 'Basically, you're out here or away at tournaments all over the lower North Island every weekend from November until March. And you've got the horses to look after—entry level is two or three ponies, but one guy in the club has seventeen.' Andy concedes that the sport has a reputation as being only for rich people, and there is money involved, especially in the bigger clubs. But Wanstead largely serves the local farming families who already have the land, and often the horses. And the culture of the club is very much a rural one, too. 'You might be drinking a beer or Pimms or bubbly in the bar, but you'd most likely still be dressed in the day's workwear. The ladies might get a bit glammed up on tournament weekends, but you won't find them wearing fascinators or anything like that!'

∗

According to Britannica[34], polo may have been played in Persia (modern day Iran) as far back as 600BC. It originated as a training game for cavalry units and was played with as many as 100 players per team, both men and women. The game spread through Central Asia to Tibet, China, and Japan, and in the thirteenth century to India. The first Europeans to play were British tea planters in Assam, in north-east India. The Calcutta Polo Club was formed in the 1860s and the first game in England was played in 1869, where it became very popular. Soon the game spread to the United States (probably Texas to begin with), then to Argentina in the 1920s and '30s where it's now the national sport.

Over the centuries the rules have gradually changed but are still pretty simple. One of the more significant involved the size of the horses. Until polo was introduced to the U.S. around the 1880s, there was a height restriction of 13.3 hands (a 'hand' is four inches). The Americans decided ponies of that size were too small and increased the limit to 14.2 hands (technically, ponies become horses at 14.2 hands, but the 'pony'description stuck). The United Kingdom followed suit, then the rest of the world. In 1919 the restrictions were lifted altogether. Modern polo ponies are mostly over 15 hands.

A full-size polo field measures 275 metres by 146 (about four hectares) if it has 'boards', or 275 by 183 if it doesn't. (The 28cm-high 'boards' are the perimeter of the playing field, put there so the ball can bounce back into play.) There are penalty lines at thirty, forty, and sixty yards from each goal line, and a halfway line. The goals consist of two posts 7.3 metres apart and three metres high. The ball is hard plastic. The stick, or mallet, looks like those used for croquet but has a flexible shaft—traditionally made from cane—and the flat side of the cigar-shaped head, rather than its end, is used to propel the ball.

There are four players to a team, and teams can be mixed male and female. Two umpires ride with the players and a third watches from the side line or stand. As with field hockey there is no off-side rule, so the ball can travel the length of the field very quickly (in fact the game was once known as 'hockey on horseback'). A penalty can be called by an umpire for a number of infringements, but most commonly they involve a player's right of way (ROW) or line of ball (LOB). You might have to do a quick Google to get those explained.

Hockey on horseback
WANSTEAD POLO CLUB

Polo is also one of very few sports that stipulate that you must hold your stick in your right hand (it's called the 'right hand rule', of course). The rule was adopted in the 1930s and was aimed at reducing the possibility of a head-on collision.

The rules I like best are that you're allowed to 'hook' another player's mallet with your own to prevent them hitting the ball, and that you can perform a 'ride-off', which to the untrained eye just looks like a bit of jostling for possession, but which is actually quite technical and an important part of the game. You could waste a whole afternoon looking at fascinating videos explaining how to execute a winning ride-off. (The ride-off manoeuvre reminds me of match-racing yachts, where both right of way and direction of travel are important factors in penalties.)

For tournament play, teams are made up of players with various playing abilities, or 'handicaps'. It's an attempt to even up the teams and make for a fairer game—a level playing field, you might say. The player's national standard is expressed as 'goals', ranging from minus-two (a novice) to ten (the best). So, a six goal player and a minus-one goal player may play in the same team. The team handicap is the sum of the players' individual handicaps. The team with the lower team handicap is granted the difference in goal credits at the beginning of the match. Each tournament has a handicap range (usually one or two goals), and each participating team's handicap must fall within that range.

In a rather quaint feature, the players' 'goal' ratings have nothing to do with the number of goals they score; rather, the rating committee of a players' home nation will consider a variety of factors such as skill, horsemanship, strategy, knowledge of polo, team play, and sportsmanship. Currently there are only around two dozen ten-goal players in the world, all Argentinian.

*

I'm sitting with ebullient 69-year-old thoroughbred racing identity Mick Ormond in his art-filled little home on the family farm, 'Mangawhero', originally part of Wallingford Station. Wallingford was established in 1853 by Mick's great-grandfather, the first of four JD Ormonds. The sprawling Wallingford homestead, which housed generations of large Ormond families, now operates as a high-end dining and accommodation offering.

There's a photograph album on the table. Mick opens it to an image of his grandfather Jack with his polo ponies, the ones he sent off to World War One. 'Jack didn't go, but the horses did.' (More than 10,000 New Zealand horses were sent to the war; only four returned.) Mick also finds a page listing New Zealand Polo Association handicaps from 1939, with his father John (who became Sir John in 1964) listed as an eight-goal handicap. John was badly injured in World War Two and never played polo again but ended up umpiring well into his later life. 'Dad was a real horseman,' Mick says. 'He loved his horses.' He also helped tutor the Wanstead team when it got going. 'Some of those young players had hardly hit a polo ball, but Dad coached them to several Hawke's Bay Dewar Cup wins.'

Also crucial to Wanstead's early success was Mike Bellerby, who'd moved into the area from the Hawke's Bay Polo Club. Mike was a reserve player for New Zealand on several occasions and his experience and five-goal handicap were a huge boon to the fledgling Wanstead Club. Tragically, Mike died of a heart attack, aged forty-two, on the Wanstead polo ground, right between the posts, when Wanstead was playing Australia.

Mick Ormond relates the setting up of the polo club, and the rural-style fundraising. 'My uncle Dave was involved, Peter and John Barrett, Jack Murphy, and a young James Dearden. They mustered wild cattle from these hills up behind us, to sell. While they were driving them back, a bull broke a leg so they shot it and barbecued it. No-one had any salt, so Uncle Dave—he was a bit of a ruffian—grabbed his hunk of beef and ran it up the flank of his sweaty horse. He had to have salt on his meat. They certainly had fun setting up that club.'

Mick also likens the club to an 1893 poem by Australian 'bush poet' Banjo Patterson, 'The Geebung Polo Club'. In the story, the rural Geebung players, 'long and wiry natives of the rugged mountainside', are challenged to a match by the Cuff and Collar Team who visit from the city with their 'natty little ponies that were nice, and smooth, and sleek'. The game is so intense that one by one the players fall off their ponies and die, and the result is called a tie. 'We've always felt like that, the country bumpkins who can rock up and take on the flash city blokes.'

While I'm leaving to head a few kilometres down Ugly Hill Road to the club, Mick can't help sharing another tale about his late uncle Dave. 'An extremely colourful character, a great team man. He worked hard and he played hard. Dave, John Barrett, Mike Bellerby, and James Dearden played as the Wanstead team for years.' The story goes that the morning of an important game in Feilding, after a big night out, Dave couldn't be found. They eventually tracked him down at the police station, still much the worse for wear. They figured the groom would have Dave's ponies ready, and they had until 'bowl-in' at 3pm for him to compose himself. 'Miraculously, he played a blinder, and they never worried about him again.'

*

The fourth chukka finishes, the laughing and shouting and soft patter of horses' hooves subsiding as the bell chimes from the clubroom. Tim and Simon trot in together, breathing heavily, beaming with satisfaction. 'It's so nice to be playing,' they say. 'Last season was a washout. In fact, in five years this is only the second time we've had an opening weekend.' The score was four goals to three to Team A, an academic result as the teams were both made up from Wanstead players (except for a visiting farm worker from Mid Canterbury). The Coddingtons' resting ponies are washed and ready to be loaded.

I hear young female voices as the other players pass by. Watching the game at a distance, and with the players heavily clad and helmeted, I hadn't thought about the makeup of the teams. 'Yes, they're Crash's kids,' Tim confirms. (Simon 'Crash' McDonald is the Club Captain.) 'They're good riders, good players too. If it wasn't for all the women playing, polo would be dead in New Zealand.'

'When I was in England, more than half the players were girls and women,' Simon adds, pulling off his knee-high boots. 'Schoolgirls, kids from pony clubs. Tons of them.' Simon's boots are looking a bit worse for wear, the long metal zips hardly holding anything together. 'I bought these twenty years ago, vowing they'd be my last pair. The helmet rules were changed a while back, so I threw mine away and stole my daughter's. I'm still not going to buy new boots. I really should put new zips on them though.'

While Charlee finishes washing Puzzles, Tim compliments her on the ponies' preparation. 'They're much better this weekend, thanks. They're performing very well.' Charlee heads off to her other job working in a restaurant as Tim and Simon load all five horses into the truck. 'Puzzles! Concentrate!' The chestnut wriggles in the wrong direction. There's a lot of stamping. Springs creak and groan, tightening on the ramp as it closes upwards. It's just a short journey to a paddock at Simon and Charlotte's place where they'll be turned out to eat and rest while players gather for the official opening of the season.

Over in the clubhouse there's already a crowd and the black-and-white walled bar is doing a good trade. Volunteers and committee members from Flemington School's Parents and Friends group have been busy setting up for tomorrow's major fundraiser—the Flemington Mud Run—and have developed a thirst. At the edge of the open room, I strike up a conversation with Sarah who explains that this is the big one for the year and should raise about $30,000. It means they don't have to be doing little events all through the terms. 'It pays for teacher aides, benefits the kids,' she says. This year's is the tenth Mud Run. It's grown from an initial 150 runners to last year's 600 and they're expecting at least that this year. 'People come from all around.' Sarah says she has friends coming over from Whanganui to run.

Jo joins us, back from collecting the school's barbecue. Jo is a past chairperson of the parents' group, and despite her children having finished at Flemington she's keen to stay involved: she'll be the MC for tomorrow's event. Both she and Sarah confess they don't know a lot about polo. 'But there's five in a team, I know that much,' Jo says. I'm happy to have very recently learned enough to correct her.

The players and supporters have gathered so Simon Coddington gets official proceedings underway. Standing by the kitchen door, a frosty Heineken within easy reach, he generously welcomes me as an outsider and explains what I'm doing here. The award for 'best presented' is well received, and there's much hilarity when a few fines for transgressions such as swearing on the field are handed out. A hearty 'Well done guys, here's to a good season,' and the brief duties are done.

I'm beginning to understand why the bar is known as the Craypot—you can get in, but it's very difficult to get out. As the little dispensary's patronage increases, so does the level of chatter amongst the gathering of polo players and supporters and fundraising volunteers. I'm introduced to a Robbie Hunter, and the name is familiar. It turns out I spoke to him on the telephone briefly when I was writing about Pōrangahau—he's from Papakihau Station, where David Aupapa grew up. (Then, I called him Rob, and he looks nothing like I imagined.) Robbie tells me about his mother who came from Scotland, who every time she went from the farm to Waipukurau she got stuck in the swamp on the 'dreadful' road from Pōrangahau, and about how the Council regularly came to pull her out. He buys me a beer.

Club captain Simon McDonald joins the circle, asking Robbie if he's 'up for chukkas' after the Mud Run tomorrow, saying he'll make the weather call at eight or nine in the morning. Simon tells me his nickname, Crash, was coined when he was about sixteen. 'Then eighteen, then twenty-nine, and the most recent one, not that long ago.' (I've also read that it refers to his physical polo playing style.) Over the hubbub, Simon says he started playing here in 2001 and had his first stint as club captain not long after that. Then a period of being secretary, and bar manager for a bit. 'Things just rotate around. Everyone eventually gets a job of some description.'

Club membership ebbs and flows, as everywhere Simon says. But like the Poverty Bay and Hawke's Bay Clubs, which have both recovered well from once being down to two or three members, Wanstead numbers are up to almost a dozen at the moment. I mention that their web page claims they're the second biggest in the country, and someone says it needs updating but five or ten years ago that really was the case. And with such small memberships, one family moving away can effectively mean losing a whole team, as happened to Wanstead recently.

In the background, expired bottles are continually dropped in a wheelie-bin by the bar. The discussion moves to how well the lambs are doing on red clover, the families who grew up around here, logging, rugby (lots of rugby), the weather, schooling. I love these communities, they're real communities, and I need to remind myself that despite the cachet some of these names have from their settler history on big stations—Ormond, Hunter, Barrett—they love a good casual chin-wag as much as everyone else.

I'm feeling the Craypot effect. But I've had two beers and I need to get back to Takapau, where my caravan is parked, before the Four Square closes. I gradually extricate myself (who said it can't be done) thanking Rob(bie) Hunter for the beer, passing by the various Coddingtons, saying maybe see you tomorrow, looking at all the Red Band and John Bull and Swanndri clad folk gathered in this humble meeting place, thinking of the Geebung Polo Club, sorry I can't stay longer.

*

The following day dawns grey and drizzly, perfect for running in the mud I think, but maybe not so good for polo. Not great for my mood, either. I had a frightening caravan tyre blow-out on the way up here and the fitted spare is low on air—I felt the slight slump on the right-hand side as I was lying in bed last night, reflecting on the day, thundering hooves still playing in my head. The locum campground caretaker, Mort, has a decent portable twelve-volt air compressor so I borrow it to inflate the commercial tyre to the required 55psi (the air hoses at many service stations won't go this high). The blown tyre still sits, shredded to the rim, in the back of the car. I make myself a bit of breakfast and head back to Wanstead under gathering clouds.

The parking paddock is packed when I arrive, vehicles lined up neat as a pin around the perimeter of the polo field. A smiling volunteer directs me around the corner through the new wooden gate, pointing to a space next to the biggest SUV I've ever seen, shiny black and Chinese. I walk towards the polo clubroom. There's a multi-coloured throng spread around the registration desk. Hundreds of people of all ages, shapes, and sizes are dressed in pink tutus, bumble bee costumes, wigs, sponsors' shirts, camo, Santa hats, bananas in pyjamas, all manner of questionable couture.

The first person I recognise is Mick Ormond, wearing grey overalls and a large brown hat. He's standing with his granddaughter, who will be running shortly. Andy Barrett— bright green from head to toe—whizzes by on a very muddy quad. Half a dozen red, white, and blue branded gazebos and associated flapping signs are concentrated around the clubroom. Spectators queue at a purple and orange coffee cart offering latte, mocha, chai.

Soon the gazebos empty and runners gather at the race start area. Jo, the MC, is wearing a striped top and something like a pumpkin on her head. She stands on a box, reading race rules through a microphone, but is having trouble being heard over the music and excited chatter. Spectators are dressed for the weather, raincoats under their arms if not already donned. I'm keeping my eye on the forecast, which isn't good.

The race is divided into three distances—ten, five, and 2.5 kilometres—and the start is staggered. Runners compete (or don't compete) individually or as teams, and as they're released by the starter they quickly head off across a paddock into a stand of trees. From my position at the start line I can see the runners as they emerge from the forest, climb a steep hill, and skid down a mud slide while being sluiced with a hose. Over the course there are tyre tunnels, bank climbs, mazes, a creek run, a bog, a stump run, the Tunnel of Terror, and mud. Lots of mud. At the finish line a two-metre-high yellow frame awaits runners who stand behind it for photos. 'I SURVIVED THE FLEMINGTON MUD RUN 2023' it proclaims.

The drizzle hasn't turned to anything more serious yet, but the MetService app on my phone is flashing orange and red

Mud-dip
FLEMINGTON MUD RUN

watches and warnings. Wary of suffering another puncture (or worse, another blowout) and getting stuck, now without a spare, in the middle of a tempest, I decide to forego any re-run of polo and the planned third night at the little private campground at Takapau and make a run for home. As I walk back to the car a young lad crosses my path, heading for the communal open-air shower. 'You finished already?' I ask. The response is quick: 'Yep. I won.'

*

Anticipating the standard look of disappointment on Pip's face whenever I arrive back from a trip early, I telegraph it well ahead. I settle up with Mort (cheapest parking with power I know of), hook up the 'van, get the cleanup done (dump station, tie-downs, double safety checks today) and chug tentatively out onto the highway. Friday's tyre drama has shaken me up a bit.

Angry clouds hover over the Ruahine Range to the west, but apart from a couple of light showers, and with a gentle northerly wind behind me, the run down State Highway 2 to Carterton and out to where we live is quick and uneventful. This is the second time recently I've curtailed a journey due to weather warnings, only for them to have come to nothing. Maybe the forecasters are a bit gun shy after Gabrielle.

And maybe—hopefully—the Wanstead Polo Club got a few more chukkas in this afternoon after all.

THE ARROW AND THE CROSS

O N A SUNNY DAY IN 2020, RETURNING FROM ONE OF Jamie Macphail's 'Small Hall Session' concerts in the tiny Mangakurī Station chapel, Pip and I decided to avoid the main highway and use Route 52. Motoring south in the early afternoon we each remarked on the leafy outskirts of Waipukurau, glimpsed the glistening Lake Whatumā in the distance, and took a fruitless half-hour side trip to look for the curiously signposted Wilder Settlement (there was nothing obvious to be found).

The former Wanstead Hotel—hub of the faded hamlet it's named after—flashed by. Ugly Hill Road loomed and passed to the right (I wondered how a hill could be so ugly it had a road named after it). Soon a sign pointed left to Blackhead Beach and the Wallingford Fire Station. Then another, indicating Wallingford Church. We weren't in a hurry so decided to investigate the church, taking a hairpin turn onto Bird Road.

On the left up a short rise, what seemed like a former school sat looking rather unloved. Opposite, a cottage and a horse truck in a paddock. A little further along the seal ended and the summer dust started billowing skyward. As the road climbed and narrowed we passed gates, cattle stops, and farmhouses, the elevation revealing ever more views over the hills to the coast where we'd been listening to music the previous evening. There was no sign of any church.

Oh well.

Just as we were pulling into some stockyards to turn back, a quad bike appeared out of the dust. The cheery farmer laughed and told us the church was right at the beginning of the road, next to the old school. Mmmm... Back down we went.

From the opposite direction a gate, partly obscured by over-hanging foliage, was a little more obvious. There was nothing to indicate what lay beyond. The latch looked like it hadn't been used for a while, rust forming on the dull zinc ring. Peering over the gate through the branches down a steep driveway we could make out a small off-white building and, yes, some stained-glass windows.

We opened the squeaky farm gate and gingerly stepped down the overgrown drive, feeling a bit like trespassers. Agapanthus spilled onto knee-high grass. A simple gabled building came further into view gradually revealing a lean-to, a small porch, and a tiny wooden cross at each end of the roof's ridge.

Around the back a black plastic water tank on a rickety timber stand was doing its best to collect rain from wobbly spouting. There was no easy view through any of the windows to the interior, and nothing of particular interest outside. Apart from

Trespassing
BIRD ROAD, WALLINGFORD

the windows and the crosses, it didn't even look much like a church. We had a quick wander around and went on our way.

*

A couple of years later I'm picking my way down the same agapanthus-fringed drive to meet Wallingford Church trustee and key-holder, Hannah Morrah. Since that first visit I've driven past the road sign on Route 52 several times and curiosity has got the better of me. I want to know why the tiny church is where it is and what it gets used for. Is it just another of those community assets that opens its doors once a year at Christmas and for the odd christening or wedding, or is there more to it?

Hannah and I played a bit of phone tag a week previous, trying to find a space in her schedule to have a chat. She's busy with three teenage children, a farm, various trusteeships and charities, neighbourhood riparian planting, an Airbnb, and fingers in seemingly endless pies (someone I speak to later reckons she'd make a good Prime Minister). But we eventually found twenty minutes to talk, and what she told me made me want to know more so we agreed to meet at the church today.

Hannah is a Southerner from Dunedin, part of the McConnon family, founders of Mainland Cheese ('Good Things Take Time'). She has married into the equally Celtic-sounding Morrah clan who farm nearby Ohineumeri Station (husband Sam is third generation). When she arrives, I'm not surprised to find she's tall and outgoing and has waves of flaming red hair. The first thing she does is wade into the undergrowth to pluck a cabbage tree flower, holding it tight to her nose, enjoying a scent which has varying popularity—some say it smells like cat pee, and I must say I wasn't overly enthusiastic when Hannah offered me the pinky-green bloom to experience.

Hannah has already told me that the building we're standing beside was not built as a church—which explains why, when Pip and I first visited, we wondered why it didn't look like one. She told me it was the original one-room Wallingford School, dating from 1881. It was turned into a church in 1960, she says, when the Department of Education built Wallingford a new school, the one that sits at the top of the drive, now itself privately owned since it was closed and disestablished in 2005.

The old building's exterior is not looking its best. It hasn't seen a lawn mower or water blaster for some time. Arum lilies have invaded the base boards. Lichen specks the heat-pump unit. It has a general air of despondency. But when Hannah opens the bishop's hat-shaped door and we pass through the tiny office, the room bursts into churchy life. Rainbows of colour stream through a dozen stained glass windows. Golden wooden pews are stacked at the front near the formal entrance porch. The altar area is covered in crimson wool carpet. A sky-blue runner stretches along the native timber floorboards from end to end. A leather-bound journal sits on a small wooden table next to the entrance—*St Peter's Wallingford, Diocese of Waiapu*, an inscription proclaims. The journal's first entry is the Dedication of the church on 19 December 1961.

The building's gabled ceiling is painted a delicious grey-blue; the elegantly triangulated trusses holding it up, a soft cream. Each window, lead-light or clear glass, is framed with natural timber. And every stick of furniture in the room—pews, altar,

Rex or Jack?
WALLINGFORD CHURCH

pulpit, Presider's chair, candlesticks, hymn board, christening bowl, side tables, even the little individual donor plaques—is by the same maker. Each piece (of rimu, I guess) is hand-adzed and bears the distinctive 'Sagittarius' mark of furniture designers and craftsmen, Rex and Jack Chapman-Taylor. It's quite a collection.

Rex and Jack are son and grandson respectively of renowned 'Arts and Crafts' architect, builder and woodworker, James Walter Chapman-Taylor. The elder Chapman-Taylor—variously known as James, Walter or 'CT'—completed 110 architectural plans in his lifetime, including *Inverness* in nearby Dannevirke in 1914, arguably one of his most elegant. In all, ninety-seven of his designs were constructed, many of them featuring in-built or freestanding furniture designed by himself.[35] A good number of Chapman-Taylor houses remain, often almost untouched, mostly around Hawke's Bay, Hutt Valley and Wellington. Twelve of them are heritage listed. By the time James Chapman-Taylor died at Lower Hutt in 1958—just before the Wallingford School was converted to a church—Rex was well established as a craftsman in his own right.

In 1940, Rex and his wife Connie built a house of his father's design on Fergusson Drive Upper Hutt (number 684 now, but there were no street numbers then). At the rear of the house was the workshop which Rex, joined by his son Jack, used for fifty years to build their distinctive wooden furniture. Rex died in 2001, age ninety-nine; Jack in 2013 age eighty-six. One of Jack's last professional tasks was to create a mantlepiece for an Aga stove in the last house his grandfather designed, built in Silverstream in 1952. Chapman-Taylor furniture is highly collectible and often copied. Aficionados can tell the difference between Rex and Jack's furniture by the length of the arrow's shaft in the Sagittarius symbol on each of their pieces.

*

St Peter's Church is on land that was once part of the great Ormond estate, Wallingford Station. The building would've been easier to find in those days—the school had a walking track and bridge over the gully further down the road, according to Mick Ormond, who I've visited at his nearby home, 'Mangawhero', to talk school, church, and polo.

'My grandfather gave the land to the Education Board,' Mick tells me. 'Then, when the new school was built above it, my father had to buy the land back to create the church. It cost him 400 pounds. He was a bit miffed.' Despite there being a school room in Wallingford Homestead, where the Station governess oversaw the early education of Mick's father and his eleven siblings, Mick's older brother Johnny and sister Caroline attended the little Wallingford school with around ten other local children. He recalls them riding there, putting their horses in the pony paddock for the day, running across the road after class to the Pōrangahau River for a swim. Mick himself went to the new school, where the river swims soon ceased—the school featured a sparkly new pool.

The school building had good bones, Mick says. 'It's all pretty original.' My walk around with Hannah reveals the teacher's office with desk and card file, a double school desk squeezed into a tiny alcove (was this the school's naughty corner?), and a room which was probably the teacher's private space—Mick tells me the teacher lived on-site. One further room contains a wooden foot-pedal organ, or harmonium, covered in a moth-eaten cloth, its pedals worn bare by the player's soles. (I realise later this was the teacher's bedroom, and the 'private space' probably the kitchen.)

The committee overseeing the conversion from school to church consisted of Mick's mother Judith (later known universally as 'Lady O'), his uncle Andrew Ormond (known as Dan), uncle Nick Wilder, and Mary Morrah, Sam's grandmother. 'A small committee is a good committee,' Mick says. Major contributors to the project were the Ormond family, who forwent the Station centennial they were planning in 1954 and contributed the funds to the cause. Mick's grandfather Jack Ormond also put aside some of his racehorse winnings for the conversion.

I ask Mick about the Chapman-Taylor furniture. 'Rex had made some furniture for Aunt Norma, and my mother had commissioned a bed and dressing table for my sister. In my mind's eye I can still see those things in her bedroom.' The Ormond ladies got on well with the craftsman, so when the question of furniture for the new church came up, Rex was given the job.

'I love that church,' Mick says. 'We bought a decent Yamaha keyboard about five years ago because the old pump organ was sounding a bit tired. Hannah went in there one day to plug it in and it didn't work—the bloody rats had got it. We had to throw it away.'

One of the early Wallingford vicars was the late Archdeacon Hone Kaa, then at the beginning of his career. Highly educated, Kaa went on to be a national figure, teacher and activist for

Māori, especially children. 'Gorgeous man!' Mick says. 'Oh yes, we loved Hone. We were very lucky to have him.' Later came Warner Wilder. 'My cousin Warner was a local farmer and a lay reader at the church. At one point we ran out of vicars, just as Warner was getting ordained. He was called Wild Man. Good polo player, confirmed bachelor for years and years, then found God. Well, he'd found everything else!'

Warner's younger brother Andrew recalls seeing forty-year-old Warner studying at the farmhouse, doing his training extramurally. 'He was very committed. To be fair, I think he always had God. It was in his bones. He'd already lived a life—seen the other side—then something clicked and he went into the church, to give back.' Warner served St Peter's and the Pōrangahau Parish for two years before moving in 1989 to the Chaplaincy at King's College, Auckland. He had a hugely popular career at King's, retiring in 2016. He married for the first time in 2009 at age sixty-two, has four young children, and is still heavily involved in the Anglican Church in South Auckland.

Andrew Wilder remembers St Peter's being very active while Warner was there. 'It was humming. We'd have church, carol services, Sunday School, right through the year. It'd be standing room only. We'd gather outside afterwards with plates and some beer and wine. I guess that was the advantage of having Warner living close by.'

*

Currently St Peter's Wallingford has no permanent vicar (and no organ). I'm walking around with Hannah Morrah as she laments the 'army of few' who look after it these days. 'Actually, I'm wondering if it's just that I haven't asked. It's such a lovely place to work around.' She feels very protective of it. It's like her marae, she says. 'It's nice to feel the generations of people who have passed through here.'

I notice some very smart plan drawings pinned to a wall. They're by Wellington architect William Giesen—another of Mick Ormond's cousins—and are dated 2017. Hannah says at that time they realised they needed to do something to bring the church to life again. 'Use it or lose it,' she says. 'It needs facilities if it's to host anything serious like a concert. It needs a smart parking solution. Water, toilets. One of Jamie's Small Hall Sessions would be perfect here, but . . . '

Building Giesen's plans is beyond their means ('Willie got completely carried away,' Mick says). Hannah and I talk about old buildings, how much life they've had through them, how they're getting harder to maintain, to sustain. She's feeling better knowing that I'm interested in this building. 'Watch this space,' she says.

Hannah must get home to the farm up the road, so leaves me to poke around a bit further. We agree to keep in touch. I spend twenty minutes gathering my thoughts, making some notes, wondering what I can do. Is this building worth saving?

I lock the door and begin the walk back up the drive. It seems to me the building is being used so infrequently it's hardly worth the effort. But then I catch myself—surely these things are always worth the effort, if you make it.

*

I'm somewhat familiar with re-purposing old buildings, although to be fair our initial Wairarapa project never got past first base.

In 2001 my little family escaped Auckland and briefly set up a basic home in a decommissioned rural school between Carterton and Martinborough. After a year or so we'd only moved the shower inside from an outside changing shed when we found a bigger challenge a couple of kilometres up the road (which you can read a bit about in the chapter *Howzat?!*). Then, the friends we sold the old Ponatahi School to gave it a fabulous Barbara Webster architectural makeover.

Our old school at least had inside toilets—rows of them, for boys and for girls—which Wallingford School did not (there were outside toilets for both teacher and pupils back in the day). And ours was a much more substantial setup when we took it over from the private Christian School who'd owned it for some years—there were more recent workshops and outbuildings scattered around the grounds and even a swimming pool buried in the courtyard, carefully reinstated by our purchasers. But, like ours, the Wallingford classroom at least got a new life, while many old buildings lie forlornly abandoned.

A couple of years ago I was poking around Pōrangahau, a few kilometres from Wallingford, and spotted a soaring roofline at about forty-five degrees attached to a building with a wonderfully Modernist zig-zag porch over the entrance. Those two features were all I could see through surrounding lush foliage (read: overgrowth). There was nothing to suggest this building was anything but a private home.

But the roofline reminded me immediately of Hawke's Bay architect John Scott's 1960 Chapel of Futuna in Karori,

Wellington, and other churches he'd designed before he died, rather too young, in 1992.[iv] I knew Scott had designed a couple of houses that were built around Pōrangahau but didn't know where they were. I didn't know of any dwellings he'd designed with such church-like features. I snapped a quick phone shot and sent it to my friend, architect and Scott scholar Nick Bevin. 'John would never design a roof like that,' came the reply, noting a particular architectural detail which meant little to me.

Later, when re-visiting Pōrangahau to research the piece *Coconut Grove* for this book, I found the non-Scott building had been divested of the botanical cloak and was now plain to see in all its glory. By then I knew it was in fact a 1960s Presbyterian church which had been converted to a dwelling, and that it had recently changed hands (the real estate listing, including photographs and sale price, is still public as I write). A sign for a professional practice was erected on the lawn. I rang the phone number. Yes, there were some plans lying around but no, I'm not sure where they went, I was told.

(The following night I got a return phone call giving me an earful for snapping a few reference shots—a porch-sitting neighbour had dobbed me in. Why would anyone want to go around taking photos of other people's houses? Strangely enough I would, I replied.)

Of course, that episode set me off on another 'whodunnit' architect quest (see also *Church with One Bell*) during which Nick Bevin, Hawke's Bay architect John Hoogerbrug (son

---

iv For context, John Scott is whānau of the Scotts at Taumata, The Longest Place Name near Pōrangahau.

So, so modern
PRESBYTERIAN CHURCH, PŌRANGAHAU, CIRCA 1962

of Len who was an early suspect), and architectural historian Dr Robin Skinner were very helpful, but ultimately it was the Central Hawke's Bay District Council who came up trumps. So, I can report that the design for the beautiful, quintessentially Modernist church came from the celebrated office of Natusch and Sons in Napier, and that those responsible for the domestic conversion are better left un-named. However, another end-of-life building which could easily have met a sticky end (not everyone likes such off-beat architecture) was successfully re-purposed. The way I see it, that's a win for everyone.

∗

In 1986 Sir John Ormond, Mick's father, spoke to Nicola Kelsey for the Hawke's Bay Knowledge Bank.[36] In the oral interview he relates how his own father, Jack, was at a Christchurch 'November Week' race meeting 'in about 1900, 1901' with the family horses (possibly 'Solitude' and 'Forty Winks'). He met a young lady at a ball. At November Week the following year he proposed to her. Her name was Gladys Wilder.

Sir John's sister Margaret Hope was interviewed at the same time and tells Nicola Kelsey, 'At first her parents were rather horrified. She seemed far too young; they knew nothing about this young man. He had to race round Christchurch finding people who knew that he was respectable; that his family were very nice people; that he would be in a position to look after a wife properly. So they were allowed to be engaged, much to the joy of Grandfather Ormond, who was enchanted with her photos, and when he met her.'

While I was sitting with Mick in his house at Mangawhero he told me this story and showed me a picture of a young Gladys Wilder. She was indeed very beautiful. He also told me about the Wilder family, how they'd arrived in Christchurch with Gladys and two siblings (three more boys were to follow), an English family from 'very good stock' who'd fallen on hard times but with enough left to buy a small farm at Rangiora. He says Gladys' father agreed to the marriage on the condition that Jack's father 'settle' the four Wilder boys. 'The old boy had plenty of land, so that's what happened.'[v]

In the Knowledge Bank interview, Sir John tells it like this: 'Jack Wilder—the youngest of the Wilders—who had worked for him, was parcelled[vi]—quite a considerable acreage was passed over, put in Jack's name. And he unfortunately got killed at Gallipoli. That land was then sold to the government. The government cut it up themselves and they sold that as a settlement, and that was called the Wilder settlement. The money from the Wilder settlement was then distributed to the other brothers of the Wilder family, and so they started farming [on] their own accord; two of them on the Wanstead side of Wallingford, and the eldest one on the Elsthorpe property, near a place called Atua.'

---

v   Andrew Wilder wrote in a 2019 biography of his father, 'Distinguished Service': 'Edmond and Maud had moved out from England in 1886 with their three older children Pearlie (Maud), Gladys and Tony ... Three more sons were to follow—Pery, John and Tim.' He also writes, 'The reasons for the move are not particularly clear...' and goes on to describe what I'd call a 'remittance man'.

vi   I'm assuming that's the same as 'settled'.

So, the Wilder Settlement. It's been bothering me ever since Pip and I took that no-result detour in 2020. Mick Ormond mentioning his Uncle Nick Wilder, chair of the church Committee. Wilders I met at the Wanstead Polo Club and saw on player handicap lists. Andrew Wilder, vicar Warner's brother. Our lovely friend Eleanor Wilder from Elsthorpe and Mangakurī Beach. Her gorgeous daughters Alice and Beatrice, our sons' ages, chips off the Gladys block. It's all starting to fall into place.

*

In its 2023 Christmas service list, published on the St Peter's Wallingford Church Facebook page, the Central Hawke's Bay Anglican Parish gives details for Waipukurau, Takapau, Ōtāne, Waipawa, and Ormondville. The post says 'There is no scheduled Christmas Eve service at St Peter's Church, Wallingford or Pōrangahau this year. Joan has retired and we have no vicar at present. Arch deacon, John Matthews of St Lukes Havelock North, has tried to find someone to take the services however has not had any luck. If people are interested we can look to hold a service in the New Year and/or Easter.'

'No vicar.' History has repeated. And no Warner Wilder to save the day. This will have come as a blow to Hannah Morrah and her community. And to Mick Ormond, I'm sure (although there was the unfortunate issue of the organ).

A few weeks after that notice was posted on Facebook, I've come up to the family bach at Taupō for a change of scenery. The air at elevation is fresh. Meg loves the swims and the river walks. I enjoy staring out the window at the Great Lake in all its moods, variously enjoying the bobbling pumice surfing up to the lawn and cursing the noisy jet skis. Occasionally I get a few words written.

I also have an ulterior motive for being here. My research has revealed that Andrew Wilder, son of church committee chair Nick, great-nephew of the beautiful Gladys, brother of preacher Warner, former farming neighbour of Wanstead Polo Club captain Simon McDonald, friend of the Morrahs, and cousin of Mick Ormond, lives not three minutes' walk down the beach from where I'm sitting. And I'm confident he can give me the definitive answer about the Wilder Settlement and, more importantly, why there's nothing in particular to be found when following the road sign from Route 52.

Andrew arrives at our humble Lockwood bang-on the appointed time of 11am. He's just a little older than me but with a superior head of curly white hair and the pragmatic manner and well-used hands of a man of the land. He's armed with some written material, including the book he's published about his father: *Distinguished Service—The Life and WWII Adventures of N.P. (Nick) Wilder*,[37] and a few typed pages, undated but titled: *Early Wallingford and it's [sic] Personalities by Sir John Ormond*.

Andrew's book is largely devoted to his father's war record. Nick had a decorated five-year tour of several theatres of combat and Andrew has dug out a tonne of detail about his heroic exploits. But there's plenty of family information, too, and at one point this: 'Here we reach a crucial point in the history' where he describes the Gladys/Jack meeting and subsequent union and, exactly as Mick Ormond relates, 'With the marriage, Ted [Edmond, Gladys' father] requested blocks of land be taken out of Wallingford to settle each of his four sons on a farm.' Further down: 'It became known as the 'marriage settlement' and . . . until quite recently Wilder Road was referred to as 'Wilder Settlement Road'.'

Sir John's document covers similar ground to the Knowledge Bank interview I referred to earlier, but with a curious variation. In the interview, he says this: 'The government cut it up themselves and they sold that as a settlement[vii], and that was called the Wilder settlement.' In the document Andrew has, Sir John says this: 'Interestingly, with Father's engagement to Mother, Mr Wilder insisted on a dowry which was a parcel of land from then on known as the Marriage Settlement.' He then relates the story, also told in the interview but with some significant differences, about how, on Jack Wilder's death at Gallipoli in 1917, the land was divvied up between the remaining three brothers.

But wait up! Hold your horses! Could this be why there was nothing to see when Pip and I went looking for the Wilder Settlement? That the 'Settlement' was a handshake between two gentlemen whose children had fallen in love? You'd think there would at least be something to look at—a heart-shaped plaque nailed to a tree or fence perhaps.

There's further confusion, of course, which somehow didn't occur to me until Andrew's visit. As you may know, there's a strong convention for naming roads which contain (or contained) the 'ballot blocks' the government gave to returning soldiers— Settlement Road(s). In fact, there are several around where I live.

---

vii I interpret this as a 'soldier settlement', balloted to returning servicemen. But I might be wrong.

According to Google Maps, the road Pip and I drove to find the invisible settlement is Wilder Road. How obvious. I asked Andrew about it. 'In the past, it's been Wilder Road with 'Settlement' written underneath,' he explained. 'But it was always known as Wilder Settlement Road, or Wilder Settlement. I just thought it was a settlement of people, but as I understand it, it was also the marriage settlement!'

'That's a nice story,' I say.

*

Nick Wilder died of a massive coronary on the family farm at age fifty-six. Andrew was eighteen. Writing his book, Andrew says, feels like he's finally got to know his father properly, after being denied the opportunity while he was alive. It is, sadly, a familiar story—the returned soldier, hampered by injury (Nick was shot in both legs), suffering in silence, dying young. Andrew says the family would often see Nick standing in a distinctive pose, rolling a cigarette, gazing into the middle distance, 'His thoughts far, far away.'

At Taupō, I'm showing Andrew the reference photos I took while I was with Hannah at Wallingford Church. He's not been there for years. The early afternoon light is bouncing off the lake; I turn my laptop around so he can see the screen. I hit the wrong arrow key and spin past shots from the Wanstead Polo Club, the meeting after the opening game of the season. He delights in seeing his old neighbours and friends, fellow polo players. He spots his daughter-in-law, Rose, in one photo.

Now we're inside the church. The porch through the window, the room with the old organ. 'Look at the walls, oh dear . . . ' The hatch from the kitchen, the stacked pews, Chapman-Taylor's 'Sagittarius' arrow. The pinned-up Giesen drawings.

We get to the church register, the Church Officer column for 1961. 'Oh, there's my father's initials, *NPW*. And *JWO*—Judith Wall Ormond. *PM*—a Morrah? And *ARWO* is Dan Ormond.'

Finally to the exterior. My iPhone snap doesn't soften the building's decline. 'Oh . . . oh no, this brings a tear to my eye. And yet, the potential. The surrounds. The lovely driveway . . . '

When I see Andrew to the gate, I'm fearful I've dragged up a few too many memories, that the current state of St Peter's Wallingford will haunt him.

The following morning I pack up the house and walk down the narrow Waitahanui footpath to return Andrew's book and documents. Cars and trucks and campers whizz by. Andrew has gone into town, but I chat with his wife, Belinda, and am glad to hear he enjoyed our conversation.

I return along the beach and put Meg in the car. We close the gate onto State Highway 1 and drive home directly, no sightseeing diversions. I count at least a dozen Settlement Roads along the way.

PERMANENT PARKING

THE RADIO HOST'S LONG LEATHERY FINGERS SLIDE the silver faders up and down a simple mixing desk. A small window is tilted open behind him, allowing the sound of passing traffic into the unadorned studio. The host is in the process of concluding a telephone interview. Adverts kick in right on cue after his guest's last words. Removing his reading glasses, the host hits the 'mute' button then pushes his headset off one ear and leans back in a black office chair which utters an angry squawk. 'I must bring in some CRC on Thursday,' he says, probably not for the first time.

I'm in the studio with Steve Wyn-Harris—farmer, columnist, and broadcaster. He's halfway through Tuesday's farming programme *The Cockie's Hour* which he has presented on Central FM twice a week since 1998. Steve and his business partners have owned Central FM since 2020. It covers Central Hawke's

Bay and the Tararua district; 'From Woodville to Te Aute, the mountains to the sea,' as Steve describes it.

The station currently broadcasts from the Civic Theatre complex in downtown Waipukurau, a distinctive building designed by the late Hastings architect Peter Holland in a 'Brutalist' style. It opened on 12 November 1981, towards the end of Brutalism's place in fashionable architecture.

The term 'Brutalist' is a bit misleading—it conjures up images of violence and ugliness. While critics of the style would suggest it's exactly that—harsh and unsightly—the description was coined from the French term for raw concrete—'béton brut'. The Civic qualifies as Brutalist for its use of this material and for its small windows, also typical of the design. But a true aficionado of Brutalism would probably frown at the building's luscious curves (having said that, Wellington's Beehive is considered to be a Brutalist building).

The Civic's raw concrete has been painted at the front in a multicoloured theme but the sides and rear still look rustically spartan, wonderfully so to my eye. As well as the radio station the Civic houses a cinema, café, and takeaway, operated by Steve's partners Donald and Sereena. Donald is also the station manager and presents the morning breakfast show.

When *The Cockie's Hour* is over Steve takes me to his favourite main street eatery—a Cambodian bakery predictably called Angkor Wat—for lunch of filled rolls and cold drinks. We eat outside on footpath tables and I'm grateful Waipukurau has a well-signposted heavy traffic bypass because although we're sitting right on State Highway 2 there aren't logging rigs and stock trucks wafting agricultural odours on our food as they pass.

Béton brut
BRUTALISM, WAIPUKURAU

Steve has been farming in Waipukurau for nearly forty years. His 360-hectare property, now co-owned with a son and daughter-in-law, hosts the Coopworth ram stud 'Marlow Genetics'. It's based nineteen kilometres from town on Hinerangi Road, in the district known as Hatumā. The Marlow operation is run over four blocks, the first and largest of which Steve and his wife Jane bought in 1985, four years after he graduated from Lincoln with an agricultural commerce degree.

We talk about the closure of the hospital and of the Tavistock pub, the viability of the only posh restaurant in town, and the pros and cons of Coopworth ewes. Time passes easily. The sparrows are hopping around waiting to pounce on the very few crumbs we've left on the table. Eventually I worry that Steve has work to do so I nudge him back to the farm and wander fifty metres to the town roundabout where there's a grassy park to sit in. One spoke of the roundabout gives birth to Pōrangahau Road and is the point at which Route 52 ends (or begins, depending on where you start).

*

Waipukurau is the largest town in Central Hawke's Bay. The origin of its name is a pool known to early Māori as Te Wai-pukurau-a-Ruakūhā. The pukurau fungus, common during the cooler months when food was scarce, was soaked in water, wai, to make it edible.

Māori settled here as early as the 1600s. Several villages, pā, were established around the area which was then heavy with bush full of birds. Waterways and lakes dotted the landscape

249

and facilitated movement for waka, and held tuna, for eating. The town's reservoir now sits on the site of the significant Pukekaihau Pā, established here because a cool spring provided a constant flow of drinking water.

European settlement began in the 1860s, essentially as a model town for which landowner Henry Russell was the sole arbiter. Russell leased sections of his land to selected residents whose house plans he would personally approve or reject. He himself built commercial and community facilities and small workers' cottages. The town site was surrounded by large farms which were later broken into smaller blocks allowing the town to expand.

By the turn of the century flax processing, sawmilling, and a meat works provided employment, and a stock sale yard soon serviced most of Central Hawke's Bay. Like its neighbouring towns Waipukurau rode the agricultural boom wave after the second world war and by 1951 its main street, Ruataniwha Street, boasted six banks.[38]

Today, Waipukurau remains very much a centre of rural support. Entering town from the south on State Highway 2 the first thing you'll notice is the amount of farm machinery for sale. Yards and yards stocked with tractors, harvesters, balers, quad bikes, side-by-sides. Surrounding the railway station—which is now a coffee shop and visitor centre—the cluster of sturdy warehouses, once used for grain and wool, now house fertiliser suppliers and truck mechanics. Trains still pass through but they're heading directly north carrying freight, not passengers.

Ruataniwha Street sports the usual array of retail outlets befitting a service town—books and stationery, sporting goods, men's and women's clothing—but like many provincial high streets it's dominated by two-dollar stores and charity thrift shops. I had to scour fully one side then the other for a simple bath towel which I eventually found in Winloves, a home appliance store (go figure).

Journalist Karl du Fresne, who grew up in Waipukurau and is still a regular visitor, remembers Winloves. He says it's one of the very few main street stores that's survived from his childhood in the 1950s and 60s. 'Everything else about the street has changed.' Except Winloves, and Story's clothing store, then known as Fulford and Holmes.

There were four menswear shops in those days, Karl remembers, serving a population of about 3,000. 'One was owned by a guy called Syd Peterkin. Syd was like the outfitter to the landed gentry. He used to drive around in a bright red Daimler sports car.

'There was a substantial menswear section in the Hawke's Bay Farmer's store too. One of the big events of my childhood was the opening of new Farmer's. It was a major occasion. I mean, it was two storeys! It sold everything you could think of. It introduced a level of glamour and sophistication unheard of in Waipukurau.' It probably sold decent towels, too.

Co-founder of Huia Publishers and former Te Aute College Principal, Brian Morris, also remembers Waipukurau's vibrant retail scene from when he grew up here around the same time.

'As music loving teenagers we'd go down to Cyril Parker's music shop, usually on a Friday when it was late night shopping. Cyril seemed particularly talkative on Fridays. I remember the HMV posters with the dog and the phonograph. He sold hi-fi equipment and had guitars hanging on the wall, but we were mostly interested in the 45rpm records stacked up on the counter.

'Being cheeky kids we enjoyed asking him for artists we just made up, which he'd promise to order in, but of course never could. He was a lovely man, a dapper dresser, always wore a bow tie. After a while we realised it was Fridays when he'd have a bit of tipple in the back room of the shop . . .

'Next to Fulford and Holmes was Beattie's Bookshop. Mum had a standing order there and every week we'd race in to get the British *Tiger* comic-strip magazine she bought for us along with her *NZ Woman's Weekly*. We were always desperate to read the next instalment of series like 'Roy of the Rovers' or 'Tough of the Track'.'

A high street retailer who looms large in Brian's recollections is pharmacist Les Grant, whose son Robert was a schoolmate right through primary school. 'Les was a lovely man. Always friendly and welcoming to everyone. I was a young Māori boy growing up in a town full of Pākehā and he'd always give me the time of day, asking how I was going.

'All those family-owned stores were institutions back then.'

The town's retail glamour and sophistication have certainly faded I muse as I pass a garish—and encouragingly empty—vaping shop. Similar provincial towns might have 'big box' retailers on their peripheries but Waipukurau is—so far—Warehouse-free. There is talk of McDonald's but the franchise has only crept as close as Dannevirke. A newly opened Dominos does a steady trade and will put pressure on the nearby pizza and kebab shop where I later waited forty minutes for an almost inedible $14 lamb doner. The wrap was so wrong on every level that I tossed most of it to the birds.

*

It's an easy walk from Ruataniwha Street to Waipukurau Holiday Park where I've installed myself for a couple of nights. The entrance features a breezy blue retro-styled sign dwarfed by a pair of gigantic Phoenix palms. Proprietor Jenette is pleasantly matter-of-fact and has a well-rehearsed welcome patter pointing out the amenities and directing me to the powered caravan sites. The Park isn't well advertised on the usual camping websites and apps and after I've found a tree to set up under, I learn why.

The Park is largely home to 'permanents', people who rent spots long-term for their own caravan, motorhome, bus, cabin, or what-have-you. They have access to the campground facilities as do visiting guests. It's a growing phenomenon in these days of housing shortages and Covid-closed borders and has made some previously enjoyable campgrounds less desirable to travellers. Jenette is at pains to stress that her Park's residents are not part of the emergency housing programme but are simply 'people who have had a change of lifestyle.' Her husband Nigel says they were ticking along nicely when international visitors were plentiful, but when Covid hit, a 'change of business plan' became necessary. They say the pre-Covid balance should be restored soon.

My immediate neighbours, though, are obviously visitors. They're not at their caravan while I'm setting up but return in a while, donned in shorts and stout shoes, walking poles swinging from their wrists. They've been all the way to an old swing bridge, one of Waipukurau's few tourist attractions, only to find it had been washed away in recent floods. It's a decent walk anyway, they say. They're retirees Neil and Liz Morris from Feilding and they're here for four nights at the end of an eleven-night trip away.

Neil and Liz look like experienced caravanners. Their compact English caravan is very well set up with a simple porch awning, coiled freshwater hose, greywater tank, portable tables, and barbecue. They're chatty and interested in my book project. Neil tells me they've been up and down Route 52 a few times in their classic MG sports car, often enjoying lunch at the Pongaroa pub. 'But we've never taken the caravan there,' he says. We agree that's probably for the best, given the current state of the road.

On my other side there's a middle-aged white campervan parked nose-in to the boundary fence. It's been mowed around and sprayed under, so I guess it's been here for a while. There's a bloke sitting in the doorway in the afternoon sun, cigarette in one hand, can of Victoria Bitter in the other. He's wearing neat blue jeans, and a peaked cap partially covers thinning hair on the dome, the rest falling long-ish towards his shoulders. He's not a big man; he looks a bit like the drummer Phil Rudd from AC/DC. He is, I discover, a rock drummer.

His cap has the logo 'ID'. 'It's the last two letters of my name,' he tells me. 'David. Not Dave. David.' David tells me his camper's motor has blown. He was on the road travelling alone for eighteen months but when the engine was diagnosed uneconomic to fix he parked up here. 'I'm not going anywhere anytime soon. Anyway, this is home.'

David grew up in Waipukurau. There was always music in the house—swing music, jazz orchestras. He fell for the rhythm. He's played in bands, rocky covers bands at pubs and parties. He's had good jobs, interesting jobs in the finance sector. He's been married three times—once for thirty years, twice for two-and-a-half. His only daughter died at forty-one, a heart attack. 'It was just lights out,' David says, making a 'tocking' sound with his tongue and stabbing a finger at the ground. His father and brother both died at sixty-eight from heart trouble. David has had heart issues too. He'll be sixty-eight in two years' time.

Later in the afternoon, on the other side of the campground, I find Pete and Colin. The two of them are sitting at a picnic table over which there's a white Warehouse pergola. On the table lays a box of bourbon and cola cans, two of which are open. Fair-skinned Colin is dressed in track pants and a casual top. A mop of grey hair erupts from under a beige trucker's cap. Pete is darker with blue jeans and wavy black hair. He has a smoker's voice and a very big smile.

The pergola is next to Pete's brown Liteweight caravan. The caravan incorporates a deck built with wooden pallets. A clear perspex roof creates a covered porch. There's a large fridge in the porch and a pot outside it growing green vegetables. The caravan is tucked in next to a hedge and partly under a weeping willow tree. I tell them what I'm doing and draw up a nearby plastic chair.

Colin tells me he's been at the campground seven years, Pete ten. They're both from around here and haven't ventured too far. Colin is on a benefit; Pete works at the local freezing works.

'I've been in and around Waipuk all my life,' Colin says. 'That's fifty-nine years.' His parents farmed at Oueroa, about twenty-five kilometres from where we're sitting. They owned the farm but had to sell it, 'because Dad was crook. He was in the war, it got to him. Shell shock. It was tough for him, for the family. We moved into town and he passed away quite soon after. He was seventy-two.

'That was nine years ago. Mum died in 2020. I lost my sister when she was forty-five, cancer. I have a brother in Palmerston North and another just out here at Hatumā, he's sixty-five. He's the one looking after me, helping me out with my payments for the caravan site and so on. He bought the caravan for me in Napier.'

Colin needs the help because recently he had a medical event himself. 'I was sitting right here, and I collapsed. This gentleman here (pointing at Pete) and a couple of others brought me around. I was just sitting here and I felt a bit squeamish and felt pain go up my chest. I was in Hastings hospital for two weeks then three days at the Waipuk Health Centre then back to my caravan. I'm not allowed to drive, it's supposed to be for a year but . . .

'I love driving trucks. I used to work for the Council maintaining roads, clearing blocked sumps. Now I sit around the caravan watching TV, doing bits and pieces. Home Care comes with my meals. I'd like to get back out there but my health's a problem.' He opens another can. 'This town is home. Everything is here, except the hospital now.'

*

Waipukurau Hospital opened in 1879 and was extended and modified many times during the following century. It closed in 1999 having apparently outgrown the needs of the town. After sitting abandoned for nearly thirty years, plans were announced in 2022 by the Council, iwi, and developers to create up to 950 houses on the site.

Meanwhile, down State Highway 2 a bit, perched on a hill overlooking the Tukituki River, is another former hospital. The Pukeora Sanatorium (pukeora means hill of health) was created in 1918 as a retreat for returning soldiers affected by mustard gas. It then became a tuberculosis hospital, and latterly a general care facility. Since 2000 the rambling collection of hospital wards, houses, and service buildings has been in private ownership as a vineyard, winery, and events centre. On the hilltop there's a bright blue lookout styled like a gateway allowing 360-degree views of Waipukurau, nearby Waipawa, and the distant Ruahine Range.

*

Pete has popped into his caravan to check a pork belly dish simmering in a slow cooker. 'I trust my own cooking, no-one else's,' he calls. Pete prepares simple solo meals most nights — roasts, chops. He's always cooked for himself since he left home in his early teens. He's been from job to job, in shearing sheds, fencing, apple picking, shepherding, and now at the meat works.

Most of Pete's family has passed away, he says — his Mum just a couple of weeks ago, Dad nearly thirty years ago. 'Dumb bugger had a barley straw up his thumb nail. He kept picking away at it, it caused a cancer. They chopped his thumb off, then his wrist, but it kept spreading. He died before he got his pension.'

Pete has a daughter in Wairoa, she's eighteen and getting married soon. 'I've got one mokopuna on the way already! Have them young, I reckon. Look after them while you're young, then when they're old enough to look after themselves you can go back to work. I had her young. Her mother is in Wairoa too, she wants to get married again. I say go for it!'

Every Sunday Pete cooks a meal for anyone from the camp who wants to gather here at his pergola. 'We might have a chop suey one week, maybe a boil up the next. We'll probably have a few beers, some music. Most people here like a drink. It's not so far to waddle home.' Everyone on this side of the camp turns up, Pete says, but not so much from the other side, where I'm parked next to David. 'They keep to themselves over there. They can come if they want, but they don't.'

Residents come and go from the Holiday Park, Colin tells me. During the apple and onion seasons it fills up a bit, and shearing crews sometimes stay. He says it hasn't been very busy with travellers like me or the Morrises lately, especially during Covid. Perhaps people coming to dog or horse shows across the road at Russell Park, say, but not so many casual campers who might enjoy being right next to the Tukituki River. Although a fence and a substantial stop-bank create visual and physical barriers from the river, there is usually enough water for a swim once you get there. 'There are plenty of eels too, great for the smoker,' Colin says.

All this talk of boil ups and smoked Tukituki eel has made me peckish, so I take my leave from the pergola and wander back

Prandial rhythm
HOLIDAY PARK, WAIPUKURAU

past Colin's rather un-loved caravan to my own on the 'other side'. Next door to me Neil is barbecuing spicy chicken kebabs on his portable Weber. I retrieve a beer and a supermarket pork pie and salad from my fridge. The camp settles in to a prandial rhythm as the sun begins to dip behind the riverbank willows.

*

The Tukituki River and its major tributary the Waipawa form the basis of what passes for Waipukurau tourism. The trout fishing is well regarded (trout smoke well too) and kayaks and jet boats navigate the ever-changing braids and riffles. Along the banks, golden crushed lime paths form a network of cycling and walking tracks named The Tukituki Trail. The tracks loop around several sites of interest, including the Tārewa swing bridge Neil and Liz Morris visited but found destroyed by recent flooding.

Over the river from the campground is the start of a track to Lindsay Bush, a stand of remnant natives where I'm hoping to find a curious tunnel the Morrises told me about. Not being a cyclist, nor having time to walk the ten-kilometre return, I drive to a loosely formed carpark on Scenic Road. There is a picnic table sitting among some weeds and an inconspicuous wire gate opening to the bush. There's no evidence of directions to any tunnel.

A group of young disabled people and their carers turn up looking for the Lindsay Tunnel too. I can't enlighten them. They leave disappointed while I open the gate and satisfy myself with a walk in the bush. The musty-smelling paths are subtly marked.

Dappled light filters down from ancient trees. The sound of the river burbles through the undergrowth. Kererū, pīwakawaka, and tūī fly about oblivious or unbothered. Human presence feels a lifetime ago.

Later I discover that the Lindsay Tunnel was easy enough to find had I been a little more patient. The 200-metre limestone tunnel was once part of a farm water race approximately ten kilometres long. It was built in the 1870s by the Harding family of nearby Mount Vernon Station. The race was tunnelled through rock to enable a gravity-fed water system from the Waipawamate stream which enters the Tukituki opposite Lindsay Bush. When Mount Vernon Station was subdivided in 1905 the water race became obsolete but the tunnel remains.[39]

*

It's time to head elsewhere so I pack up and say farewell to my new campground friends. A courier van is dropping supplies at the camp office when I stop for a quick chat with Jenette. I tell her I've enjoyed her clean and tidy campground, that the 'permanents' are friendly, and that I'll no doubt be back.

I leave town thinking I'll take the back road to Takapau, through Hatumā near Steve Wyn-Harris's farm. Heading east on Pōrangahau Road it's hard to miss the old Waipukurau Hospital Steve and I talked about. I stop to clamber over a collapsed security fence for a nosey around the site. Plenty have beaten me to it. There's graffiti art, just plain graffiti, rubbish, and a big dangerous vandalised mess strewn in and around the overgrown complex. The buildings themselves are evidence of

Still sturdy after all these years
DEAD HOSPITAL, WAIPUKURAU

why demolition and development has taken so long—they're so well-crafted, exemplars of when things were built properly, still anchored firmly in the landscape.

The journey past Lake Whatumā and around the back blocks to State Highway 2 is Central Hawke's Bay at its most picturesque. I feel a bit of a cheat not continuing south via Route 52 but this road is better. It snakes around bends, rising and falling like a Mediterranean tide. In verdant fields, grazing cows swish their tails. Distant mountains shimmer in the heat.

An old kiwi caravan dances along the road glinting bronze in the midday sun.

ANCESTRAL PATHWAYS

IT'S ALMOST A YEAR SINCE I VISITED AND WROTE ABOUT Waipukurau, the northern full-stop on Route 52. I had a nice enough time. The weather was sunny and calm. The campground was quiet and clean. I met some interesting people. I ate some terrible food. And I found a cool Brutalist building which housed a radio station and I got to sit in the studio and talk to the host after which we went to lunch and talked some more.

But I was a bit disparaging about the town's visitor attractions—essentially, I said there weren't any. And that's been bugging me. I keep feeling like I must've missed something.

A bit later, needing some more personal detail for my story, I spoke to Brian Morris. Brian grew up in Waipukurau in the 1950s and 60s. He was a young Māori living in a predominantly Pākehā town. He gave me some good quotes for my story, painting a picture of what his life was like. He told me about the

264

record shop with the tipsy-on-Friday proprietor; recalled the booksellers where his mother bought him *Tiger* magazines; and spoke fondly of the schoolmate's father who kept a pastoral eye on him, a fish half out of water.

Brian also told me about his friend and teaching colleague Patrick Parsons. In 1999, Patrick wrote a book, commissioned by the local Rotary Club's Book Committee, titled 'Waipukurau— The History of a Country Town'.[40] 'I tried to encourage him to change the 'The' to an 'A',' Brian told me over the phone. 'He showed me the chapters on the Māori history and I said, Patrick, you're trying to compress centuries of history into three chapters while you spend nine chapters on the last 150 years. Mathematically, that doesn't make sense!'

(The minute we finished our conversation I opened my own Waipukurau story and furiously typed a still-criminally-brief couple of paragraphs on its Māori history.)

As is my wont, before I called Brian I did a bit of a Google on him. Pretty high powered! Treaty negotiator. Chair of Rākautātahi Marae. Former Principal of Te Aute College and co-founder of Huia Publishers (as I've already told you). And a key instigator of a significant Waipukurau cultural tourism venture, Ngā Ara Tipuna.

Wait.

What?

Waipukurau tourism? Ngā Ara Tipuna? Why had I not heard of this? Why didn't I find it while I was snooping around? How come my campground neighbours didn't tell me about it? Did I not ask the right questions? Was I just being lazy? Or, worse, racist?

*

Sometimes what you think will be a ten-minute phone conversation to check some facts or grab a bit of detail turns out to be five times that. Brian had just got home to Lower Hutt from a tangi at Takapau, and had mokopuna excitedly jumping on and off his knee, but graciously gave me twenty minutes on the subject of Waipukurau's main street. Then I dropped the Ngā Ara Tipuna question.

Brian told me he'd sat down with his elders to talk about the title of his friend's book and they weren't happy. Well, he'd told them, Patrick is sticking to his guns and there's nothing we can do about it. It's up to us to tell our own stories. 'That's what had steered me into publishing. How do we tell our own stories? For a long time our elders didn't want to share their stories. They didn't trust other people with them.'

Later, Brian and his brother Phillip formed a small group of local hapū elders who met regularly to discuss what they were going to do about all the history essentially locked up in people's heads. Brian says they were encouraged greatly by a kuia called Ahi Robertson. 'Ahi was brought up by her grandfather, Ihaia Hutana, who as a boy was present when the Waipukurau Block was sold in 1851. So she knew what her grandfather had told her, and was our primary source of information. She was key to the group.'

During one meeting a Central Hawke's Bay councillor came to talk to them. 'She said, "We want to do something to acknowledge the pā site known as Hunter Park". We said, well that's nice to know, but you need to understand that the site, which we know as Pukekaihau, doesn't exist in isolation. It was part of a network of pā designed to protect the food resource, which was the two lakes. She said, "Two lakes?" We said yes, there used to be two lakes—the one we all know as Whatumā, and one across the road, across Route 52, called Ongātoro. It's not there anymore because it got drained.'

Brian is on a roll here and I'm listening intently. I learn that at times of flood, like during Cyclone Gabrielle, Ongātoro returns. I hear that there are seven important pā sites in Waipukurau and that the town was built on and around Pukekaihau Pā because it had—and still has—a freshwater spring at its summit. He tells me the councillor's visit opened up a conversation about how the simple sign she was suggesting could be expanded to the network of pā. And as the digits on my voice recorder ticked towards thirty minutes, Brian tells me about coming across a project which gave him the idea for what has transpired.

*

Forty minutes' drive from Kerikeri in the Bay of Islands is Rangihoua Bay. According to the brochure for what became a Heritage Park in 2014, here you can 'Travel back to a pivotal moment in New Zealand's history to the place where Māori oversaw the first permanent Pākehā settlement in Aotearoa'. As part of his work for Huia Publishers, Brian found himself at Rangihoua one day, walking the Marsden Cross Pathway. The track leads to a lookout over the beautiful bay, skirts around the pā site perched on a cliff top, and then circles the site of Samuel

Marsden's settlement of missionaries. It eventually arrives at the cross itself, a monument in stone to the first Christian service held in our country, on Christmas Day 1814.

Along the Rangihoua trail a dozen points of interest are marked by timber framed information boards, etched Corten steel maps, and wide-lensed illustrated scenes—'sculptural markers', according to the concept's designers and creators, a company called Locales.

'I found Locales was Wellington based,' Brian tells me. 'So I went to see them.' Excited by the company's work and what they could offer, Brian took his idea back to the expectant Waipukurau group. A presentation to Council followed, demonstrating how the Rangihoua concept might be applied to telling the story of the pā network and developing a quality visitor experience. They lapped it up. The Locales team developed a detailed concept plan. Everyone loved it. A partnership was established between the Council and the Tamatea taiwhenua in Waipukurau. It was all go.

'Timing is everything in life,' Brian said to me. 'At that time, Council were looking for an opportunity to build a relationship with local hapū, marae, and the Taiwhenua. We saw this project as an opportunity to tell our story at a significant scale. And from within the coalition government, Shane Jones had money in his Provincial Growth Fund. So to cut a long story short, we applied to the PGF and were successful. Other funders came on board too, and we met as a hapū to discuss what it was we wanted to share, what we were happy to be published.'

In the eyes of Brian Morris, Ngā Ara Tipuna (Ancestral Pathways) is a big step for local Māori. For so long, he says, his parents' and grandparents' generations were silent about their own stories. There was a general aura of mistrust. 'If we ever asked them, they'd tell us bits and pieces, but they didn't really see any value in talking about it. There was a lot of residual . . . I guess, hurt.'

But the time is right, he says, to present the first real piece of cultural tourism in Waipukurau. 'These stories have been sitting here all along. It's time to bring them out into the open.'

∗

From my earlier visit to Waipukurau, I've remembered passing a signed pā site on Scenic Road as I was looking for the Lindsay Tunnel. I didn't stop—I had a date at the radio station and was flustered. Retracing my steps recently, I pulled off the road at the bend where a hillock rises slightly to a pocked moonscape, then falls away to a stream bed. The signage says it's Kaitoroa Pā, first stop on the Ngā Ara Tipuna Driving Tour.

I pull out my phone and browse to the Ngā Ara Tipuna website[41]. Tapping on the Start the Tour button, a smooth male voice reads an introduction. I stand gazing at the view, and listen:

Nau mai, haere mai. Welcome. On our tour today we'll travel across the Waipukurau-Takapau rohe (or tribal area), inhabited by Māori for hundreds of years. This rohe was renowned for its rich sources of food. Lakes, rivers, streams and springs once spread across this region. Today, these have been much reduced, due to drainage to acquire farming land and stop-banks to control flooding. Prior to European settlement, there were also extensive podocarp forests—a valued source

of birds, berries and wood for the tīpuna (or ancestors). Travel with
us along the braided Tukituki River. We'll visit Lake Whatumā: once
this area's most prized natural resource. We'll stand atop the Pukeora
limestone cliffs. We'll see several pā sites where the tīpuna lived, and
places of early interaction between Māori and Europeans. Continue
the tour to hear kōrero—stories—about this land from mana whenua:
the tribes with authority over the Waipukurau-Takapau area.

I click on the link to #1, Kaitoroa Pā. A video preview shows an aerial view of the pock-marked pā I'm looking over. I hit the 'Start' arrow and Brian Morris magically appears. He's sitting in a wharenui, behatted, nicely lit, looking just off-camera. For a minute and a half Brian explains that this pā was a seasonal food-gathering camping place, that the river, pre-stop-banks, used to run right past here, that food was gathered from the water. He tells us that flax, harakeke, a plant with a multitude of uses, was in abundance here too. I listen as I gaze through the cutout in the metal sign which frames the area he's referring to.

Another video, a little longer, features Brian talking about trade with the early Europeans. He tells us that timber, and ropes made from the flax, were in high demand with settlers arriving in ships. And that nails, animals, and certain European foods were prized by the Māori, who also began leasing land to these Pākehā arrivals. Professor Roger Maaka then appears and explains how trading changes the dynamic of a society, because suddenly people are working to create surplus, not simply enough for local needs. That's something I hadn't given thought to before.

The effect of standing looking at the place where people came to camp under the stars and gather simple resources hundreds of years ago, while being told about it by their descendants who appear like apparitions on a hand-held telephone, is strangely unsettling. But it makes me want more, so I set off to #2 on the tour, Te Waipukurau Pā.

Te Waipukurau Pā is a major and more recent pā, on flat land, and also by the river. Brian and Roger tell us how it was the hub for news and trade, about the Anglican missionaries who had such an impact, and about the 'dream of pastoral productivity' whereby Māori and Pākehā agreed to live alongside each other and develop a farming economy. They explain how their tīpuna were briefly run out of the area, 'beaten around' by tribes who had acquired muskets. We also learn about the relationship between Donald McLean—Governor Grey's land purchasing agent—and Te Hāpuku, a prominent Ngāti Kahungunu chief, and the sale and purchase of more than a quarter of a million acres of Māori land. It's fascinating stuff. Stuff I should've known more about.

There are five more sites on the Ngā Ara Tipuna Road Tour and I spend the next couple of hours driving, stopping, looking, reading, watching, listening. It's an immersive experience, and the pā pop up in surprising places—due, I suppose, to the landscape being quite different before Pākehā started fiddling with it. Then I head to the railway station where a small shelter, a whare kōrero, protects 3-D landscape maps that serve as a launching pad for the experience. From here, one can stroll to the 'main course', the pā that started it all, Pukekaihau.

*

271

Perfectly framed
FROM PUKEORA SCENIC ROAD

It's actually not that easy to find the first stop on the Pukekaihau site tour (suggested time one hour), it's kind-of tucked around behind a couple of workers' cottages opposite the railway tracks. But if you know the site is officially named Hunter Memorial Park, a small plaque on an iron gate will lead you in the right direction.

A quick look on the Ngā Ara Tipuna website will show you why an hour is suggested for this one—there's a lot to get through. Firing up the mobile phone tour takes you step by step through the four information stops as you climb the lime path up the hill towards the spring, the reason for the pā's existence, now the town's reservoir. The climb is enough to raise the heart rate slightly, and the summit is surprisingly elevated. Along the way, palisading created from native trees and branches indicate a defence system just as it would have existed back in the day. Space-age Corten steel information boards, or pou, stand at lookout points, cut-outs framing view shafts of significant features around the Waipukurau landscape.

Once again Brian presents several of the videos which, together with the information on the pou and several illustrated panels, tell the many stories of the thriving community that lived here up to 600 years ago. The stories I might've missed out on had I not done just that little extra bit of digging earlier.

*

Writing this during a general election campaign that veers wildly between hilarious, frustrating, kick-the-TV dumb, and just plain repulsive, the gentle and respectful presentation of oral traditions, facts and opinions along the Ngā Ara Tipuna trail is a salve for the soul. That so much of it has only now been committed from memory to a physical form for this project speaks of what Māori—and, increasingly, Pākehā—call mana. It's a significant, prestigious endeavour.

Along the way there was probably—like any project of governance—some compromise, frustration, maybe even a bit of niggle. I don't know and I'm not going to ask. The only thing of importance is that it ended up, I think, a major work of cultural art.

GOOD DAY FOR DUCKS

IN MARCH 2019, GERMAN CYCLIST SUSANNE FRANZ WAS enjoying the twisty, hilly pavement of Route 52 as she continued north on her solo tour of Aotearoa. As well as the welcome challenge of some ups-and-downs and side-to-sides, she was finding the road peaceful and picturesque, away from the roaring tyres and acrid exhausts of the busy State Highway 2.

Aotearoa may have been just another item to tick off on a long list for the 45-year-old from Munich, not one she intended to linger on. Other exotic locations awaited, to add to Cuba, Sardinia, Croatia, and others she'd pedalled her heavy old mountain bike around over the years. Susanne started travelling a little later in life because as a youngster she engaged in professional sports ('judo and football—without the money') and travel didn't fit with training programmes. In Dominica she coached the national women's football team.

Having completed a circumnavigation of the South Island and then the rail trail from Wellington over the Remutaka hill to Featherston and Greytown, Susanne was now intent on hugging the eastern side of the North Island through to Auckland, then heading off to French Polynesia. At least that was the plan until she rode into the tiny Central Hawke's Bay township of Waipawa.

*

The quirky settlement of Waipawa is a mere few minutes' drive beyond Waipukurau, the official northern end of Route 52. It's no more than a hop skip and jump, and the two are more-or-less joined at the hip—in fact I've heard Waipawa residents refer to their southern sibling as simply 'the other town'. There's even a concrete walking and biking track called the Shared Path that runs parallel to the highway joining them. So in my mind I've stretched Route 52 by seven kilometres.

Don't ask me why but for some time I've had a curious affection for Waipawa. Perhaps it's the nineteenth-century villas clinging to the sides of hills reminding me of the Wellington I grew up in. Maybe it's the fact that this is where you turn off State Highway 2 to get to beautiful Mangakurī Beach where we used to spend long, languorous holidays with friends and our combined kids and dogs. Possibly it's just the great fish'n'chips you can get at the takeaway joint opposite the museum carpark.

Waipawa is the seat of the Central Hawke's Bay District Council and is the region's second biggest town with a population of a snick over 2,000. Apart from a few shops changing hands, nothing much appears to have happened here for decades. The landmark clock tower is rendered a little less visible by encroaching trees, but that's about it. Occasionally one hears how it is CHB's go-ahead town, but I couldn't find a lot of go, nor much ahead. In fact, other than a fancy new butcher and a flashed-up fuel station the only sign of recent progress is a High Street shop selling vinyl records and the analogue equipment required to play them. Oh, the irony.

Paddy McCloskey runs the River's Edge Holiday Park in what's known as 'lower' Waipawa, on the edge of the Waipawa River. It's a quiet spot with flat campsites, old-school facilities, and a gate directly to the river's stop-bank where dogs and their humans can roam unleashed. A guitar enthusiast, Paddy will happily pause laundry or lawn duties to discuss the merits of Gibson acoustics versus Takamines, or to show you the instrument he made himself a few years ago based on the old Guild jumbo in his collection. Paddy has owned River's Edge for thirty years and has a reputation in online camping app comments sections as a friendly and relaxed host.

I first stayed at River's Edge around the time Paddy bought it from the Council. It was a trip with the Wellington Flyfishers Club, which I'd joined to get some tips after deciding to take up the sport. I don't really do clubs—I'm too much of a lone ranger—but the club captain, Gordon Baker, had been a Design School student of my father's and I'd seen his intricate illustrations of trout flies, like the Hare & Copper, and Pheasant Tail, complete with instructions on how to tie them, in the club's monthly magazine.

I recall pitching my little tent outside the campground's old wooden Scout Hall where everyone else was sleeping marae-style (not only am I unsociable, I don't do marae-style—but no-one seemed too phased). It was a crisp, sunny, and calm weekend. There were large rainbow trout snapping at our artificial nymphs everywhere in the deep pools and rapid riffles and I had some considerable success, even being asked to guide a couple of other newbies for a morning. It was big water and lots of walking at that time; I'm not sure I could do it these days. An angler drowned on the Waipawa River a few years ago, a guy about my age.

This visit I'm parked up alone in my caravan for a few days, experiencing the aftermath of Cyclone Gabrielle on Paddy and his remaining 'permanents', the people who call River's Edge home. I arrive as a swamped house bus is being winched and lifted from its muddy site, off to be reinstated somewhere else. Resident Fiona and her son Harley are looking on.

Technically the camp is closed but there are a dozen residents here, plus me, making do in the patched-up facilities. There was very big water right through the campground six months ago, waist deep, when the stop-bank failed up-river. The upper township was spared the deluge but below the highway and road bridge there was carnage. People grabbed pets and whatever else they could before hurrying from their submerged homes. In the campground, caravans, awnings, and cabins tumbled and bashed and bobbled their way downstream. Fiona's motorhome was one of them—she's now living in a cabin she relocated here after it got blown off her land outside Pōrangahau. Another chap's tent vanished, along with everything inside it. Campers were rounded up and evacuated to the local community centre.

Storm haulage
CYCLONE RECOVERY, WAIPAWA

Paddy is putting on a brave face as he rebuilds the kitchen and ablution block, knowing there's months more of waiting, cleaning up, dealing with insurance companies and builders, replacing furniture, curtains, heaters. There's a pervasive smell of mud and damp. Skill saws screech as campers re-build their timber awnings and tiny homes. Dehumidifiers whir in soggy campervans. The grass is gradually poking through the silt and sand. The tent-dweller has a replacement, already patched with duct tape. Life goes on.

*

The road between Masterton and Waipukurau—Route 52—is well known to both local and visiting cyclists as a decent touring route. For hardy locals it's a challenging ride, taken either as the entire 183 kilometres over a couple of days or as day rides from peripheral towns and villages. For visitors it's a way of taking the path less travelled and enjoying some rural landscapes and Kiwi hospitality.

The route is signposted at both ends with the distinctive Ngā Haerenga New Zealand Cycle Trails logo. Ngā Haerenga is a network of trails all over Aotearoa and the Route 52 trail is perfect for linking with those in Hawke's Bay or, by extension, the central North Island. It's what's known as a 'connector' ride, and the Ngā Haerenga website lists it as a '202km Grade 3 ride over 2-3 days'. It's essentially a continuation of the Remutaka and Wairarapa Valley trails which Susanne Franz had just completed.

The website also says, 'Road bikes or touring bikes are suitable for the terrain', a detail Susanne either didn't notice or chose to ignore before piloting her heavily laden mountain bike over the trip. It doesn't seem to have slowed her down though, as she easily managed the seventy-six kilometre ride from Greytown up to Alfredton in one day.

Leaving the Greytown Camping Ground early on a frosty morning she grabbed some breakfast in Masterton, then headed east along Te Ore Ore Road before turning left into the Te Ore Ore-Bideford Road, past the marae and left again onto Whangaehu Valley Road. The valley is quite picturesque, albeit a little shaded in parts as it snakes alongside and occasionally over the river. Susanne says the road was in quite good condition then, but I know it has deteriorated significantly since.

Susanne had done her homework and, knowing there was nothing to be found in Alfredton by way of shops or cafés, she was carrying three days food and water in her swollen panniers. Finding only a school, sporadic housing, and no people from one end of Alfredton to the other, she was surprised when I told her later that Alfredton was once a bustling little settlement complete with a hotel, post office, and two stores. She set up camp for the night at the Alfredton Domain, shared with an older Kiwi couple in a motorhome. The Domain shows up on most camping apps and websites but is sparingly used; it's free but has no facilities other than a basic toilet block. She reported a quiet night at the Domain, with calm weather and a restorative sleep.

Next morning was very cold and foggy as Susanne set off. From Alfredton she more than completed her target of around seventy to eighty kilometres per day by pedalling the eighty-eight (give or take a kilometre) to Wimbledon. 'I don't remember much wind,' she told me when we met in Waipawa.

(Route 52 is known for its wind.) 'It's a pretty road. It became a nice day. I loved the ride, it was hilly. I was exhausted when I arrived.' She took lots of scenic photos, which she showed me on her cell phone. 'On a bike you can easily stop to take photos. The road was good. It was strange that no-one else was there, I had it all to myself.'

The Wimbledon Tavern is a very attractive colonial two-storey wooden hotel right on the road, seemingly in the middle of nowhere. It was built in 1886. There's a scattering of farmhouses and sheds to give the pub some company, and a turnoff which follows the Wainui River to coastal Herbertville ten kilometres away. The tavern's new owners were happy for cyclists or other travellers to park vans or put tents up in their grounds; Susanne returned the favour by eating in the bar, a seafood basket which she remembers as rather underwhelming. It was very quiet, she reports, with maybe just a couple of truckers passing through, and no locals in the bar.

The next day she headed off with the intention of getting to Waipukurau Holiday Park, sixty-four kilometres. This would've meant she'd completed the entire Route 52 ride, and more if you include Greytown to Masterton, as a solid three-day pedal.

On the way she passed the Longest Place Name sign and, as is obligatory, stopped for a selfie photo. 'Of course I stopped!' She made the short detour into Pōrangahau for her customary pie and cold Coke from the dairy. It was only a relatively short day so when she got to Waipukurau she considered carrying on to Waipawa, only an extra seven kilometres. Checking the online camping apps on her phone, she liked the look of River's Edge Holiday Park. It was further off the main road than the

Waipukurau camp, and close to the cycle lane. And commenters were reporting a friendly host called Paddy.

'So that's how I ended up here,' Susi told me as we chatted in the kitchen of the on-site villa she now shares with Paddy. The large old house he relocated here some years ago is slightly elevated from the camping area, and it escaped the worst of the cyclone, although water reached the floorboards and some repair of carpet and vinyl is necessary. That's not bothering their German Shepherd, Harvey, however, who is flopped in front of the electric heater, hiding from the wintry elements outside.

Susi's plan was to stay one night in Waipawa, then go to Napier, and carry on to Taupō. 'But I stayed two nights. Then went to Napier. Then came back.' She spent another three days at Rivers Edge then continued her planned travel up to Auckland, and to French Polynesia briefly. . . . Then came back. 'We met in Auckland and did a road trip for two and a half weeks and talked about how we could make this work. I said I wanted to go back to Munich for a year because I had my school job and I couldn't just say I'm not returning. So we agreed we'd visit each other over that year and see how it worked out. And if it did work out, I'd come back here.'

But they hadn't planned on Covid and all the hurdles the world-wide pandemic presented.

Paddy and Susi are an easy-going pair, active, fit, with a positive outlook on life. They would need all those attributes to navigate the obstacles they faced in the two years it took them to get a visa for Susi to come and live in Waipawa with Paddy. She now has residency. 'Once I was here it was no problem, really. Just the getting here was. All the problems were only because of Covid.'

Life is totally different, she says. 'I grew up in a small village like this so that's not such a big upheaval really. But first I had to find my role here. Everything is new, including my job—I'd never even mowed grass before. Cafés close at 3pm. There are no restaurants.' Worse, she still hasn't had a proper summer. 'Paddy promised me hot, dry, Hawke's Bay summers. He hasn't delivered.'

Susi might get lucky now that the weather pattern has apparently shifted from La Niña—which has been bringing the wet rubbish from the east—to El Niño, supposedly a drier, westerly system. From coastal, northern Wairarapa, up through Hawke's Bay and Gisborne, the last couple of years in the east have been unrelentingly soggy. Wet. So wet. And then Cyclone Gabrielle.

Paddy grew up in Waipawa and remembers as a child seeing the river rise almost to the top of the stop-bank, beside what is now his home and business, and feeling perfectly safe. 'We always believed that the stop-bank would protect us from anything the river threw at us. We never imagined we were ever at any risk. But last year it got even higher and fiercer. People started wondering how safe we really were. And then this year Gabrielle happened. It's created a lot of fear—will it happen again? We always believed we could fix things, but this is something we don't know we can fix.'

Paddy sometimes wishes he still had one of the two houses he owned on the hill, in 'upper' Waipawa, but he's long since poured those assets into his campground. Customers from all over the world have become friends. He loves getting his band The Monotones together to play Pink Floyd covers and a few originals at the local pubs. He and Susi have plans to get away a bit, but they feel a big responsibility for their residents and guests. The river is constantly on their minds. They don't sleep well when it rains.

*

Susi recently ditched her mountain bike for a road cycle and joined the local club. Her competitive nature means she's already been out racing on the local roads. One of her clubmates is Tony Ward from the High Street record shop, a road cyclist from way back. Tony and his wife Catherine moved from north of Auckland to Waipawa in 2010 to be closer to her family. He regularly uses the Shared Path to cycle the seventeen minutes from their lifestyle block to the shop, the only way to do it, he says. He had an accident during a race a while back which has slowed him up a bit. 'Six of us came down doing forty kph. If it wasn't for my helmet I wouldn't be here.'

Tony has had his shop 'Passionate About Vinyl' for eight years and is a real enthusiast for Waipawa and his High Street retail colleagues. He says they were virtually unaffected by Cyclone Gabrielle, an observation echoed ruefully by Paddy McCloskey. And it certainly feels like a town of two halves as I walk the short distance up from the Holiday Park.

It's Sunday afternoon and I want to catch a photographic exhibition before closing time. It pelted down last night—so much so I thought I'd wake up floating—and it's still raining steadily as I pick my way around the puddles on the unmarked walkway from river level, up a flight of steps, over the uncontrolled railway crossing *(LOOK BOTH WAYS!)* and into the public carpark beside the Central Hawke's Bay Museum.

The museum is housed in what was, until 1986, a BNZ bank. The grand black-and-white building is impossible to miss, sitting smack in the middle of town with an invitingly wide tiled footpath and a striking collection of vintage farm machinery arranged outside. The small provincial museum is known for being well run, with a full-time director and paid staff. The smiley chap behind the counter tells me they normally get around 5,000 visitors a year but that the recent removal of the $8 entrance fee ($5 for locals) looks like increasing that number substantially. He said they've recorded 900 in the first four free weeks. I take a relaxed meander through a busy warren of pioneering exhibits, eventually emerging in an expansive, white-walled gallery space.

In 2009, Taupō photographer Jeremy Bright was travelling through Hawke's Bay to an assignment in Wairarapa when he happened upon the disused Waipukurau Hospital. It was destined for demolition. I'd found the site myself during a recent stay in Waipukurau, when it was almost all gone, and couldn't help sneaking through the fence for a closer look at one remaining building. Jeremy's website suggests he has an interest in end-of-life objects—one portfolio is called 'Abandoned', another 'Chernobyl'—so this was right up his alley. He snapped a few shots at the time and then re-visited the hospital sporadically for the following twelve years to document its further decline, until there was virtually nothing left of it. The result is 'Ghosts of the Past', a darkly beautiful collection of work and a treat to find in such a small town. Uplifted, I drop a banknote into the museum's donation box and head back out into the drizzle and gloom.

*

In Nelly Jull Park, the 'Ladies Rest Public Toilets' are embla-zoned with a whimsical artwork of their own. A colourful, skilfully painted mural covers entirely two sides of the cottagey concrete block facility. A wader-clad angler stands thigh-deep playing a leaping rainbow trout. A pair of brown ducks tread water nearby—one is bum-up, pecking at the water weed. A Paradise duck swoops overhead. A cabbage tree emerges triumphant from the riverbank. Green hills in the background are topped by blue sky and fluffy white clouds.

Around the corner a '*STOP! 3WATERS*' sign shouts from the gunship-grey Farmlands and Equestrian Central building. A nearby window poster advertises Friday Film & Food in the CHB Municipal Theatre, 'May Fools—a French Classic!'. Swamp Tree Workshop—which makes and fixes guitars, ukuleles, and furniture—is closed ('please phone or text'). The library is shut, too, but its window says it's 'encouraging imaginations'. Tony's record shop is open, Fleetwood Mac spilling from a speaker on the footpath. Goat Horn café still has a few customers; Index is waiting a bit longer for women to buy their clothing.

The 4-Square supermarket is being re-built after it burned down in 2021. Kingfishers Gifts is where you buy party things, sweets, Christmas crackers, and where you'll find the town's postal services. It's run by Meredith Drake. Waipawa Fish Supply has a painted sign saying 'Come In, Haere Mai, Kia Ora' and opens at 4.30pm. It's run by Mark Drake.

There's a poster for an annual fundraiser to raise money for Starship, the highlight of which is a race between dozens—

hundreds?—of yellow plastic waterfowl let loose on the Waipawa river. The beaked toys are sponsored by local businesses like Tony's, and you can put a bet on the result. It's called Duck Day, and it's organised by the Drakes. I'll leave that right there.

I'm back at the fish'n'chip shop at 6pm. The windows are all steamed up. There's urgent activity at the deep fryer, lively chatter out front. A young lady takes my order: One battered fish, one hot dog, two potato fritters please. The phone rings incessantly. Ding goes the door, ding again, people collecting orders. 'Thanks Mark.' Soft drinks being liberated from the chiller. Till ringing, EFTPOS terminal beeping. 'Thanks, Mark.'

I collect my order. 'Thanks, Mark.'

It's that kind of town.

THE FORLORN FOUNTAIN

ABOUT HALFWAY THROUGH WRITING THIS BOOK— halfway in content that is, certainly not in time—I hit a snag. Well, a creeping series of mini snags actually which, when added up, suggested I had a problem. Namely that the whole premise of my endeavour had sort-of evaporated. Or, rather, had become buried in a mire of storms, earthquakes, politics, and pines. It suddenly seemed to me that Route 52—and therefore my book—had ceased to exist.

These days I'm reluctant to take my old caravan back onto Route 52—the culmination of Cyclone Gabrielle, seismic activity, slips, deferred maintenance, logging trucks and general neglect has caused rivets to pop and bits to fly off my fifty-year-old 'van every time I venture onto it. But I still need a way to access the communities on and around Route 52 I'm writing about. To feel some connection, some immersion. To park up somewhere, prop up a bar, see what comes my way. Doing long day trips from home or sleeping in musty motels was not what I had in mind.

But a photograph saved my bacon. A simple iPhone image I took while wandering idly through Pahiatua's intriguingly named Carnival Park Scenic Reserve one crisp March afternoon, heading north, stretching my legs, searching for inspiration.

I stepped through the green wrought iron gate into the Reserve and chose a course to my right. The meandering forest-floor path is unformed, spreading like tentacles through the dense undergrowth of mahoe and nikau palms. Tawa, rimu and tōtara stretch skyward, their resulting canopy blocking all but a dappled light. Direction is indeterminate in here, but when I reached what felt like full-circle the curve of the walkway revealed a bright green clearing. A grassy dell, ringed by trees and ferns. A large camelia tree. It was like finding a remnant of a fantastical film set. I pictured nymphs and elves dancing, playing flutes and zithers, with pointy-toed shoes and conical hats. I imagined water, a forest, curling tree vines climbing up tall trunks. Poetry. Singing. Merriment.

The scene formed in my mind during the time it took to pull the phone out of my pocket, then—c-click—it was gone. All that was on my screen and in front of my eyes was a feature-less clearing. The image had an air of abandonment—like the future of my book project.

On closer inspection however, there were signs of life. A couple of yellow plastic drums had been placed inside a multi-faceted concrete bund with hooped wire edging—perhaps the remains of a pond? Outside the bund in a small, muddy, leafy patch of ground stood a three-tiered metal object covered in

Abandoned assemblage
CARNIVAL PARK, PAHIATUA

dense moss. It had heavy square-section tubed feet and what looked like a brass connector at its base. A fountain. Around it in the mud there were kid-sized footprints, and a small green plastic object sat in one of three dishes.

I took a picture, left the Reserve, and continued my journey.

*

It's a few weeks later. I've found the picture while scrolling through the albums on my phone. It's given me an idea.

I've set up my caravan at Carnival Park Domain—right next to the Scenic Reserve—for a night, maybe two, to do some thinking. A mobile writer's retreat. I've camped here before—it's quiet, secure, and close to town (and to a good fish'n'chip shop). The circular grassy domain is dotted with huge specimen trees—oaks, copper beech—planted over a century ago to mark various occasions, like the town's first church service. I'm parked under one of them. There are wooden park benches and solid picnic tables, a kids' playground. Nearby is a black shed with a penguin, a moa, and other creatures painted on it, the purpose of which is not immediately apparent but which I find out later is known as the Pavilion.

A couple of caravans are parked on a sealed area on the edge of the Domain. A 'tiny house' on wheels is on the grass not far from me, but distant enough, lights already on, bleeding dully through the tinted glass. The brick-clad custodian's house has large windows overlooking the campground; they're netted, but I can see movement inside. (It's a bit of a fishbowl for them, I think.)

The custodian is gathering up large sawn rounds from a felled oak tree near to me, heaving them onto a trailer for splitting back at his shed. As he pulls away the trailer clips a wooden park seat, knocking the edge off a slat. He soon returns on foot with a drill and screws to fix it, his tricolour foxie pup on a recall lead. We talk briefly about training the wilful, intelligent breed, and how I should bring Meg for a playdate next time.

As dusk settles around the Park I drive the two kilometres to Hills Diner for my standard takeaway order—one battered fish, one hot dog, two potato fritters. (For some reason I figure renouncing the traditional scoop of chips for the fritters will be kinder on my waistline. I know, I am a misguided fool.) There isn't anybody in the 'diner' section but, by the counter, three or four people sit flipping dog-eared pages of ancient *New Idea* magazines, waiting for their newsprint-wrapped dinner.

While my order is being prepared I take a stroll along Pahiatua's main street. The streetlights are starting to take effect. The hardware store doors are shuttered. The car dealers have locked up their offices and gone home. Muffled bar chatter and the brash bells of pokie machines filter out from the Club Hotel. The New World supermarket is doing an after-work trade, rattly trolleys coming and going on the entry and exit ramps; I duck in to buy milk and wine.

The last children have deserted the Harvard Adventure Park, so named because it features a bright yellow WWII Harvard aircraft up on stilts with a slide coming out of it. The playground is situated on a wide centre strip between the north- and south-bound sections of the highway—this grassy divider was designed to accommodate a railway line which was never built here but located to the west of the town.

Pahiatua is unarguably on State Highway 2—I'm walking on it right now, back to the diner. But it's no further off Route 52—closer actually—than other places I've written about, places that consider themselves 'on' Route 52. It's the nearest town to several of the Route 52 settlements. I don't want to take the 'van on R52 anymore, but equally I'm reluctant to give up on this book. I take the warm packet of questionable nutrition back to the caravan, stream a 'chilled out' Spotify playlist to the Bluetooth speaker, pour a generous plastic tumbler of pinot gris, and begin mulling my dilemma.

The debate with myself doesn't last too long. By the finish of the second tumbler the 'easiest route' side of myself is nudging ahead. Halfway through the third it is surely winning. And when the wine's finished and it's time to find my toothbrush it's pretty clear the geographical boundary of Route 52 is my own construct and I need to get over myself.

By the time my head hits the pillow it's settled—from now I will forgo my purist ideals and use Pahiatua (or Dannevirke or Eketāhuna or Takapau or wherever) as bases from which to collect my stories.

And to find out more about the mysterious clearing in the Reserve and the fountain in my photograph.

*

William Lints was a New Plymouth hairdresser, gymnast, skater, and water polo player. He was also inclined towards theatrical and musical endeavours. William grew up in Whanganui with Scottish parents. In modern day terms, William was a bit of a polymath.

Lints is credited with devising and organising the first ever 'Queen Carnival', held in Whanganui in March 1914 to raise money for the war effort. Lints' idea was that the carnival would take place over a month or so and might include a theatre revue, a sports match, an auction, talent show or an orchestral performance. It would feature several women sponsored by various local businesses or organisations—the Queens—who would solicit paid votes from the public, costing maybe a couple of pennies. The Queen with the biggest total of donations would be crowned Queen of the Carnival.

The Whanganui carnival was a huge success and Lints would very soon be hired to organise further events all over the country. True to his many skills and passions, a carnival's multitude of performances would often be by his own travelling company. There would also be contributions from local talent to give the events a parochial flavour.

On a website dedicated to the World War One Centenary Programme (WW100), in a piece written in 2016, Manawatū historian Margaret Tennant offers some detail and opinion of the carnivals.[42] Tennant describes the crowning of twenty-year-old Joyce McKelvie at the Rangitikei fundraiser in September 1915 which raised £15,563 for wounded returning soldiers. (As a comparison, a similar Carnival in Auckland raised £251,000.) The caption to a wonderfully detailed photo in her story reads: 'Elaborate preparations were made for the coronation of Joyce McKelvie (seated centre and wearing a crown). Local seamstresses would have outfitted her retinue of page boys, ladies-in-waiting and courtiers. A local magistrate and barrister lent their wigs for the occasion too.'

Joyce's crown was a replica of those worn by English monarchs, Tennant writes, and 'The wartime charity queen carnivals were a form of public drama which referenced tradition, patriotism and loyalty to empire, but also allowed for merriment, ridiculing of authority and challenges to social norms. Young women sold kisses on street corners, 'khaki-clad maidens' paraded in processions, carnival books caricatured politicians and local notables were tried in mock courts for various offences. Respectable women allowed themselves to be on public display as potential carnival queens and voted for in coinage, though these were not beauty contests as such—mature married women and local worthies were as likely as pretty young women to be among the candidates.'

Queen Carnivals took many forms over many years but were always held for the purpose of fundraising for a good cause. As it was for the Queen Carnival held at Pahiatua in June 1914.

*

Pahiatua (god's resting place) was settled in the last remaining part of what was known as the 40 Mile Bush (Te Tapere Nui o Whātonga). Unusually, there was no government involvement in this settlement; rather, in 1880, the Wellington Land Board put 12,000 acres of the bush up for sale.

The land was taken up and subdivided over the following few years by various now-familiar Pahiatua names—Sedcole, Mann, McCardle, Wakeman. It's said that the first settlers were John Hall, who arrived on 28 February 1881, and John Hughes who followed the next day, and that they and their families comprised

Pahiatua's population that summer.[43] 51-year-old John Hall's purchase of several hundred acres of the bush was to have tragic consequences for himself, but ultimately a great gift for Pahiatua.

In May, John Hall's wife and three sons joined him, and they set about clearing the bush. The following year, when there were just a few acres to do, their 24-year-old son John Henry was hit by a falling tree. His injuries—reportedly both legs broken in several places and his skull split in two—killed him instantly. As a memorial to John Henry, that area of bush was left undisturbed.

The Halls' land was known to be of good quality, and they farmed it successfully for the best part of twenty-five years. In 1906, by now in their mid seventies and intending to retire to Levin, they put it up for sale. On 12th December an advertisement in The Wairarapa Age read:

IMPORTANT LAND SALE AT PAHIATUA. An important sale of suburban land at Pahiatua will be held on Wednesday next, December 19th, when Messrs Abraham and Williams, Ltd., will offer in the Olympic theatre, the property known as the John Hall Estate, which adjoins the town of Pahiatua, and is within five minutes' walk of the Post Office. The block contains 365 acres of the finest land in the colony and has been sub-divided into areas ranging from ¼ acre up to 37 acres, thus giving business and residential sites as well as sufficient areas for small dairy farms. The terms of sale, which are remarkably easy, together with plans of the sub-division, can be obtained from the auctioneers on application. [44]

John Henry's memorial bush block, plus an adjoining four-acres of the Halls' estate, were purchased by a group of local businessmen who, eight years later in 1914, offered them back to the community for £800. The Pahiatua Progressive Association decided to hold one of William Lints' Queen Carnivals to raise funds for the purchase of this land. The carnival raised enough for the transaction and the so-called 'People's Park'—the combined bush block and what came to be known as the Domain—opened on the 26 December 1914. But it wasn't long before trouble was brewing, and problems are still bubbling away 110 years later.

*

For over a century, the twelve-acre memorial block of virgin bush has been available to the good citizens of Pahiatua—and passing visitors like me—to enjoy easily and at no cost. Within months of its purchase, water had been found or donated and a pond formed in the bush around which were dotted hydrangeas and camelias. According to local historian Paul Francis Lea, writing in 2021, the park was proving very popular with locals. 'It was reported at the time that children's voices sounded through the People's Park on a Thursday afternoon during the annual picnic of the District High School. 'Committeemen, teachers, parents and pupils spent a pleasant time'.'

Lea continues, 'By 1915 the People's Park had a name change to Carnival Park and was a much-loved beauty spot well known by travellers throughout the country. For decades to come, beautiful flower beds surrounded the open central area around the goldfish-stocked lake. Ducks and swans were a common sight. It became a popular spot for wedding photos, often used by clubs, churches and schools for their picnics and social events. The bush walk and lake was a peaceful wonderland.

The People's Park
PAHIATUA

Early advertising described Carnival Park as 'A pleasant Picnic destination'. Newspaper ads promoted Carnival Park, like this example from the 1920s: 'Come and Picnic in the beautiful piece of Native Bush that skirts the grounds. The shade of the sheltering palm is as nothing compared with the sweet and seductive charm of Carnival Park'.'

Through the decades Carnival Park has been kept afloat by various entities. But as early as 1917, just three years after it was formed, there were issues.

Lea again: 'Within a few years the upkeep funds were slowly but surely depleting, and concerned locals lent a helping hand. On 22 Sept 1917 it was reported: 'Dr. Dawson has donated a fiver to the People's Park fund. Milton Alpass promises five guineas and some swans. He has already given some water for the lake'.'

'20 Feb 1919: 'Matters in connection with the Carnival Park have got to such a stage financially that a public meeting has been called, to decide what had best be done'.

'22 Feb 1919: 'Four young swans have been placed on the lake in the Carnival Park. There has been a lonely old bird on the lake for some time now'.

'On a brighter note,' Lea continues, 'a March 1919 news-paper article said: 'The black swans and the cactus dahlias are particular attractions just now at the Carnival Park. The park is in splendid order and visited by many'.'

But in April 1920: 'A profit of £20 was made on the late flower show, and this will be donated to the Carnival Park Board, which is very hard up.'

Paul Lea writes that by Aug 1921 water was obviously becoming a problem for the lake, when it was stated that 'A water diviner has been employed with a view to finding a spring in the Carnival Park with a more plentiful supply than the present one'. And that in May 1928 the question of water 'has engaged the attention of the Board for some considerable period.' He says the diving showed promise but the cost of drilling bores was prohibitive, and that there were ongoing problems over the decades through drains blocking and the pond leaking.

Improvements continued on the Domain side with the building of an 'accommodation shed for motoring tourists' in 1930. The building contained a kitchen, fireplace, open dining-room, and shower bath, 'and is electrically lighted'. The Pavilion became a great asset for the public attending A&P Show days at the rugby ground next door – visitors filled Thermos flasks and picnicked in the grounds. This was the birth of the Carnival Park campground, and later that decade a children's playing area was added.

In the 1960s a new ablutions block was built with toilets, showers, washing facilities and a cooking and lounge area. Under the supervision of the Council's Domain Board, the camping ground has continued to flourish and now provides a peaceful and safe haven from the madness that is presently the outside world. A good place to think.

Unfortunately, just through the wrought iron gates in what's now known as the Scenic Reserve, things are once again not so rosy.

'For most of the 20th century, with very limited resources, through two world wars, the Pahiatua Borough Council managed to keep the Reserve looking beautiful,' wrote Paul Lea. 'But it went into decline when the Council was merged into the new Tararua District Council in 1989. The Reserve suddenly became surplus to requirements, and it was 'given away' to the Department of Conservation.' Lea says DOC have neglected it ever since and have discouraged local groups from attempting to maintain it, wondering if they've been concerned about 'health and safety' liability. 'Over the years various community groups have tried to get it back to its former glory, but each time DOC have forced them to down tools and leave.

'The People's Park is now DOC's neglected bush.'

*

In 1965, freshly graduated teacher Judy Gleeson arrived at Pahiatua School to take up her first posting. Within five years she had married a local and settled on a small farm on the edge of town, adjacent to Carnival Park. Judy retired from Pahiatua School three years ago. Fittingly, she is on the local Council's Domain Board, responsible for overseeing the operation of the camping area and its facilities.

The brick-walled, cattle-stopped gateway to the property Judy now shares with her partner of twenty years, Bryan Doherty, is almost taken over by a profusion of trees and shrubs of many varieties. The driveway is tight, native branches trimmed to within an inch of where a vehicle might come into contact. Getting out of the car I feel like I've stepped into an aviary; dozens of tūī are flapping around waiting for Judy to feed them. It's nippy July outside but toasty warm in their lounge—26C, I'm told—very welcome as I've come direct from a few days at an uninsulated lakeside Lockwood.

Judy is a bubbly septuagenarian with a shock of grey hair. We sit in facing armchairs while from a third chair Bryan watches an Ashes series cricket replay, TV sound off, headphones on. Occasionally an involuntary exclamation suggests a wicket or a boundary. Judy has the presence of a lifetime classroom teacher and an engaging conversation style so that not once in an hour do I manage to sneak a glance at the screen.

Judy's personal association with Carnival Park goes back long before she moved here, when she inherited a postcard her grandmother had sent from Pahiatua back in the Park's heyday. 'Grandma was a tailor in Wellington and used to come here with her employer once a year. They'd stay in the Club Hotel and make new-season dresses for the women from the country.'

When Judy started at Pahiatua School she found that the three local schools all used the Carnival Park Reserve for nature study, and the Domain for picnics and sports. So it wasn't long before she was taking her own class there. 'The dense bush is quite an intimidating experience for children,' Judy says. 'We used to take little five-year-olds in there, they'd be clutching my raincoat. We'd do some weeding, identify plants, I'd even get them to write some poetry. They'd lie on their backs in the ferns, looking at the canopy for inspiration.'

Later, through the 1980s and 90s, Judy's school groups and parent working bees grew Kōwhai seeds and planted trees to attract the birds and keep the Reserve in some sort of shape. But by now the Council had run out of money for maintenance, and the previously picturesque pond with its gliding swans, gulping goldfish, and three-fronded fountain was falling into serious decline.

The pond had dried up once again, Judy thinks, as a result of tile drains on nearby farmland—her own included—collapsing. The inlet was still visible, she says, but nothing was emerging from it. A group called Friends of Carnival Park concreted the pond and filled it from a well they found in the park. 'It looked lovely for about a month,' Judy says. 'Then the Council discovered there was a discrepancy in their water meter readings—the pond was emptying faster than the well's pump could fill it. They came knocking and we had to turn it off.'

The Domain Board then tried a few more things to retain the water in the pond but eventually gave up. 'And anyway, DOC had found out what we were doing and we were 'talked to' and told that the pond was not in their plans. They said the camelias and hydrangeas had to go, the karakas had to go, the pond could stay there but they weren't fixing it. They did sanction us doing some native planting, and the kids had fun doing that with the help of the Regional Council.'

By the end of the 1900s the pond had filled with lovely rich compost from the forest's falling leaves. Happily sprouting from it were ferns, weeds, seedlings. The pond had been reclaimed. Bit by bit it faded from sight.

'You can only see it now,' Judy says, 'because about five years ago St Anthony and Pahiatua Schools had a big clean up. We took away trailer loads of gunk. There's no way we'll ever get the Reserve back from the Crown. That just doesn't happen.'

So, my fountain lies there with seemingly no future.

*

On a drizzly day in June 2022 a community open day took place at Carnival Park. Huddling under umbrellas and raincoat hoods were manu whenua, DOC, members of Treasure Carnival Park, the Domain Board, local conservationist Peter Russell, and Explore Pahiatua Incorporated (EPI)—the visitor arm of Tararua District Council. Judy Gleeson was there in several capacities, as was Stan Wolland, Carnival Park supporter for half a century; Karolyn Donald—committee member of both EPI and Treasure Carnival Park—mentioned them both in her address.

The occasion was a big announcement about an agreement between DOC and EPI to 'enable community restoration of the site,' according to a DOC media release. 'The open day formally celebrates the establishment of this agreement and seeks to get community feedback and involvement in the next steps.' [45]

A year later, this agreement seems to have come to nothing. The DOC ranger who said at the time she was 'excited about helping restore the reserve to its former glory and reintroducing endemic species' has now informed EPI that they will 'probably see less of her going forward'.[46] Large cypress and wilding pines inhabit the boundaries. Possums munch on native leaves, insects, and bird eggs. The pond remains devoid of water, folding back into the forest floor.

Meantime, funded by EPI, Peter Russell has been diligently beavering away in the forest, weeding, identifying noxious plants, working on an ongoing maintenance and restoration plan. Morale elsewhere is tangibly low as volunteers run out of steam. During my stay here I'm witnessing The People's Park turning in on itself again.

I guess whatever happens I can continue to visit the immaculate campground which, Judy Gleeson tells me, is earning its keep nicely. I can park here under a beautiful tree, take Meg for a walk with her new foxie friend, eat fish'n'chips, and wander around searching for my dancing elves. The fountain won't rust away quickly—it's stainless steel—and maybe the inexorable growth of its vivid green mossy coat will render it even more photogenic. I can unhook the 'van, leave it here, and drive to 'proper' Route 52 places. Find a café or pub, snoop around, see what comes my way.

The road has sprung back to life.

A BIG LUMP OF
COUNTRY UNKNOWN

AN ENTRY IN MY CARAVAN JOURNAL DATED 24 AUGUST 2020 is titled 'Mākurī Mistake'. It describes returning from a trip to Te Awanga, intending to stop off at Alfredton for a night, taking a wrong turn in the evening gloom, realising that the caravan's driving lights were not working, and ending up at Mākurī. 'In the middle of nowhere,' the post reads. 'Very showery and cold. Pitch black. No-one around. Feeling a bit vulnerable.'

I'd somehow found my way to the Mākurī Domain and pulled up behind a rather piecemeal building ambitiously signed 'Country Club'. It was surrounded by large trees, dripping and swaying as the squalls passed through, and I could hear a stream gushing by behind the undergrowth.

A welcome port in a storm
MĀKURĪ DOMAIN

'Pissed with rain overnight, woke me up at 3am for a while,' the journal continues, in crisper handwriting. 'Very windy this morning, should be a fun trip home ☺. Nothing much to recommend Mākurī Domain other than flat hard ground and a basic toilet. Still, I'm glad it was here, I was tired, and it would've been dangerous driving any further.'

The rest of the trip home was indeed 'fun', getting smashed by the gales and sheeting rain as I retraced my steps for twenty-three kilometres, down through the narrow gorge, over several one-way bridges, back to the highway. The weather refused to let up as I hurried south to safety.

*

I'd been to Mākurī once before, deliberately, briefly, many years earlier, with someone else driving, in search of trout. The fish in the Mākurī River can be large, we were told, particularly below the school. Easy enough to spot, but not so simple to catch. We soon discovered all three things were true, quickly moving on to more promising pickings on another stream.

This time I'm making a day trip alone on a cloudless blue-sky day with no caravan in tow, and no intention of fishing. The narrow metal Pori Road climbs away from Route 52 just north of Alfredton, up the Puketoi Range to an elevation of 564 metres. *'NOT SUITABLE FOR TRUCKS WITH TRAILERS'*, the sign at the bottom says. Not suitable for trucks at all, I would've thought.

My ears pop as I gingerly steer heavenward, catching an occasional glimpse of the vertical fall over the fence, tucking as close into the hillside as possible, hoping nothing is coming down. Manoeuvring past another vehicle on a road little wider than a farm track would be even more heart-stopping. The view from the top is otherworldly.

The Puketoi Range lords over much of Route 52's central length, protecting (sort-of) the settlements around Tiraumea, Pongaroa, and Waione from the worst of the westerly. This is limestone country, outcrops jutting through surprisingly green surrounds. It's a dry February kept looking lush by large stands of native forest, a decent rainfall, and the many springs that dot the range. Talk to farmers around here and you'll find water is not an issue.

As Pori Road drops rapidly towards Mākurī on the western side of the range (more ear popping), I keep my eye out for Mount Marchant, the farm owned by Daniel and Louise Bowie. Lou has recently been appointed (rather, volunteered army-style) President of the Mākurī Country Club and I'm keen to revisit it in better circumstances.

I find the Bowies and their ten- and nearly-nine-year-old children George and Lucy in the yards, far below the homestead, a quartet of dogs clipped neatly along a fence waiting patiently for their next piece of action. The family is drafting lambs for the 'works'. Lou grabs the keys to the Club and hops in my car. They've been farming Mount Marchant on their own for nine years now, buying it from Daniel's parents who retired after thirty years on the property. 'So we knew exactly what community we were moving in to,' Lou tells me, sliding a cigarette from a half-empty packet as we pull up by a wooden picnic table in the sun.

Mid-Canterbury-raised Lou is the person the word 'irrepressible' was coined for. Small in stature, big in energy, Lou has for most of her life competed in elite level show jumping. 'I came up to the North Island looking for more competition. I found myself a husband too.' As well as Country Club duties Lou is chair of the village social committee, a member of the local catchment group, on the fundraising arm of the school, and no doubt has other roles she doesn't mention. 'I'm very much a 'yes' person,' she says. 'And I like a party.'

But the time has come to hang up her jodhpurs, she feels, at least for now. 'I just sold my truck. I had four competition horses, and I recently retired the last one. When the kids were younger I'd be away every Thursday to Sunday; now I don't want to leave them.' While hinting at 'never say never', you get the feeling that she's just making time to do more around the community.

On this still and shiny day, the Country Club building and surrounding Domain feel a far cry from the 'mistake' nearly four years ago and I've forgiven it already. Fashionably rusty Corten steel signage announces the complex at the gate. Grass clipped for a school fundraising event a few days earlier is now being grazed by a dozen fluffy white sheep. Exotic trees glow with fresh green foliage, sunlight filtering through their leaves.

Lou explains how the idea of the Club originated in 1983 when the little timber and breeze-block pub in the village closed and the licence transferred to a Wellington tavern.[47] That pub was built in the 1950s after the original, 1897, two-storey hotel burned down in 1949.

The Club started off as a single room, she says, a small bar built by local farmers. Gradually a kitchen was added, a fireplace, and a larger extension about fifteen years ago, then the covered porch. All with volunteer labour. At the same time a nine-hole golf course was laid out on the domain and surrounding properties as a means of obtaining a liquor licence. The course fell into disuse some time ago but has recently been partially revived.

Operation of the not-for-profit Club bar is also entirely voluntary, rotated between eight committee members on regular Friday night openings. 'We're never quite sure how many are going to turn up,' Lou says. 'It might be two, it might be twenty.' The cooler months tend to be more popular, she says. 'Mākurī winters are very long, wet, dull. It's a good place to get together, talk about farming. Or, more likely, talk about not farming.'

In the summer the Domain hosts a good number of campers and motor homers, maybe around ten at any one time Lou estimates, many of them regulars. It's getting more popular, and they're mostly here for the fishing that's literally right on the doorstep.

*

One of those visitors is Masterton angler Nick Jolliffe. Nick is around my age and has been fishing for as long as he can remember. He's been plying the Mākurī River for over forty years. A natural storyteller (he's a career salesman) Nick entertains me over a long black and a flat white at Masterton's Trocadero Café with the history of his relationship with the waterway. He's pleased I'm writing about the river—he's not one to keep fishing secrets—and about the area in general. 'Good on you,' he says. 'Fame for Route 52 is long overdue. It's a big lump of country unknown.'

Family farms
COUNTRY CLUB, MĀKURĪ

Nick tells me that in 1981 he was twenty-five, just moved north from Christchurch, and had a sales job with BP Europa out of Palmerston North. Many Friday afternoons he'd meet up with a fellow rep at the Pongaroa pub. 'One time I was driving through Mākurī to get there and thought I'd better have a crack at this piece of water one weekend.' A few Saturdays later he found himself casting to a fish he'd spotted from the riverbank but was unable to see from his wading position in the water.

'A voice from above and behind me said, 'You're six feet short and you need to be another three feet out.' I followed the stranger's instructions, struck when he told me to, and had a nice fish on the line.' Discussing how they'd share the river, the two anglers agreed to spot for each other pool-about, working their way upstream. After a successful morning's fishing they went their separate ways.

That night Nick's flatmate suggested they go to see a friend of his play in the band at the Armada Bar in the infamous Fitzherbert Hotel. 'During the band's break the drummer wandered over to our table. Before my flatmate could introduce us, I said, 'That's the guy I was fishing with this morning!' From then on Earl and I fished the Mākurī almost every opening day for nearly thirty years.[viii] We had a huge fishing partnership over that time, on dozens of different rivers, but it was all built around fishing the Mākurī.'

Nick tells me the Mākurī River is what the British would call a chalk stream. It has a limestone bottom and is spring fed, and very

---

viii This was Earl Pollard, who played for decades with popular Manawatū country and blues acts Legal Tender and Bullfrog Rata. He died from lymphoma in 2011.

rich in life—koura, insects, even shrimp. It rises in the Puketoi Range at an area called the Cascades where there are some deep channels and waterfalls. It winds down the valley for about ten kilometres until it gets to Mākurī township, where it disappears into a very steep gorge. 'Most of the fishing is done above the gorge—you'd have to be a maniac to fish down below, it's all slippery boulders and deep water and fast runs. Very, very hard.'

Past the gorge the river wanders down to the Tiraumea and into the Manawatū. Access on this part of the river is difficult but Nick thinks for this reason it plays an important part in keeping the fish population healthy further upstream. His theory is that because this lower section doesn't get fished a lot, it holds a good population of large trout. He's pretty sure that when fish numbers drop in the higher reaches these downstream dwellers simply move up to replace them. This means that despite the relatively large number of anglers on the river ('pressure' in angling terms) there are always plenty of good-size fish available, both browns and rainbows, averaging around five pounds in the old language.

There are also some real monsters in there, Nick says, but as I found out myself on that first visit, the chunky ones don't get that way by being stupid. 'On one particular corner there was always a big jack sitting in a pool. We called him George. George just treated us with contempt. We only managed to hook him twice in ten years.' Then one spring he wasn't there anymore.

As Nick tells it, the Mākurī is known as a 'three trip' stream. 'The first time you fish it you go wow, this is wonderful, this is great, look at all those trout—and you don't catch anything. The second time, you've got a plan, you know what you did wrong last time, you execute the plan perfectly, and you go home with nothing. The third time, you've adjusted your plan, you fish all day, and you still go home empty-handed. So you don't go again.'

It's a stream that requires perseverance, he says. 'I got lucky bumping into Earl on my first trip. Earl was a natural. I'm an okay fisherman, but nowhere near in Earl's league. Fishing with him was a delight. We had a heap of fun, and we caught fish. He was mates with the local schoolteacher, who would pour rum and Coke down our throats for breakfast if we were staying with him. A real hangman.'

Fishing friendships are special, and Nick spends the next little while in the café topping up his coffee, reminiscing, relating 'Earl' stories—the ones that got away, those that didn't, the cuppa tea breaks to watch the top-dressing planes buzzing overhead, his distance-running adventures and flying escapades, the music, and eventually his illness.

'One day we were up around Takapau, fishing the Tukipō, not having any luck. Earl was tired—he was very sick by this time—so we went to a spot he knew near Ormondville. Earl hated electric fences, so he went to find a gate while I jumped the fence. I found a fish sitting right below me in the pool. By the time Earl arrived I'd hooked the fish, so he jumped in the water and threw it out onto the bank, something he'd done for me a million times.

'We went and sat on a log in the late afternoon sun, both of us staring into the stream, knowing without speaking that this was our last trip together. I said, there's another one in there, Earl. He said yep, got into the water, hooked it, I got in and threw it

out for him. We sat down with our fish each. And that was it.'
Nick goes quiet for a moment. 'Sad. Y'know, I've been back to
that spot a few times, and I've never seen another fish there.'

*

The Mākurī River follows the twisty Coonoor Road from its
source to the village. According to Wikipedia the name Coonoor
(generally pronounced ku-nor) was first used for an early sheep
station and was later applied to the place at which four roads
meet near where the river rises. The name was also given to a
school on the road which opened in 1896 and closed in 1968
when the roll had dropped to seven.

Wikipedia also tells us Coonoor is a municipality of the
Nilgiris district in the Southern Indian State of Tamil Nadu.
It has an average elevation of 1,650 metres above sea level and
features a sub-tropical highland climate. It's famous for its tea
production and for Sim's Park, a botanical garden spread over
an area of twelve hectares with a collection of over 1,000 plant
species. Most interestingly, in 2011 the town had a population of
45,494 with a sex-ratio of 1,058 females for every 1,000 males,
much above the national average of 929.

According to former Mākurī resident Bill Murphy, as quoted
in the 1994 publication *Makuri School and District 100 Years Plus,*[48]
a British soldier by the name of Charles Parsons was wounded
at 'some place called Coonoor, he came out to Aotearoa and
drew a section in the Valley as an original settler and he named
the district Coonoor'. The publication claims that the word
Coonoor means 'high country' in Indian; my research says it

Mountain village
MĀKURĪ

could also mean 'jagged landscape' or 'grazing slopes'. Put all three together and I'd suggest Mr Parsons got it bang on. (There is also a Coonoor Road in the Timaru suburb of Watlington but it appears to have none of those attributes.)

Fourth generation Coonoor Road farmer Patrick Diamond has been eating a lot of curries lately he tells me when I pop in to see him and his mother Agnes at her house on the edge of Pahiatua. The reason, he says, is that his sister Maree Diamond and fiancée Cushla Paton are not long back from a holiday in India, during which they felt compelled to make a side-trip to Coonoor. 'We thought we couldn't go all that way and not go to see it,' Cushla told me on the phone later.

The tour they'd taken finished at Fort Kochi in Kerala. On the map, Coonoor looks like an easy enough trip from there, just 260 kilometres, so they hired a driver and set off. Six hours and scores of twists and turns later, they arrived. 'We could see immediately why Charles Parsons named our little district after the place where he was injured. The approach to the town, with its steep climb and hairpin bends, is very much like here, but with tea bushes growing rather than sheep grazing.' Cushla describes driving past limestone outcrops, springs and water-falls, and plenty of camelias and rhododendrons. 'It's cooler up there, too. One day we were completely covered in a blanket of clouds, which can also happen in Mākurī.'

The 365 hectare Diamond family farm 'Glenmornan' has boundaries on both the Mākurī and the Mangatoro Rivers, which bubble up from the same spot at the Cascades. Patrick has never tried his hand at the angling art, but Cushla has fished a bit around Taupō. The river is pretty narrow on their property, and the bottom a little muddy, so it'd be a walk or drive downstream to get somewhere fishable. They're very happy to see so many people using the river, though. 'There's plenty of access, even without crossing farmland,' Patrick says. 'We know several of the fishers by name, the locals all get a wave, they all seem to be very well behaved.'

*

Another long-time Coonoor Road resident is retired teacher Jane Seymour. Along with her farmer husband, Alastair Fetch, Jane lives on 518 hectare 'Waimarara' and operates the Mākurī River Retreat. The couple met when Jane came to Mākurī in 1981 to teach at Mākurī School, which in those days had around sixty children, and where Jane has spent a large part of her teaching career. (Farmers often marry teachers, Agnes Diamond told me. Or dental nurses.)

Waimarara's white-gated, tree-lined entrance leads almost immediately to a substantial castellating steel bridge crossing the Mākurī River. To the right a very large pond—a lake, really—is elegantly planted with long-established natives and exotics. A pair of fibreglass dinghies—one blue, one yellow—are tied up awaiting paddlers. On the left a pretty white farm cottage with a sign—'*Retreat*'. A substantial stream tumbles noisily along the side of the drive towards the river, evidence of a very productive spring further up.[ix] Everything is green, lush, quite

---

ix   In fact, there are two large waterfalls upstream— *Waimarara* means scattered, or cascading, water.

unlike most other places in the wider district at this time of the year—mid-February.

The sun is shining and the birds are singing as Jane emerges from a neat-as-a-pin white homestead to greet me. Wide verandas with black railings, several sets of French doors, white roses and pastel hydrangeas all lend an 'Arts & Crafts' look. Jane has our seating determined at a wooden dining table. Alastair passes by to introduce himself, and heads back out to the farm.

Jane confesses to being a bit 'wary' of me, and she's obviously discovered I'm easy to find on the internet. She's been misquoted in the past, she says. But we quickly discover we were both at Wellington Teachers' College at the same time in the 1970s—Jane was a year ahead of me—and the conversation flows easily.

Reminiscing about that time always gives me true pleasure. They were the best three years of my life, I like to say, and Jane feels strongly about it too—'It was special.' I was in an experimental student cohort which essentially side-stepped most of the boring bits (professional development, physical education, maths) in favour of the good stuff (music, ceramics, language, drama). The philosophy seemed to be: Turn this bunch of crazy, hairy young people into decent creative adults, then let them loose on the kids and see what happens. Three years of spending five days a week playing with clay and words and Moog synthesisers with such legends of arts education as George Webby, Laughton Pattrick, Robert Bennett, Laurie Lord, Dorothy Carmody, Ralph McAllister . . . what's not to like?

With me rabbiting on about myself, ten minutes pass before Jane gets a chance to tell me she taught Patrick Diamond's sisters (the younger ones) when she first arrived at Mākurī; that the village wasn't really any bigger back then, but the families were (and there were more of them); that the community has had to fight hard to keep the school (at one point it got down to four students); and that Waimarara Station climbs right to the top of the Puketoi Range where, over the ridge, there's a lovely bush reserve.

I also learn that the big green blob of pine trees assaulting one's senses on the way out from Pahiatua was previously a very successful sheep and beef farm called Tuscan Hills; that both long- and short-tailed bats (pekapeka) live around here (there's an extensive cave network on the Puketoi Range, well known to speleologists); and that in 1975 Alastair's uncle Bill Fetch was the driving force behind the hugely popular Martinborough Fair in South Wairarapa.

Then we get to talk about what I really came to talk about—the fishing.

*

Mākurī River Retreat is a delightfully simple farm cottage, possibly built around the 1950s for a previous owner's mother, Jane thinks, although she suspects the mother never actually lived there. It's appointed in a farm cottagey way with the original green Shacklock wood range still in situ, a bricked-in bath, and classic period furniture. Over the years the cottage was used by visiting family and friends, but increasingly Alastair was being approached while he was working around the farm by fishers wanting to lease or rent.

'We got it painted and anglers came and stayed and enjoyed it,' Jane tells me. Now the visitors book features entries from regulars such as a famous Finnish musician, a group of French medics, some professionals from Wales, and a miscellany from Wellington.

They come from all over to fish the Mākurī, enjoying the cottage's direct access to the river, its peaceful location, the country hospitality, and the challenging fishing. Jane's early marketing efforts have paid dividends, and the Retreat is as busy as she wants it to be. 'Have a look at my Facebook page, I hardly put anything on it these days. In fact, that reminds me, a fisherman gave me some photos, I should upload those soon . . .'

Meanwhile, downstream, in the less-often-fished stretch between the gorge and the Domain, it looks like, along with the caddis and mayfly, plans for a new venture could be hatching.

*

When 71-year-old George Ross was a nipper his father managed Te Mai Station in the remote hills east of Tinui, out towards Castlepoint. It was so isolated, George says, there were thirteen gates between the farmhouse and the road. Consequently, he did his first four years schooling by correspondence.

When he was nine, George's family moved to NgaToii on Range Road, in the foothills of the Puketois near Pongaroa. Here he was able to go to school—to Pongaroa School, then thriving with a roll of about 160 (currently it's a third of that and falling). George recalls the Pongaroa-Pahiatua road then being completely unsealed and very rough. 'We had Vauxhall cars,' he tells me. 'In the winter, Dad put Land Rover tyres on them so we could get to town. There were endless slips and mud. It was a real challenge.'

Today, living in Mākurī, George can travel to either Pongaroa or Pahiatua on sealed tarmac. But he's still had to navigate ten kilometres of no-exit metal getting to and from his farm on what's known as the Woodville-Aohanga Road. 'My father bought the land there in about 1970. It was 800 acres of mostly scrub. I was leaving school at the time and went shepherding and shearing and fencing around the district and saved up a bit of money. When I was twenty-three the government was dishing out eighty-five per cent loans through the Rural Bank, so I bought Dad out and he bought more land closer to Range Road. Then I got to work and cleared the land. I chopped about 100 acres a year with a brush saw, farming it as I went.'

Revealing his entrepreneurial spirit, George bought some adjoining land during the 1980s 'Not a good idea. The interest climbed to twenty-eight per cent. Just as well I was single.' Then another bit fifteen years later. 'Nervously. I had little kids by then, I didn't want to make another mistake.'

But he needn't have worried—a property boom was just beginning, the scaled-up farm's cashflow was good, and gradually he was able to buy some more paddocks and a couple of houses in the village to make life easier for his wife Sue and the children.

Having been here for half a century and involving himself in just about everything—he was squeezing our chat in between sorting out an issue at the town's top-dressing landing strip and setting up the Pahiatua dog trials starting the next day—

everyone knows George Ross. Likewise, Sue is someone everyone mentions, too. 'She's the village matriarch,' George says proudly.

Their son Dougal now runs the farm. After shepherding on Tautane Station, at Cape Turnagain, Dougal came back home about a year ago. George says, 'I don't want to be one of those fathers who gets in the way, which means I'm often jumping out of bed in the mornings without a purpose. So I bought some bare land in Hawke's Bay.' He's now working on selling some of the village property to fund his new project.

Part of what the Rosses are selling is some river flats and a couple of terraces below their house, in the section that flows between the domain and the gorge. And as I'm snooping around town, I learn a deal has been concluded which could lead to the already world-famous trout stream getting even more popular.

*

Dave Wood is often the name on anglers' lips when asked to pick Taupō's top fishing guide. A senior guide at exclusive Poronui Lodge for the last two decades, and full-time professional for many years before that, Dave has fished and mentored wherever there are trout in Aotearoa. He's accompanied beginners and experts from all corners of the globe—he has a regular client from Alabama with whom he's spent over 450 days exploring the country's many and varied streams and rivers.

While perfectly happy chasing double-digit rainbows on the big water of the Central Plateau, Dave is at heart a dry-fly aficionado. He likes nothing better than being on a stream in March or April, when the water is cooler and the fish are in their

Tiger country
BELOW THE BRIDGE, MĀKURĪ

best condition, watching a brown trout rise to the surface to gently sip a little mayfly or caddis imitation. 'It's trickier,' he tells me by phone just after flying out from a heli-fishing assignment somewhere. 'More skilful.'

Dave leased Waitahanui Lodge on the shores of Lake Taupō for several years and has been looking for a riverside spot of his own for some time. In April 2023 he was guiding a group of clients—including his Alabaman regular—around the many very fishable Tararua District rivers, basing themselves at Mākurī River Retreat. 'On the Friday, Jane invited us down to the Country Club. While there I met George Ross, we got talking, and I discovered he had a bit of river flat he was interested in selling. Next morning I went for a look, a couple of weeks later I came back with my wife Sofia, and things happened pretty organically after that. It's a lovely little village, a nice tight-knit community, we're looking forward to being part of it.'

River access on Dave's new block is not as straightforward as further upstream—'In the trade we'd call it 'tiger country''. But for him that's part of the attraction; that, plus the area is relatively new turf, although he has fished here several times. 'I'll be back down with my eldest son soon, we'll spend a couple of weeks just looking around, finding the little streams, doing a bit of research.' Dave's slightly reluctant to describe exactly what he has in mind for the place, but he does give me some hints. 'It'll be flash, but it won't be big flash. One or two cabins, a little lodge building . . . '

With his Taupō commitments it'll be a split existence, Dave says, but I get the feeling the split will work well for him. As Lou Bowie said, winter in Mākurī can be long, wet, and dull, so spending those months guiding around the Lake could work out perfectly. And where better to spend the warmer evenings than around Mākurī village, sitting under a tree in the Domain, listening to the cicadas?

*

I haven't picked up a fly rod for the best part of a decade, since I decided Fish & Game were no longer getting my hard-earned licence money. Their intractable (and I thought unreasonable) attitude towards a youthful misdemeanour on the part of my teenage son really ground my gears, and cost him a sizeable chunk of his student allowance. I figured that would be all the revenue they'd get from my family for a while.

To be fair, I'd somewhat run out of steam with the fishing anyway. Moving to Wairarapa had distanced me from regular fishing buddies—at least those who weren't developing arthritic ankles or spending more time at The Great Lake. The Taupō rivers were getting too busy, and blindly pitching ten-weight lines with leaded globugs attached into the turbulent Tongariro had long since lost its appeal.

The Wairarapa move had also plonked a river right in my daily view, and you know what happens then? When your mind says you can fish any time you like, somehow your body never gets around to it. The stretch of the Ruamāhanga above and below the Kokotau Bridge (the scene of the crime) can occasionally be quite productive, and I gave it a reasonable working over for the first few years we were here. But kids' sport on weekends, and earning a living the rest of the time, began to take precedence.

When I first got my little caravan—the season before my last fishing licence ran out—I'd potter up to the Pohangina or Mākākahi for a night or two, but I found I was happy enough just going for a stroll and seeing what I could spot.

However, the Mākurī is attractive on many levels. It's a comfortable enough day trip from home. Access is good and gentle. The fish are a decent size. Above the village it's a low and steady flow, not too physical. All adding up to being quite suitable for someone slip-sliding past middle age with a bad back and dodgy hips.

But I need to get past the 'three trip' syndrome. And get over my gripe with the licensors. I could do with shedding a few pounds to take the pressure off those painful joints. And perhaps, maybe, one of my new-found expert friends, with their knowledge and experience, might take me under their wing, at least briefly, on a calm sunny day, to offer practical advice from the riverbank above.

To be my Earl.

PINE HILLS

FROM THE MĀKURĪ SCHOOL JUBILEE BOOK 1995–2020:

Ernest W. Hansen 'Pinehills'.

*Although 'Pinehills' is not geographically in the Makuri district,
Mrs Sonia Mackenzie (daughter) would like it acknowledged because
of the involvement her father had with the district.*

*Ernest Hansen, his father and two brothers Norman and Otto
began farming in 1913 until he married Winnifred in 1931 and they
bought out the Partnership.*

*Ernest served in the Home Guard and was on the Makuri
Committees of the Hall, Horsesports, Jubilee, Church and Golf Club.
He also built the School Archway for the 50ᵗʰ Jubilee.*

*Their daughters Elfreda and Sonia had Correspondence School
from their mother who was active in the Church Guild and Golf Club.
They sold 'Pinehills' to their daughter Elfreda and Bruce Fogden in
1961 and was resold to Davidsons in 1966.*

*

When the Hansen family began developing a nineteenth century 200 acre ballot block high on the eastern side of the Puketoi Range, below the Mount Butters summit at the junction of Rimu and Rākaunui Roads, little did they know that 125 years later the name they gave the property would be so prescient.

Pinehills, which eventually grew to 1,000 acres, was so named for the trees planted to provide some relief from the persistent westerly that blows over the hills at that altitude (there's currently talk of a big windfarm development close by). But of course, like most of the farms around there and elsewhere, the rest of the land was scorched earth—the 'scrub' (native bush) having been cleared and grassed to graze sheep and cattle.

I'm familiar with these pioneering Hansens a little. Sonia Mackenzie—born Sonia Hansen at Pinehills in 1935—is the wife of my mother's cousin, the late, lamented, elaborately-moustachioed Jock Mackenzie. Jock had a sister, Jean, to whom my mother Jacquie was very close. Jean and Jock were really the only cousins Mum had—she was effectively an only child, her father's first wife having died in childbirth, Mum arriving ten years later when her father Wynford Beere married Jean and Jock's aunt, Mavis Ross. (Are you keeping up?). My own father Ron was very fond of Jean, too—they were both sticklers for grammar and spelling and I have a memory of them talking on the phone endlessly. No-one in the Burt family was allowed to pass through Hawke's Bay without calling in to see Jean, and her mother Iris while she was alive, at 419 Hastings Street South. That address is etched on my brain.

At altitude
PUKETOI RANGE

Jock and Jean grew up on historic Olrig Station at Maraekākaho where their father Alec was manager. Jock joined the Air Force as a sixteen-year-old (he lied about his age) and was still flying for a living when he met Sonia, who was ten years younger, at a party. Not long before they married, in 1956 when Sonia was twenty, Jock had an accident while aerial top-dressing. He sustained damage to his face, particularly his top lip when the compass bowl sliced through it. This led to his famous luxurious moustache, enhanced from the existing standard-issue pilot's version to hide the scars. It became part of family folklore.

The newlyweds lived in Hastings township during which time Jock was forced to retire from flying when his hearing was failing, so they moved to a small farm in Marton. Later they bought Mount Cameron at Dartmoor, inland from Hastings. They had five children—Catherine, Kenneth, Anna, Kirsty, and Sarah.

When I was a kid we'd go to Mount Cameron as a family, puttering gingerly up the island from Wellington in one of the old cars Dad was always crawling underneath to keep it running. We loved the farm animals, the horses, our little second-cousins, and Jock's jokes. We were also highly amused by his kilt. (Sonia, Jock, and Jean were instigators of Clan Mackenzie in Aotearoa; Sonia became its first and only female lieutenant.)

It was a busy home. Sonia always had time for others as well as her own brood and there was invariably a houseful of local farmers' offspring running around with hers. It was my London-born, city-dwelling father and his townie children's chance to experience a bit of genuine, rural, metal-road Aotearoa.[49]

The reason I mention all of this is a couple of coincidences.

Firstly, Jean told me in a 2001 letter (she loved writing letters) that the Hartgill family, who farmed at Akitio and whose big old Dannevirke house I now live in (you can read a bit about that in the chapter titled *Howzat?!*) used to buy rams every year from Ernest Hansen's Romney stud at Pinehills.

Then, while I was writing about shearing contractors and farmers Dave and Rebecca Buick for the chapter *Colour Code,* I discovered that back in 2016 they'd bought Pinehills. Their idea was to use it as a breeding unit and fatten the progeny on their Pongaroa farm, Taraora. But with the proliferation of forestry, Pinehills was soon completely surrounded by trees so they sold it to help fund another, larger property, Te Rau, a breeding and finishing unit, again on the edge of Pongaroa.

After a century-and-a-quarter of providing for a decent handful of families, Pinehills is now 400 hectares of pine hills. Smothered from top to bottom in a single shade of dark green gloom.

A NEW CHAPTER?

IN MARCH 2024 PIP AND I DECIDED TO ATTEND A FRIDAY night concert in Whanganui by the Wellington-based 'dream pop' band French for Rabbits. I suggested we take the caravan and Meg and make a weekend of it, maybe park up at a beach and get some ozone. The weather was looking good. She agreed.

Other than a couple of WOMADs and the odd occasion when we've taken the 'van to a local wedding or party to avoid having to drive home afterwards, Pip hasn't spent much time away in the little mobile bach. To be fair, a lot of my trips have been for the purposes of this book, some for other writing projects, a couple of fishing trips, and plenty just for the hell of it or when I needed some space. Also, I've spent an awful lot of static time in this caravan (almost every word of this book was written in it) so the alone-to-with-Pip ratio is heavily skewed. And anyway, she always refers to it as 'your caravan' rather than as matrimonial property (I don't know whether to be worried about this or not).

We got a bit lucky at the Kai Iwi Beach Holiday Park, snaring a cosy site with a glimpse of the ocean. The five-minute walk to the beach is easy, either down a grassy track from the camp-ground or along a quiet road through the Mowhanau settlement with no footpath but wide grass berms. Along the way Norfolk Pines abound and tumbledown old baches are jumbled up with modern homes. A fantastical playground sits right in the sand, a little stream running through it, a flying fox and giant wooden pirate ship the main attractions.

Meg loved the beach, roaming high up the crumbling cliffs chasing rabbits through the undergrowth, paddling in the tide, racing along the black sand doing the foxie zoomies. Pip enjoyed sitting in the 'van, sun streaming in, working on her own writing project—the artist floor-talk for an exhibition of her 'Boro' collection, opening imminently at Te Manawa in Palmerston North[50]. The concert in the stunning St Peter's church in Gonville was good. The fish'n'chips from the campground store were even better.

Me, I wasn't quite myself. A bit jittery, feeling like what's usually my own space wasn't. So on Saturday morning I took myself off to find a sourdough loaf at the riverside market and for a bit of house-spotting around Castlecliff. I've long thought I could live in this city when it's time to move, but I suspect I'd be on my own—Pip gives the impression of intending to go nowhere.

On Sunday morning, noting the number of the site we were camped at for a possible return visit, I wound up the stabilisers, unplugged the power, and hooked the 'van to the tow hitch. We made our way out, dropping the barrier-arm swipe card at the office with our thanks for a pleasant stay.

The other coast
KAI IWI BEACH, WHANGANUI

*

It's a reasonably easy drive from Whanganui to home—about three hours with the 'van on the back—but perhaps half an hour longer than I like to do in one leg, so we stop in Pahiatua for some tempura and nori roll from Joy Sushi (so good). I also want Pip to see the remains of the little lake I wrote about in the chapter *The Forlorn Fountain*, so on the way out of town we turn into Halls Road, then into Glasgow Street.

The narrow tree-lined street soon takes a kink and a leads through the entrance to Carnival Park Domain. Only a couple of visiting caravans are parked up on the grass, and a few 'permanents' on the seal—I recognise them from my stays here. Meg jumps from her travel crate, toetoe tail going a million miles an hour. We open the white gate to the bush reserve and meander through vague trails leading this way and that. Nothing much has changed since I was last here, I think. The empty pool is still full of leaves. The mossy fountain hasn't moved. The volunteers' weed bins remain full. There's perhaps a little more evidence of pest control—pink ribbons tied to branches, multi-coloured plastic triangles pointing here and there. Meg has her nose to the ground, zigzagging among the trees.

After a little while we close the gate and walk back to the car. The midday sun streams down through the glorious oaks and conifers. Birds tweet. The autumn colours are beginning to show. We're only an hour from home.

I'd love to come and stay here for a couple of days, Pip says.

Domain with large trees
PAHIATUA

NOTES

1   https://street-stories.nz/street/te-ore-ore-road/

2   https://rangitaneeducation.com/wairarapa-history/ and
        https://library.mstn.govt.nz/wairarapa-stories/our-places/the-eight-year-house/

3   https://paperspast.natlib.govt.nz/newspapers/WDT18880121.2.13

4   445.154 hectares—Aotearoa switched to metric in the 1970s

5   Kernohan, David, *Wairarapa Buildings: Two Centuries of New Zealand Architecture*, Wairarapa Archives, 2003

6   Edmonds, June (compiled by), *Alfredton: The School and the People*, Roydhouse Publishing, Carterton, 1987

7   Fowler, Michael, 'Young, William Gray', *Dictionary of New Zealand Biography*, *Te Ara—The Encyclopedia of New Zealand*, 1998 (updated 2012)
        https://teara.govt.nz/en/biographies/4y3/young-william-gray/print

8   'State housing in New Zealand', https://nzhistory.govt.nz/culture/
        state-housing-in-nz, (Ministry for Culture and Heritage), 2014

9   Ramsden, Jill, *State Houses, A Roadside View*, Ram Publishing, 2021

10   McKay, Bill & Stevens, Andrea, *Beyond the State: New Zealand State Houses from Modest to Modern*, Penguin New Zealand, 2014

11   https://www.ruralnewsgroup.co.nz/rural-news/rural-general-news/
        stuffing-the-good-out-of-wool

12   Lineham, Peter J.,'Elliott, Keith', *Dictionary of New Zealand Biography*, *Te Ara—the Encyclopedia of New Zealand*, 2000
        https://teara.govt.nz/en/biographies/5e3/elliott-keith/print

13   Weir, John (Ed.), *The Poems of James K. Baxter*, Oxford University Press, 1980

14   https://natlib.govt.nz/records/42683834

15   http://www.sciascianz.com/docs/Nicola_Sciascia_Story.pdf

16   https://www.nzgeo.com/stories/dancing-down-the-decades/

17   https://www.davidwardmusician.com/wheel-of-experience.html

18   Papers Past—Bush Advocate, 22 November 1907

19   Humphries, Toby, *The Main Road: Growing Up at Akitio*, Astro Copy, 2005

20   Cowan, Muriel, *Twenty-six Men from Last Century*, M.Cowan, 2002

21   Archbold, Rick and McCauley, Dana, *Last Dinner on the Titanic*, Allen & Unwin/Madison Press, 1988

22   Wilson, John, 'European discovery of New Zealand: Cook's Three voyages', *Dictionary of New Zealand Biography*, *Te Ara—The Encyclopedia of New Zealand*, 2005
        https://teara.govt.nz/en/european-discovery-of-new-zealand/print

23   Clip of Sam Hunt introducing and reading Naming the Gods on Youtube
        https://www.youtube.com/watch?v=xrgC5yxU9Q4

24   https://www.nzherald.co.nz/nz/wilder-ways-not-a-handicap/
        YVCVE4LFN2MHFCPXT5K7N2TSNY/

25   https://www.rnz.co.nz/programmes/black-sheep/story/2018794417/
      escape-artist-the-story-of-george-wilder

26   Ansley, Bruce. *Wild Journeys*, Harper Collins, Auckland, 2018

27   https://www.scoop.co.nz/stories/CU1511/S00219/
      poems-stolen-from-george-wilder

28   https://www.rnz.co.nz/national/programmes/mediawatch/
      audio/2018939547/midweek-mediawatch-justice-for-herbertville

29   https://paperspast.natlib.govt.nz/newspapers/dominion/1916/11/07/6

30   From *Shot at the Somme* published by Weaving the Strands 2021

31   https://www.chbdc.govt.nz/our-district/walking/

32   https://natlib.govt.nz/he-tohu/learning/learning-activities/
      new-zealand-place-names

33   https://thelongestplacename.co.nz/history/

34   https://www.britannica.com/sports/polo

35   Siers, Judy, *The Life and Times of James Walter Chapman-Taylor*,
      Millwood Press, Wellington, 2007

36   https://knowledgebank.org.nz/audio/ormond-sir-john-davies-wilder-
      gladys-margaret-margaret-hope-memories-of-wallingford/

37   Wilder, Andrew, *Distinguished Service; The Life and WWII Adventures of N.P.
      (Nick) Wilder*, Andrew Wilder, Taupō, 2019

38   Pollock, Kerryn, 'Hawke's Bay places—Waipukurau', *Dictionary of
      New Zealand Biography, Te Ara—The Encyclopedia of New Zealand*, 2009
      https://teara.govt.nz/en/hawkes-bay-places/print

39   https://www.tukitukitrail.com/lindsay-tunnel

40   Parsons, Patrick, *Waipukurau: The history of a Country Town*,
      Waipukurau Rotary Club, Waipukurau, 1999

41   https://tour.ngaaratipuna.co.nz/#/intro

42   https://ww100.govt.nz/rangitikei-queen-carnival

43   https://en.wikipedia.org/wiki/Pahiatua

44   https://paperspast.natlib.govt.nz/newspapers

45   https://www.doc.govt.nz/news/media-releases/2022-media-releases/
      community-collaboration-to-restore-local-treasure/

46   https://api.tararuadc.govt.nz/TDC/minutes/pahiatua/05-04-2023.pdf

47   Mākurī School and District 100 Years Plus ISBN 0-473-02597-3

48   Champion, Rae & Smith, Lyn, *Mākurī School and district: 100 years plus*,
      The School, Mākurī, 1994

49   Sources: Meech, Bernadine, 'The Hansens of Pine Hills', *Under the Puketois*,
      Pahiatua, N.Z. : B. Mech, 2004; Interview with Sonia Mackenzie:
      https://knowledgebank.org.nz/audio/mackenzie-sonia-
      winnifred-mary-interview/; Sarah Crysell and Anna Mackenzie

50   https://www.temanawa.co.nz/wp-content/uploads/2021/03/BORO-
      Discovery-Time-24-April-2020.pdf

ACKNOWLEDGEMENTS

Brian Morris, Pūangi Ltd, for Māori Language and Cultural Editing.

The Estate of James K. Baxter for permission to publish the poem 'At Akitio' by the late James K. Baxter.

Wairarapa Lifestyle Magazine for permission to re-purpose commissioned stories 'At Akitio' and 'Soldiers in Monochrome'.

Permission to publish the lyrics of the song 'Cape Turnagain', words and music by Barry Saunders © Copyright Concord Music Publishing ANZ Pty Ltd All print rights administered in Australia and New Zealand by Hal Leonard Australia Pty Ltd ABN 13 085 333 713 www.halleonard.com.au Used By Permission. All Rights Reserved. Unauthorised Reproduction is Illegal.

While every effort has been made to obtain permission of copyright material reproduced herein, the publisher would like to apologise for any omissions and will be pleased to incorporate missing acknowledgements in any future editions.

From the author:

This book was born from a coaching session I had with author Catherine Cooper, who planted the seed in the very first hour. For that I thank her, as I do the dynamic Mary McCallum for valuable early assistance and ongoing encouragement. I'm grateful to my publisher Deborah Coddington for her unwavering belief, and for suggesting, when I bought the first caravan, that a journal of its travels might come in handy one day. It did.

My occasional and member-fluid writers group, the Cronutters, has provided supportive company, and both Karl du Fresne and Redmer Yska have generously offered sage advice from their lifetimes of experience. I thank Barry Saunders for the inspiration for 'One More Circle' and use of his words; Nick Jolliffe for unwittingly providing the subtitle; everyone who read a draft or chipped in an idea; and my little family—Pip, Oliver, and Lucien, and Meg, of course.

Most importantly, 'Cheers!' to the dozens of people around Route 52 who I met, picked up, quizzed, stalked, badgered, and wrote about— without you, etc . . .

First published in Aotearoa New Zealand
by Ugly Hill Press 2024
70 Karāpiro Road, Karāpiro, Waikato,
Aotearoa New Zealand.

ISBN 9781838583614

All photographs © Simon Burt except
 p. 134 photograph © Olivia Robertson
p. 181 photograph © Ellen Baxter
p. 196 photograph © Shine Krishna (Fotographian)
p. 238 *Pōrangahau church, Hawke's Bay* (Detail). Winder, Duncan, 1919-1970:
Architectural photographs. Ref: DW-0885-F. Alexander Turnbull Library,
Wellington, New Zealand.

Edited by Jemma Moreira

Designed and typeset by Keely O'Shannessy

This book was printed on FSC® certified paper

Printed in China by Everbest Printing International Ltd

Simon Burt was born in England in 1954 and spent his first eleven years between London and Wellington. Despite a dismal high school record he was accepted into Wellington Teachers' College from where he graduated in 1975.

After a brief teaching career Simon has been a maker of corporate videos, a television commercials producer, tourist newspaper publisher, advertising features writer, web developer and copywriter, magazine contributor, father, and farmer. He lives on a Wairarapa 'lifestyle' block with his wife, textile artist and educator Pip Steel, and their fox terrier Meg. They have two adult sons, Oliver and Lucien.

Route 52 is his first book.